PATHS *of* POLLEN

D1603154

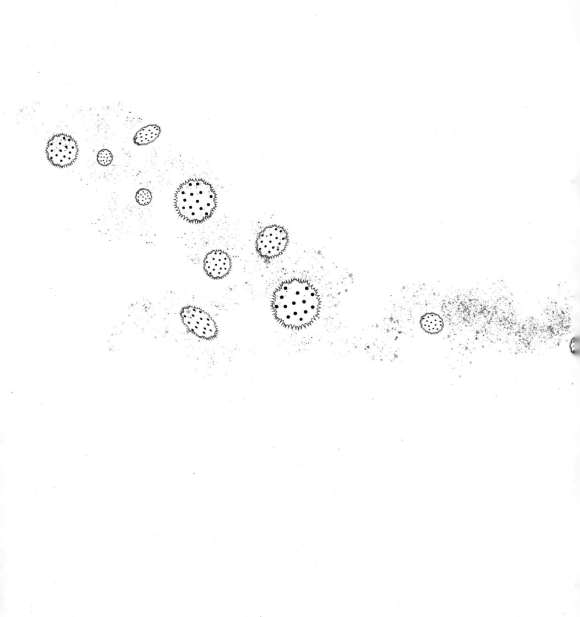

PATHS *of* POLLEN

Stephen Humphrey

McGill-Queen's University Press
Montreal & Kingston · London · Chicago

© McGill-Queen's University Press 2023

ISBN 978-0-2280-1897-1 (cloth)
ISBN 978-0-2280-1960-2 (ePDF)

Legal deposit fourth quarter 2023
Bibliothèque nationale du Québec

Printed in Canada on acid-free paper that is 100% ancient forest
free (100% post-consumer recycled), processed chlorine free

Funded by the   Financé par le
Government   gouvernement   Canadä   Canada Council   Conseil des arts
of Canada   du Canada   for the Arts   du Canada

We acknowledge the support of the Canada Council for the Arts.

Nous remercions le Conseil des arts du Canada de son soutien.

cip to come

Set in 11.5/14 Filosofia
Book design & typesetting by Garet Markvoort, zijn digital

CONTENTS

ILLUSTRATIONS

ACKNOWLEDGMENTS

This book has been an expedition of learning, involving numerous teachers. I was privileged to receive so much knowledge firsthand from world-class scientists and naturalists. All persons I've quoted in this book were inestimably generous with their time and knowledge. I hope I've done justice to their insights.

Thanks to Elmer Zumwalt for sparking my passion about bees and Sheila Zumwalt for throwing me numerous lifelines during this project.

Thanks to Sarah Peebles for helping me experience the diversity of bees and to see (and hear) them as living works of art.

Thanks to Sara Wolch for helping me refine my interviewing and critical listening skills, and for teaching me that no part of any process is the easy part.

(Thanks to anyone else named Sarah I might have forgotten.)

Thanks to Gary Humphrey for driving me all the way to Vancouver Island, to recite five-line bee poems, and not throwing me off the ferry.

Thanks to the Vault writers group for reading my chapters and not complaining (much) that they weren't fiction. Thanks to Heather Wood for her timely advice.

My writing efforts were generously funded. My thanks to the Ontario Arts Council, to the Canada Council for the Arts, and for the tail end of an NSERC Strategic Network grant. This book is NSERC-CANPOLIN contribution #150.

Thanks to Pippa the cat for instructing me to relax and take breaks. Thank you Christina for your green thumb, compassionate listening, and unwavering faith in me. I love you.

Finally, let me thank the pollinators, who taught me that labour is comingled with beauty and that there's value to even the briefest lives.

PATHS *of* POLLEN

Pollen's Progress: Where's It All Going (and Where Has It Been)?

Pollen's job is to go places. It is an organism with no limbs, physical senses, or consciousness, yet it's nonetheless tasked with a do-or-die mission to accomplish one of nature's great errands: plant reproduction. Plants don't move, and mostly they don't need to. They are nourished by their own alchemy of water, CO_2, and sunlight, so they don't need to roam around searching for food. Sex is another matter. Since plants are immobile, they can't go out and search for mates. Instead, they release pollen grains, tiny portable vessels which deliver their sex cells to other plants. This act of remote conception is called pollination. When pollen consummates this vegetative union, a fertilized plant makes seeds.

Plants exchange pollen, frequently but not always assisted by animal agents (sometimes wind is their only ally). A range of different animals pollinate plants, including birds, reptiles, a few mammals, and scores of insects. This diverse cast of creatures all bear the title "pollinator." Pollen is small and transportable, but it doesn't know where it's going and can't move under its own power. Since animals are built for mobility and inclined to move around, they're natural helpers. Not that they know they're helping. Pollinators go to flowers for reasons relevant to themselves, not plants. They arrive seeking food, shelter, spots to lay eggs, or places to mate. Their plant-bound journeys just happen to coincide with a plant's need to spread pollen. Pollen is spread through networks of self-interested, mutually dependent stakeholders. However, when pollination succeeds, these unwitting partners help far more than themselves. They benefit much wider webs of life. Plants could not perform their ecological roles if they did not reproduce, so pollination is necessary to ecosystems. Crops require pollination, so it's essential for agriculture. The world would be less green, and hungrier, if pollen could not get where it needs to go.

However, like other systems in nature, pollination networks are vulnerable to stress. Nature is currently beset by many kinds of ecological stress, and signs point to overstress across living communities. Notably, there are upticks in species extinctions. Die-offs have gotten so extreme, some ecologists suggest Earth is facing its sixth mass extinction. Mass extinctions involve rapid drops in biodiversity. When key species disappear, webs of interdependence collapse, dragging more species to oblivion. Given time (millions of years), life recovers and repopulates, but things don't come back just like before, and numerous things are gone forever. No-one has seen a *T. rex* since the previous mass extinction, except in movies and museums.

No living thing is guaranteed permanence. Nor has any form of life always been here. If we look back one billion years, we'll see nothing alive on land – no animals or plants, not even soil, just bare virgin rock. Half a billion years later, when plants started greening the world, there was no such thing as pollen. For millions of years plants propagated with spores, but when pollen arrived, it brought certain innovations, such as the creation of seeds. Like pollen, seeds were tough, portable, and more resistant to moisture loss than spores. Millions more years passed before flowers and their by-products, fruits, came along. Up until 140 million years ago, land vegetation had nothing to show but greenness. Yet by the time plants finally revealed their colourful, "flowery" side, scores of species had vanished in four mass extinctions and several minor extinction "pulses." Flowers, themselves, were not safe from going extinct. Fossil evidence from mass extinction number five hints that the largest lineage of flowers, along with their pollinators, came close to disappearing (see chapter 6). Had history followed a different path, flowers might not exist today. For all we know, the next mass extinction, or the one after, will finish off flowering plants, once and for all.

How the next round of extinctions proceeds might well be in humanity's hands. The human race's impact on nature has intensified since *Homo sapiens* first began to exploit nature's bounty. Some experts even propose calling our current geologic epoch the Anthropocene. Environmentalists fret over the prospect that human actions (and inactions) may drive nature to inexorable "tipping points." A tipping point is where an event, once set in motion, become unstoppable, like a roller coaster hurtling over a rise. Past a certain point, gravity takes over, and the rest is downhill.

If anything is going up these days, it's the planet's temperature. As we burn through fossil fuels, greenhouse gases released into the atmosphere push global temperatures ever higher. According to America's climate-monitoring agency, the National Oceanic and Atmospheric Administration (NOAA), the ten warmest years on record have occurred since 2005, the last seven since 2014. Even if greenhouse gas emissions hold steady or decline, computer models predict the Earth's average temperature will rise between 2.4 and 5.9 degrees Celsius by the end of this century. Those numbers may not sound large, but the last time world temperatures approached this level was 56 million years ago. That dramatic warming event, called the Paleocene-Eocene Thermal Maximum (PETM), was especially hard on marine species, killing more than 90 per cent of ocean life. Greenhouse gases, from volcanoes most likely, saturated the air over 20,000 years, a geologic eyeblink. That period of "rapid" heating was slow compared to now. By recent estimates, human activity pumps CO_2 and other compounds into the atmosphere nine to ten times faster. If emissions keep to their current rate, Earth could match the PETM's levels in 140 to 259 years (five to ten human generations), a hundred times faster than the PETM.[1]

Pollen plays a fascinating part in researching past climate events such as the PETM. Among its climate-monitoring tools, NOAA maintains a global pollen database. There, pollen extracted from sediments all over the world helps scientists infer past climate conditions without "direct observational data."[2] Pollen particles are useful for this sort of analysis because they age well as fossils. Pollen grains are strong as well as small. The sex cells inside them stay viable for just a short time, but their outer shells remain intact for millions of years. "Pollen" derives from two Greek words: *"paluno,"* which means "to sprinkle," and *"pale,"* meaning "dust." Leftovers of this once-living dust hint at how long pollen has played its role in nature's story.

Pollen can also teach us about climate history – if we look very closely, more closely than the naked eye can manage. It takes powerful lenses to examine these durable little grains. In 1682, when microscopes were relatively new, English botanist Nehemiah Grew first discovered that clumps of "bee bread" from honeybee hives were made up of individual grains.

He called these "globulets."[3] Grew conjectured, correctly, that pollen's purpose was sexual in nature. Their hardy shells harbour gametes, or reproductive cells, within them.

Grains of pollen may have simple-looking designs, or might be geometrically complex, even sculptural. From species to species, they present a range of forms. Grew was the first scholar to notice that grains of pollen are different-looking, depending which plant they come from. Pollen grains are like fingerprints for plant species. Their distinctiveness makes them useful to NOAA's climate researchers. By extracting pollen fossils from sediments, scientists can deduce which plants used to live in a place and how plentiful they were. To researchers, pollen grains are like tiny time capsules, in situ records of which plants perished and which ones persisted through ice ages, droughts, and global heat waves. This knowledge helps to model future climate trends.

Which plants will flourish as the world warms up? In the near term, probably lots of plants will. At first, longer growing seasons and more carbon dioxide (which plants consume) could make the world leafier. But there can be too much of a good thing. Plant leaves vacuum up CO_2, turning carbon into sugars, which plant metabolisms use, while releasing oxygen, which animal metabolisms need. However, plants can only suck in so much carbon. Research shows some rainforests, the so-called "lungs of the planet," have begun emitting, rather than absorbing, CO_2.[4] With so much carbon floating around, will the world keep getting leafier, or will plants wither and wilt, overwhelmed by their new global hothouse?

Plants have plenty of problems already. In 2019, scientists announced 571 plant species had gone extinct over the past three centuries.[5] Climate change was not even the top cause. Other human-led factors did more to trigger declines in plant diversity, such as plants losing habitat to industry and cities, invasive species out-competing local plants, and pollution – climate-warming and otherwise. Meanwhile, humanity's need for plant products keeps growing. Demand is trending up for plant-sourced goods such as food, medicines, fibres, wood and other construction materials, and biofuels. In 1960, the world had 3 billion human beings. In 2022 Earth's population officially reached 8 billion, according to the United Nations' *World Population Prospects* report.[6] That number is up from 7 billion in 2010. We could reach a projected 9.7 billion people by 2050. One survey predicts that global food demand will rise by 35–56 per cent between 2010 and 2050; complications from climate change could bump up this figure to 62 per cent. The United Nations Food and Agriculture Organization (FAO) says food production will need to increase by 70 per cent within that timespan to keep up with consumption.[7]

Pollinator populations also look to be trending downward. In 2016, a panel of experts filed a report for the United Nations commission on biodiversity, the Intergovernmental Science-Policy Platform on Biodiversity and Ecosystem Services (IPBES). The document, titled "Assessment Report on Pollinators, Pollination and Food Production," concluded that 75 per cent of food crops and nearly 90 per cent of wild flowering plants depend to some extent on animal pollination. It also found that pollinators were increasingly under threat, as "Nature across most of the globe has now been significantly altered by multiple human drivers."[8] While pollinators exist across the animal kingdom, the majority are insects. Bees get most of the press, but flies, beetles, butterflies, and wasps pollinate as well. Unfortunately, population data for insects points to steep declines in their numbers. A *New York Times* article in 2018 announced, "The Insect Apocalypse Is Here."[9] The piece referenced a European study published in 2017 that warned the world has 75 per cent less insect biomass since 1989.[10]

Still, pollination is not merely a numbers game that measures so many pollinators versus so many plants. It is webs of different species mutually adapting to changes in their environments. Pollination networks, being complex, are vulnerable to change; but they also have some flex. They might lose plants or pollinators might go away, but the networks themselves stay intact — up to a point. Attrition happens in nature, it's nothing new, but living communities can crash if too many species vanish. At some point, too much is too much.

In 2020, scientists at the Georgia Institute of Technology looked at fossil pollen from over the past 20,000 years. They were testing for "landscape resiliency" of plant communities in North America. They found that North America's landscape resilience is at its lowest since the so-called "end-Pleistocene megafaunal extinctions," when the continent's biggest mammals died out, 40,000 to 50,000 years ago. What worried the researchers was the present-day ratio between "residence times" and "recovery times." The longer plants reside in places, the more diverse they become and the faster they recover from disturbance. Sadly, say the

Living dust: "Pollen" comes from two Greek words: "paluno," which means "to sprinkle," and "pale," meaning "dust." Pollen grains in this image, magnified 500 times, are from sunflower (*Helianthus annuus*), morning glory (*Ipomoea purpurea*), hollyhock (*Sildalcea malviflora*), lily (*Lilium auratum*), primrose (*Oenothera fruticosa*), and castor bean (*Ricinus communis*). Their distinctiveness makes pollen grains like fingerprints for different plant species. (Dartmouth College Electron Microscope Facility)

scientists, right now too many habitats are too young. We have forests, but not as many old forests. We have grasslands, but those grasslands are less biodiverse. It is harder for younger, less diverse ecosystems to build back up when they're knocked down. The scientists warn of "foreboding potential extinctions to come."[11]

The good news is while plants have the potential to go extinct, they also have the capacity to bounce back. Plants spring from seeds in just weeks. A grain of pollen forms over a day or so. People know how to plant seeds. They've done it for thousands of years. We can declare plants or pollinators endangered and make plans to protect them. But how do we protect *pollination*, which is not a species but an ephemeral network of organisms? Preserving networks requires stewardship, which is not just action but habit. After you plant a garden, you need to keep tending it. Stewarding takes time, and also learning. Like a garden, knowledge too needs tending. Pollination is complex ecologically, and difficult scientifically. As a topic, it's a moving target, in no small part because plants, pollinators, and the natural world keep changing. But before we race further into pollination's (potentially daunting) future, let's pause for a moment to peek into the past, where innumerable adaptations led to life as we now know it, and somehow resulted in the little vessel of life called pollen.

CHAPTER 1

A Prehistory of Pollen

Pollen Zoom

Pollination's origin is kind of a chicken-and-egg story, one with a very old chicken and a very small egg – or rather a very small shell with something squishy inside. The story runs through several extremes of large and small, so we'll need an elastic sense of perspective. To stretch our minds sufficiently for that, let's start with one of my favourite science films. In 1968, animator Eva Szasaz created a short film for the National Film Board of Canada, *Cosmic Zoom*. The film starts with a boy and his dog in a boat, rowing on a lake. The view expands until we're shown Earth from space, then our galaxy, then the entire cosmos. Next, we zoom back in until a mosquito on the boy's arm fills the whole screen. We zoom in more, until we're looking at blood cells, then protein molecules, and finally, atoms. The film's visual poetry illustrates how much goes on in the world that is larger and smaller than what we usually perceive.

Events at such radical scales are not just interesting abstractions; they shape our lives, even when they're too large or too small to see. Planet-wide weather systems collude to make it rain on our picnics. Viruses too small for human eyes to discern can potentially disrupt the whole of human affairs. If only we could get a proper look at these things. But of course, we can. Using satellites, we can witness Earth's climate as one interconnected system. We can view viruses less than one micron in size with scanning electron microscopes. Current technology turns *Cosmic Zoom*'s revealing fantasy into visible reality. Still, when these radical views reach human eyeballs, it's the human imagination's turn to wrestle with what we see.

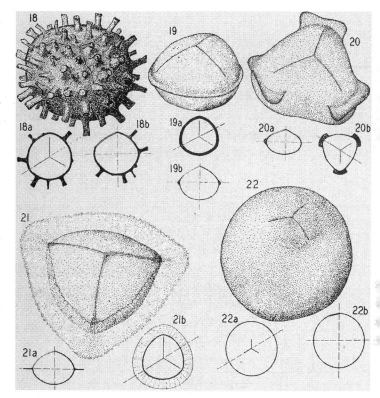

Not shown actual size: Under magnification, these spores from extinct plants have an alien appearance. They might not be from space, but they are time travellers, in a way. The spore in the upper left corner came from *Raistrickia*, a fern-like species that lived during the Carboniferous Period, around 300 million years ago. The spore in the upper right came from *Lepidodendron*, a Carboniferous tree related to present-day clubmosses. (Illinois State Geological Survey)

My own imagination does strange things when I try to make sense of grainy, greyscale images that were photographed through microscope lenses. One image makes me recall fuzzy tabloid pictures I once saw of triangular UFOs. At its true scale, the object in the photo could fly right over my city and I'd never notice, since it's only fifty microns (0.05 millimetres) across. Another specimen is roughly spherical and spiked with numerous blunt points. Massively enlarged, it could pass for a World War II naval mine. Scaled down, it might be the new variant of some flu-like virus. Shown actual size, the spiky ball would look like a pebble next to a boulder if you put it beside a grain of sand. These cryptic objects are in fact fossils of plant spores, extracted from ancient sandstone.

These spores have names that sound like aliens took part in naming them. The spikier spore belongs to *Raistrickia*, an extinct genus of fern-like plants.[1] The plant has been extinct too long for biologists to nail down its precise species. They can only settle on its general type. "Genus" means "type" in Latin, the language of biology. If families of organisms were branches on a tree, genera (more than one genus) would be smaller twigs growing from the larger branch of their family. *Raistrickia*'s entire limb on the tree of life, with all its offshoots, is long dead. The plant the spore came from has no living descendants, but the lineage of ferns survives. Ferns have graced every continent, even Antarctica, back when that landmass was tropical. The lineage of ferns is so ancient, if you went back 300 million years, you would find them still carpeting forest floors, in the shade of Earth's original woodlands.

Hiking through Fossil Forest

Over a 60-million-year span known as the Carboniferous Period, swampy forests covered landmasses we wouldn't even recognize today. There are fossilized remnants of such woods on Canada's east coast. The Joggins Fossil Cliffs are one of the most intact relics of Carboniferous forest on Earth. Tourists can wander rocky beaches at the foot of these cliffs and see fossilized tree trunks jutting from cliff faces. Some former trees are petrified hollow stumps where early reptiles once laid eggs. Dragonflies with two-foot (sixty-centimetre) wingspans once hummed overhead, and millipedes more than two metres long perambulated through mud, leaving tracks, the only trace left of these long-vanished invertebrates. The Appalachian Mountains loomed over this rainforest, back when they were taller than the Himalayas. Africa and Eurasia were close continental neighbours, since all the world's landmasses were shoved together as one supercontinent, Pangea.

The Joggins Cliffs are now in the Bay of Fundy, where they encounter the world's highest tides. The beach beneath the cliffs, where I've joined a guided tour, will be underwater an hour later. As high tides lap at the cliff face, it erodes, dislodging fossils, which tumble out. The beach is strewn with fossil fragments like smashed pottery. Things that were once alive kept their shapes through a process called "permineralization," through which rock replaced their tissues, cell by cell. We pick up pieces of permineralized tree bark, to marvel at them, and then put them back. The Joggins Cliffs are a UNESCO World Heritage Site, so no souvenir-hunting is permitted. Some of these clay-coloured shards have thorny diamond

Still standing: Lycopsid fossil at Joggins Formation, Cumberland Basin, Nova Scotia. Trees like this once stood up to fifty metres tall in a swampy rainforest during the Carboniferous period. (Michael C. Rygel via Wikimedia Commons)

shapes, like flattened pineapple skins. They were once the bark of *Lepido-dendron*, an extinct genus of trees that looked like fifty-metre dust mops.

Lepidodendron's much shorter descendants, the club mosses, are nick-named "ground pines" for their needle-shaped leaves. Club mosses are not pines, nor are they mosses. They are from an ancient lineage that spawned some of the first trees and possibly the first "vascular plants" — plants with stems that contain specialized tissues called "xylem," which draws water upward, and "phloem," which moves nutrients around like vessels transport blood. Without this internal plumbing, no plants, cer-tainly not trees, could ever grow tall. Trees in the Carboniferous further supported their fantastic growth with lignin and cellulose, which made them woody, like all trees ever since. On the beach at Joggins, we pick up

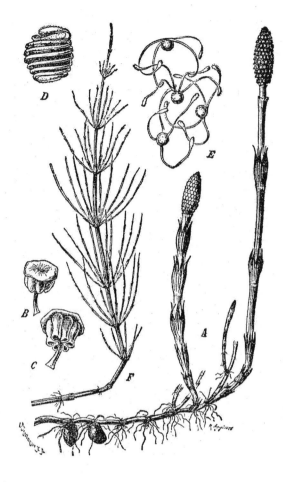

Spore factory: Horsetail (*Equi-setum arvense*) in its various life stages. Its club-like strobilius (a) contains spores. Spore-bearing organs on the strobilius called sporophylls (b) open up to release the plant's strange, mobile spores (c). Appendages called "elaters" close (d) and open (e), reacting to small changes in moisture, which allows the spores to "walk" and even "jump." When the plant is not releasing spores, sterile "vegetative shoots" (f) with spiky leaves shoot up. These earn horsetails the nickname "scouring rush." (Encyclopædia Britannica)

preserved bark that's textured like corduroy. This was the skin of *Cala-mites*, another primeval tree. *Calamites*'s living descendants, field horse-tails, barely reach a grown person's knees. Dana Brown, our guide, says locals called horsetails "scouring rush" while he was growing up, and used them for scrubbing pots and pans.

"It was like the first SOS pad," he jokes.

Walking Spores, Swimming Sperm

Even present-day horsetails look out of their time, with their ridged stems and toothy, upcurving shoots. One less visible sign of their pre-historic nature is a lack of pollen. Their towering ancestors, *Calamites*, existed before pollen or seeds could evolve. Instead, *Calamites* propagated with spores, as horsetails still do. In their reproductive phase, horsetails are crowned with brown, club-shaped growths called "sporangiophores," which are covered in clusters of spores. While some plant spores look like alien spaceships, horsetail spores more closely resemble tentacled aliens. They are tiny spheres with four ribbon-like appendages called "elaters," which coil and uncoil, reacting to small changes in moisture. This unconscious flexing powers a spastic sort of motion. The spores seem to walk, even jump at times – a few centimetres at most, but enough to catch wind currents and ride them short distances.[2]

When horsetail spores finally walk, sail, or bounce someplace with adequate light and moisture, they germinate into spiky, green mini-plants called "gametophytes." Though they all started as asexual spores, each tiny plant could end up male, female, or hermaphroditic. Their job is to produce male or female sex cells, called "gametes." Male gametes behave much like animal sperm. They have tails, and swim through droplets of water, blindly seeking female gametes to fertilize. Should fertilization succeed, an asexual plant, called a "sporophyte," will germinate, grow tall, and release spores. For primeval plants such as horsetails, spores are like small, simple seeds, or "propagules." Each spore contains a single cell, which generates a new plant. This cell is kept safe by a shell made of tough material called "sporopollenin." One botanist called this natural polymer "the most resistant organic material of direct biological origin found in nature."[3] Spore shells are tough enough to stay intact for millions if not hundreds of millions of years.

Spores to Seeds

If someone shot a sequel to *Cosmic Zoom* in the Joggins Cliffs, their camera might zoom in on the cliff face, to reveal fossil spores embedded in sandstone. Say the camera kept going, magically penetrating layers of rock. It would find even older spore fossils, and older ones still the deeper it went. Sediments tell stories this way; the past is buried under what came after it. Layer by layer, these enduring particles drop hints about plant evolution. At points, they reveal major breakthroughs, such as when pollen started appearing. This signals a serious leap forward for plant reproduction. Pollen grains resemble spores in many ways: they have tough shells of sporopollenin and come in many shapes. However, the job pollen does is different. Instead of sprouting into a plant, it supplies sperm to fertilize a plant's female organ, the "ovule." This union produces a plant embryo and a layer of starchy tissue around it called "endosperm," the new plant's built-in food supply. The ovule's outer skin hardens into a "seed coat." The total construct is a seed.

There are fossils of the first pollen-producing "seed plants" at Joggins. Seed ferns are another dead lineage; there are no more around. But if you reversed time and looked at them, you'd see something like ferns sprouting from tree trunks. Those extinct plants are called "seed ferns," but they were not ferns, despite their fern-like leaves. At least the "seed" part is accurate, since they grew from seeds. There are fossils of those seeds, which resemble petrified nuts. When they were viable, the seeds contained living plants, preparing to sprout. In a sense, pollen grains shelter versions of tiny plants, themselves. The cells inside them are highly reduced versions of male gametophytes, the single-sexed plants that sprout from spores. The gametophytes within pollen shells have no leafy parts, but they do produce sperm.

No-one knows how abbreviated male plants got into spore-like shells. But fossils of primitive pollen hint at the stages early pollen evolved through. Strictly speaking, pollen from seed ferns wasn't completely pollen, say evolutionary botanists. They call it "prepollen" because it lacked some features of "true" pollen. Receptacles for this primitive pollen were more basic too. Pollen grains fell into female vessels more like cups than flowers.[4] The seed fern's male "flowers" were longish sacs dangling from leaves.[5]

The Coming of Cones

Despite the coming of pollen, no flowering plants bloomed during the Carboniferous. However, some plants evolved cones. The class of trees known as "conifers" still exchange pollen this way. Present-day conifers, such as jack pines, eastern white pines, and balsam firs, occupy forests near the Joggins Cliffs. Their male cones have features called "scales," which resemble roof shingles. The scales open up to discharge pollen, which wind carries off. Pollen grains from modern pines are weirdly intricate. Each grain has two hollow bladders to keep it airborne. When one of these bulging pollen grains blows into a female cone, it slowly extends a hollow tail, its pollen tube, and sends sperm to one of the cone's ovules, which hold the plant's version of eggs (see chapter 15). When pine ovules grow into seeds, female cones expose them by opening *their* scales. These exposed seeds are not enclosed by fruit, like seeds from flowering plants. They're naked to the world. Conifers are called "gymnosperms," which means "naked seed" in Latin. The oldest known fossils of pine pollen were found in a gypsum quarry near the town of Windsor, Nova Scotia. They're 140 million years old, which is young by Joggins standards.[6]

Fossil pollen grains from more primitive gymnosperms are found in the Joggins Cliffs. These don't have fancy extras like aerodynamic bladders. Their appearance is decidedly simpler. Pollen from an extinct conifer genus, *Potonieisporites*, looks like a half-eaten hard candy mashed into a date. *Illinites unicus*, another extinct tree species, had pollen grains like oblong rocks.

Coal Age Microfossils

These early conifers perished, along with seed ferns, in the Permian mass extinction, 250 million years ago. During this unprecedented die-off, 95 per cent of marine life and 70 per cent of life on land ceased to exist.[7] In the lead-up to this tragedy, volcanic eruptions, caused by continental movement, saturated the air with greenhouse gases. Runaway global warming likely laid waste to the trees at Joggins.[8]

The ruins of this forest do not hold many intact remains. Even before the Permian die-off, time took its toll. There were storms and fires, like in modern forests. Trees sometimes pitched over because of top-heaviness and shallow roots. They might have been crushed by titanic siblings, which fell on them afterward. These fallen giants lay where they fell, unable to rot away since bacteria hadn't yet evolved to decompose wood. Time marched on, and sediments buried them over three hundred million years. Very few came through all that in one piece. However, pollen and spores remained intact. These tough little grains are sometimes the only evidence certain plants ever lived. This makes them fascinating to a subset of researchers called "palynologists," who study spore and pollen fossils. They are paleontologists, but not the kind who unearth huge beasts like mastodons and dinosaurs. Nothing these fossil hunters collect measures more than a couple of millimetres.

To reach microscopic fossils embedded in rock takes powerful drills, like those used for coal exploration. Some of the first Carboniferous fossils ever found came from coal beds. The term "Carboniferous," coined in 1822, means "coal-bearing," since four-tenths of all coal can be traced to this geologic period. Brittle chunks of soft bituminous coal litter the beach at Joggins. They crumble when I pick them up. More than sixty coal deposits can be counted along the cliff face. Dana Brown points to burnt orange patches where disgruntled coal workers, protesting mine closures in 1961, set fire to coal seams, which superheated the sandstone to terracotta.

"When I grew up here, it still was smouldering," says Brown. "It smelled like sulphur."

There is so much coal in this fossil forest because coal is made from forest. Over time, trees and other plants transformed into peat, then into coal.[9] While they were alive, Carboniferous plants pulled so much CO_2 from the air that the so-called "coal age" had 15 per cent more oxygen than now. Much of that age's stored carbon is now back in the atmosphere. In 2021, the World Energy Agency calculated that coal supplies a third of the world's power and contributes 72 per cent of its fossil fuel emissions.[10] Some palynologists help coal companies find this combustible rock. The distinct shapes of spore and pollen fossils reveal which plants became coal in ancient peat mires. Experts use this knowledge to predict coal quality.[11] Microfossils point the way to fossil fuels.

Oil and Flowers

Oil companies have their own uses for palynology. They keep palynologists on staff to make on-site determinations about where to drill, based on microfossils of ancient plant and marine life.[12] The viscous tar-like liquid called "bitumen," from Alberta's oil sands, formed at the bottom of inland seas. These waters once deluged western Canada during the Cretaceous Period, around 100 million years ago. There are many dinosaur fossils in Alberta, documenting their presence during that period. After the Cretaceous, dinosaurs that did not become birds dropped out of existence. Flowers, on the other hand, had just gotten started.

Fossils found near Dawson Creek, British Columbia, and Milk River, Alberta, show the increasing presence of flowers. Some of the first flowers had blossoms so small scientists didn't recognize them at first. Such flowers were simpler, often incomplete by today's standards. A number went extinct, becoming evolutionary dead ends. Once they really got going, though, flowering plants spread rapidly, reproducing at rates we might call "weedy." Flowering plants currently make up 90 per cent of land plant species. With no ability to move themselves, flowers have gone practically everywhere.

Flowers broadcast incredible beauty and biological variety into the world, but their reproductive mechanisms are mostly unseen. A flower's pretty-looking petals enclose its ovaries, where seeds (and fruit) are formed. "Angiosperm," the scientific term for flowering plants, means "hidden seed." Yet for all they keep hidden, angiosperms are some of nature's biggest show-offs. Flowers burst forth colourfully from leafy sameness.

Many people are passionate flower fans who enthusiastically cultivate favourite breeds. But humans are not the only, and certainly not the first, species to notice flowers. During their rapid campaign to conquer the world, flowers recruited the services of innumerable insects and small flying animals to spread their pollen. Insect fossils offer ancient snapshots of early pollinators. Some insects met untimely ends when tree resin suddenly engulfed them, and then hardened over time into amber. Some Cretaceous insects, entombed in the smoky yellow rock, had flower pollen stuck to their bodies, even partly digested in their stomachs. Luckily, enough bugs kept clear of tree fluids to fertilize flowers. Prehistoric pollinators helped angiosperms spread and diversify faster than any plants before them.[13] Flowering plants persist, and flourish, thanks to pollinators. Likewise, pollinators persist because of flowering plants. Bees, which appeared during the Cretaceous, arguably exist only because of flowers.

Let's picture the camera's omniscient eye from *Cosmic Zoom* closing in on a bee. The view tightens, to encompass one of the bee's bristly, complicated hairs. Stuck to that hair is a pale yellow pollen grain, covered in

Pollen grain: A single pollen grain of rockcress (*Arabis voch*), a flowering plant in the mustard family. Pollen is a durable and transport-able vessel for plant sperm. (Marie Majaura)

crusty, curvilinear shapes reminiscent of brain coral. The grain is an ir-
regular sphere dimpled in three places for pollen tubes to come out. This
is one possible shape for pollen, since pollen grains are as diverse as the
plants that make them.

The bee doesn't see pollen as portable sex cells, but as food for her
young. Still, it's in the plant's interest for the bee to find this protein-rich
bounty, since her food-gathering spreads pollen. Thus the forms of flowers have evolved to attract bees and other pollinators. Flowers stand out
visually to humans as well. We like looking at them. But flowers send specific, targeted "messages" to pollinators. Our appreciation of flowers is so
secondary, some floral signals are invisible to us. Next chapter we'll discuss the visual language of flowers, and how pollinators decode it.

CHAPTER 2

Pollinators Painted the World

The Scandalous Sexual Displays of Flowers

When American artist Georgia O'Keeffe first exhibited her larger-than-life portraits of flowers in 1925, she inadvertently kicked off a perpetual conversation over the supposed sexual message of her artworks. Critics likened her voluptuous, outsized renderings of flowers to female anatomy, an association still hard to shake a century later. One writer for the UK's *Guardian* newspaper put it this way: "There are few artists in history whose work is consistently reduced to the single question: flowers or vaginas?"[1]

O'Keeffe herself denied the paintings had any sexual intent. During one of her rare interviews in 1970, she retorted, "When people read erotic symbols into my paintings, they're really talking about their own affairs."[2]

In fairness, flowering plants are highly sexed and completely shameless about it. Not only are a flower's genitalia on full display, they are located in the most visually striking part of the plant. While viewers of O'Keeffe's works may see vulvas in the whorls and folds of flower petals, they might fail to notice the flower's actual sex organs, dangling in plain sight. It is very human to mistake advertising for the product.

One of O'Keeffe's artworks portrays two spotted lilies (*Lilium lancifolium*). Each flower in the painting waves around six mallet-like anthers, the male organs that make pollen. They surround the lily's female organ, its stigma, a little button shape atop a slim appendage called the style. The lily's petals, with their suggestively anatomical whorls, may stir sexy thoughts in art enthusiasts, but such saucy musings can distract from the flower's actual, overt pansexuality. Like most flowering plants, lilies are hermaphrodites. Only 6 per cent of angiosperms have fully separate sexes.

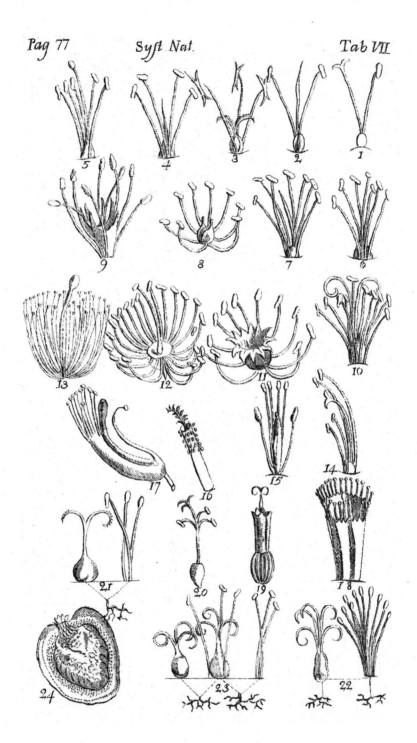

The Swedish botanist Carolus Linnaeus scandalized eighteenth-century Europeans with his observations about flower bisexuality and other complex truths of plant reproduction. He inflamed scandal just by asserting that plants reproduced sexually. Linnaeus pioneered modern taxonomy; the system biologists use to classify living things. "Taxonomy" comes from two Greek words, *nomos* ("law") and *taxis* ("arrangement"). It is the science of identifying plants, animals, microbes – anything alive – and working out where they fit in the many-branched "tree of life." Linnaeus set out to classify all living things according to his naming method, binomial nomenclature, which gave each organism a first and last name, in Latin. (He prized this scholarly language so much he Latinized his own name.) He made Latin the basis for his naming system in his 1735 publication, *Systema Naturae* (*The System of Nature*). The book categorized plants and animals within a descending hierarchy of kingdoms, then phyla ("divisions"), classes, orders, genera, and finally species.[3] Biologists still use this system.

In 1751, Linnaeus courted controversy with his method for classifying plants in his botany textbook, *Philosophia Botanica*. He divided plants into twenty-four classes, based on their number and arrangement of sex organs. Linnaeus, son of a Lutheran minister, chastely referenced male and female sexual parts as "husbands" and "wives." He called the calyx, the leafy structure supporting the flower, a "marriage bed."[4] Despite Linnaeus's modest word choices, detractors such as German botanist Johann Siegesbeck fumed over the "loathsome harlotry" of Linnaeus's "sexual system." Linnaeus retaliated by naming a weedy plant for his offended colleague. *Sigesbeckia orientalis* remains Siegesbeck's one lasting claim to fame. This act of scholarly vengeance shows how much licence is taken with Latinizing species names, and how thinly disguised in-jokes find their way into science.

In any case, Linnaeus's classification system survived its detractors. So did the saucy reputation of plants. In 1789, Charles Darwin's grandfather – naturalist, physician, and poet Erasmus Darwin – made plant

Flower genitalia (OPPOSITE): Swedish botanist Carolus Linnaeus courted controversy in eighteenth-century Europe for classifying plants according to their quantity of sexual organs. This illustration from his 1751 book, *Systema Naturae*, shows various sets of stamens, the male organs of plants. (Carolus Linneaus)

Bee as marital aid: The iris's stigmatic lip "kisses" pollen off of a nectar-seeking bee. As the bee backs out, male anthers rub pollen onto the bee, to cross-pollinate other irises. (William Hamilton Gibson)

sexuality the theme for his collection of botanical poetry, *The Loves of the Plants*. This popular volume teaches plant reproduction through playful, bawdy verse, while defending Linnaeus's theories in footnotes. The poetry's innuendo might seem tame by present-day standards, but the poems still make teachable points about plant sex. Consider this stanza, where Darwin compares the mating habits of hollyhocks (*Alcea rosea*) and irises (genus *Iris*).

With vain desires the pensive ALCEA burns,
And, like sad ELOISA, loves and mourns.
The freckled IRIS owns a fiercer flame,
And three unjealous husbands wed the dame.[5]

The "three unjealous husbands" are the iris flower's trio of anthers, which lurk beneath an equal number of female parts, the flower's three "style arms." The style arm is built into a canopy-like petal with a fiery-looking, upturned crest. When a pollinator shoves its way beneath the petal to reach the flower's nectar, a part of the style arm called the "stigmatic lip" kisses pollen off the insect's body. An "unjealous husband" patiently waits its turn before rubbing pollen on the departing insect as it backs out of the flower. Pollen is now on its way to fertilize another iris's female parts. If anthers and stigmas are "husbands" and "wives," as Linnaeus describes, it's better no-one is jealous, because the marriage situation is clearly an open one.

The notion of marriage itself falls apart pretty fast, though, since anthers and stigmas on the same flower aren't married to one another any more than my fingers are married to my toes. They're parts of the same complicated life form. Even all this spicy talk about plant polyamory overhypes the drama of plant sex, which is fairly undramatic. There is no foreplay, no climax, just some grains sprinkled on a sticky pinhead. Like many seductions, the exciting part is courtship. Flowers have been powerful tools for human courtship. They spark associations with sex, romance, and marriage in people's imaginations. But flowers don't bloom with our amorous moods in mind. Despite our passion for them, flowers are signalling other receivers.

To get a sense of how flowers actually look to their "intended" viewers, let's consider Georgia O'Keeffe's 1951 canvas which she titles "Lavender Iris." The artwork is like a cropped photographic blow-up of the complicated, visually arresting flower. The flower looms large, as if viewed from a tiny approaching aircraft. Whooshing down from the iris's centre are petal-like parts known botanically as "sepals," more specifically as "falls." The iris has three falls, each filigreed with veins, and a splash of white and yellow down its centre. For a pollinator on approach, these might look like well-marked landing pads. The flower even raises flags to alert them. Three petals, called "standards," furl upward like pennants.

When a pollinator, say a bee, lands on an iris, she is searching for food. She wants pollen for her offspring, or nectar for her energy needs. The iris needs the bee to rub against its sexual parts, and to make sure she finds them, it offers visual guides. Those splashy patterns on the iris's sepals point the way to nectar. En route to her nectar reward, the bee facilitates plant sex. Mission accomplished for everyone.[6]

The Better to See Flowers With

Bees are good at memorizing patterns that lead to food sources, even strange ones. Proving just how strange, Australian scientist Adrian Dyer trained honeybees (named *Apis mellifera* by Linnaeus in 1758) to recognize human faces. He used sugar syrup to convince bees that photos of human faces could reward them like flowers do. Dyer even trained bees in his lab to associate certain people's faces with sweet rewards. News about Dyer's work prompted an ominous visit from the United States Air Force with questions about bees and facial recognition. Since that visit, nothing has surfaced yet about any kind of "spy bee" program — at least that anyone's heard about.[7]

Bees don't interpret human faces like humans do. In Dyer's experiment, people's likenesses were unorthodox floral patterns, not individuals. Conversely, humans don't regard flowers like bees do. Yet what we do have in common with bees is visual organs to view faces and flowers. Our different animal orders each have some form of sight. Human eyes, inherited from fish, are squishy, liquid-filled spheres that swivel in several directions and focus like camera lenses. Insects have compound eyes inherited from underwater crustaceans. These contain clusters of light-gathering parts called "ommatidia." Compound eyes can't roll around like ours, but their field of vision is much wider. Imagine seeing in front of you and to both sides at once. This is handy for flying, and why it's hard to sneak up on flies with a swatter. Bees also have three simpler additional eyes, called "ocelli," on top of their heads to detect light, dark, and motion. Their two larger, more obvious eyes have cone cells with colour-sensitive pigments, as human eyes do.

German biologist Karl von Frisch was first to prove that bees saw colour. This perceptive scholar won the Nobel Prize in 1973 for discovering honeybees had symbolic language based on dance. He also made

The better to see flowers with: Bees, like humans, have eyes to see with, but human and insect eyes have evolved differently. Bees, like other insects, have compound eyes. They also have three simpler, dot-shaped eyes on top of their heads called "ocelli," which can sense light, dark, motion; and the polarity of light. Bees also see different light wavelengths than humans do. (Gilles San Martin)

historic strides in understanding bee perception. He proved the extent of their colour sense in 1916 using sugar syrup and cardboard squares laid out somewhat like squares on a checkerboard. After training honeybees with syrup, von Frisch removed their sweet reward to see whether they returned to coloured squares instead of grey-tinted decoys. In this way, he proved floral colours were visible to bees.[8] Von Frisch's research also revealed limits to bee colour vision. He learned that bees could not distinguish the colour red. They treated red squares no differently than non-coloured squares on his grids. On the other hand, bees picked out blues and purples with subtlety and speed. Many plants pollinated by bees have blue or purple blossoms. Bees also see yellow quite well, hence their interest in yellow-petalled flowers.

Yet von Frisch's experiments did not explain why bees showed interest in deeply red flowers, such as red poppies (*Papaver rhoeas*). No-one could

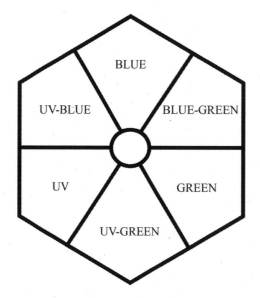

Colour wheel for bees: In the 1990s, German bee scientist Lars Chittka designed a colour opponency system for bees and other insects that takes into account their lack of red vision and their ability to see ultraviolet. Colour opponency was first theorized by physiologist Ewald Hering for human beings. (Lars Chittka)

work this out until the 1920s, when another German zoologist, Alfred Kühn, learned that bees sense shorter light wavelengths; ultraviolet is visible to them. It was known, from early photographic research, that some flowers reflect ultraviolet light. At least a quarter of flowering plants do this.[9] But no-one knew bees saw such colours until Kühn did his own version of von Frisch's experiment. He irradiated small cards with ultraviolet light, which he produced by shining arc lamps through glass prisms, and then tested those cards on bees.[10] Red poppies, it turns out, are deeply red and vibrantly ultraviolet, but no colours in between. Humans and bees are each half-blind to red poppies, for opposite reasons.

In the 1990s, Lars Chittka from London's Queen Mary University worked out a colour opponency system for bees, adapting research by German physiologist Ewald Hering a century earlier. Hering theorized that humans distinguish colours through comparison to their opposites: blue versus yellow, red versus green, black versus white. Chittka adapted this system for bees by pairing off different colours – blue, green, and an in-between colour he called "blue-green" with three colours invisible to human eyes, "ultraviolet," "uv-green," and "uv-blue."[11] There is no way to describe in human terms what these "invisible" colours look like.

"We can't actually imagine the colours that an insect sees," he admits. "No more than I can figure out how you personally perceive blue or green or red."

While it's intriguing that bees see colours we don't, Chittka says there is nothing inherently strange in it. "In an evolutionary sense, it isn't anything necessarily more special than blue or green sensitivity. It just appears special to us because we lack that sensitivity."

Ultraviolet vision is shared by most arthropods, animals with segmented exoskeletons and compound eyes: insects, arachnids, many-legged myriapods such as centipedes, and crustaceans such as crabs, shrimp, and lobsters. Arthropod eyes could see ultraviolet colours, underwater, millions of years before flowers existed on land. This strongly suggests that floral colours are adaptations to pollinating arthropods.

"Pollinators arguably painted the world," Chittka writes in an article for the scientific journal *Annals of Botany*.[12] "Most vegetation," he elaborates, "was just plain green before plants had the 'idea,' so to speak, of employing insects or other animals as vectors."

German poet and polymath Johann Wolfgang von Goethe was the first scholar to notice the artful transition of leafy greenness to colourful petals. In his book *Metamorphoses of Plants*, published in 1790, he described what looked to him like "leaves of the stalk become transformed into petals." He enthused over how living things exhibit "the most varying forms through the modification of one single organ."[13] While learned and gifted, Goethe was not a scientist. However, he strongly believed in looking closely at nature and took pride in his observational skills. "The eye was above all others the organ by which I apprehend the world," he declared in his autobiography.[14] Using his favourite sense, Goethe observed that tulip petals resembled leaves, but with different, more "flowery" colour schemes. More recent forms of analysis confirm Goethe's assertions about leaves as the "archetype" for petals and other flower parts.[15]

The basic green of plant leaves is a by-product of light collection. Plants steal energy from sunlight to fuel an extraordinary process called "photosynthesis." They "synthesize" their own food from water, taken up through their roots, and carbon dioxide, sucked from the air through tiny pores called "stomata." Specialized organelles (organ-like parts in cells) called "chloroplasts" split these molecules and convert them to energy-storing carbohydrates. Leaves gather energy for this operation with light-sensitive chemicals called "pigments," which absorb red and blue wavelengths, but reject green, the colour we see.

Most land plants are a similar waxy green, but aquatic flora, called algae, come in many colours. Algae are not strictly plants, although they share ancestry with land plants. Algae range from single-celled protists to huge, leafy-looking masses comparable in scale to trees. The pigments they use to photosynthesize reflect (and absorb) various different colours. There are red algae, yellow algae, brown algae, and even pink algae, along with green algae, which land plants evolved from. Did land plants absolutely have to be green? Not necessarily. Some botanists think red-leafed plants could have dominated the land, but for some bad evolutionary breaks.[16] Sometimes green-leafed plants turn red. This happens every fall; leaves change colour as the green-reflecting pigment chlorophyll breaks down, revealing other colours.

"Even today's plants that do not have flowers have the same kinds of pigments," says Chittka. "They're in the leaves, they're used for various processes, such as protection from herbivores or incident light and so on. You just need to bring them to the fore to generate flower colours and subtract, to some extent, the chlorophyl from them to bring them out. So the plants already had such pigments. They just needed to accumulate them in the flowers." The colours and patterns they developed, he explains, signal pollinators. "Plants needed to find ways to generate signals to these pollinators."

Chittka clarifies that plants do not, to anyone's knowledge, have ideas, strategies, or thoughts of any kind. They simply respond to evolutionary pressures. But if plants don't exactly "think" about bees, I ask (wondering if it's a silly question), do bees think about flowers? After a momentary pause, Chittka mentions experiments in the 1950s by Martin Lindauer, a former pupil of Karl von Frisch. Lindauer apparently "overheard" late-night conversations among honeybees.

"He sort of peered into beehives and found some bees would display these dances in the middle of the night, which of course is entirely outside the normal foraging process." Normally, honeybees dance in the daytime, since their movements communicate distance and direction to flowers, based on the sun's position. "There's no point in doing that in the middle of the night."

Nonetheless, Lindauer found bees performing their dances long after dark. When decoded, these dances gave the correct positions of flowers.

"We have no idea what these dances' significance is," says Chittka. "It's my interpretation that there might be a kind of offline thinking about these locations. So that's one kind of insight that's interesting, in that regard – whether they're thinking about flowers."

As someone who's spent his career watching bees solve problems and process information, Chittka exhibits a certain respect for their tiny brains, which he describes as "exquisitely miniaturized bio-computers."[17]

While simpler than human brains, bee brains are still complex enough to boggle researchers.

"If they were *simple*, we would understand them by now, and we're a very long way from that."

Eavesdropping on Ultraviolet Signals

It might be a stretch to say Canadian biologist Daniel Hanley studies how bees think about flowers, but he is certainly interested in how bees, as well as birds, respond to colours and patterns as signals. A "signal" in nature, he explains, means something specific: there is a sender and a receiver. Even an unconscious sender, such as a flower, is legitimately signalling if it gets a message across.

"In the case of the flower it might be, 'Here is my pollen,' or, 'Here is my nectar reward,'" says Hanley. "It has to be able to be received by the intended recipient – maybe a bee, maybe different kinds of pollinators. They have to receive that information and understand what it means and behave in the right way. If all those things happen, then it can be considered a signal."

For human researchers to perceive ultraviolet "signals" from flower petals, they need cameras with special filters. In ultraviolet photography, flowers seem otherworldly and psychedelic, like they're being viewed under blacklight in nightclubs. The "trippiness" of such images results from false colours used to depict hues that remain imaginary for us. Assembling such pictures involves three monochromatic images, each filtered for one bee colour, layered together.

"We have a two-dimensional image that makes sense to us," explains Hanley, who studied visual art prior to becoming a scientist. "But independent of that, the way it would be perceived by the bee is entirely different. There are other things that go on in a bee's eye that are totally different from us."

Like Chittka, Hanley says ultraviolet colours are not necessarily special, but because Earth's atmosphere blocks so much UV light, ultraviolet colours are rare on Earth's surface. Flowers "use" the rarity of ultraviolet colours for different messaging than so-called "visible" colours. Ultraviolet "nectar guides" send signals to pollinators, based on where ultraviolet is not.

"The interesting thing is that those nectar guides are where the UV is missing, not where it is present," says Hanley. "UV is strongest on the edges of petals where it's bright and then at the centre it's usually UV-dark."[18]

These contrasts turn out to be valuable for helping insects navigate flowers. Jana Vamosi, a botanist at the University of Calgary, studied ultraviolet messaging in yellow monkey flowers (*Mimulus guttatus*). This spotted flower reminds some people of a theatre mask, while others see a monkey's face. Spots on its petals paint a trail leading to the flower's nectary and reproductive parts. A peek into the ultraviolet spectrum unmasked more surprises in the flower's coloration for Vamosi. She found ultraviolet patterns that looked like additional guides. The markings not only led bumblebees to nectar and pollen, they also helped the bees position themselves on petals. When Vamosi coated flowers with sunscreen to inhibit UV reflectance, some bees landed facing the wrong direction. Confused bumblebees left altered flowers unrewarded. Afterward, they were less willing to return.[19]

In 2019, scientists performed an experiment very much like Vamosi's, where they daubed sunscreen on the petals of flowers in West Africa to block UV light – some partially, others fully. Bees started to abandon the sunscreen-painted flowers. Interestingly, flies kept coming back.[20]

Most days, flowers don't get visits from scientists with suntan lotion. However, plants around the world might have been part of an unplanned experiment decades in the making, which changed the UV colouring of some flowers. Research out of Clemson University in South Carolina revealed that commercial chemicals might have made flowers less UV-reflective. In the 1970s, scientists discovered atmospheric pollution was coming from a can. In those days, chlorofluorocarbons (CFCs) were widely used as refrigerants, solvents, chemical agents for making poly-mers, and propellants for aerosol sprays. Unfortunately, these chemicals also catalyzed the breakdown of ozone (O_3) in Earth's upper atmosphere. There, a thin layer of ozone molecules blocks large amounts of the sun's ultraviolet light. While ultraviolet might be just another colour to insects, too much of this energetic light can damage cells. The loss of Earth's ozone layer was potentially devastating for life on the planet.

A global treaty known as the Montreal Protocol was drafted in 1987, banning CFCs worldwide. The ban seems to have worked. The ozone layer is slowly repairing itself. However, some plants show signs of long-term effects from missing ozone in the upper atmosphere. During the de-cades when more UV than usual was reaching plants, certain flowers went "darker" in the UV spectrum, protecting themselves with pigments that absorbed, rather than reflected, UV light (like human skin does by tan-ning). This was especially true in bowl-shaped flowers with very exposed anthers, such as cinquefoils and other species in the rose family. Such flowers sent less clear signals in the UV spectrum, the US study showed.[21]

That effect is not universal for all plants. Flowers with less open shapes are less vulnerable. Also, it remains to be seen how flowers that were affected will respond as ozone holes repair themselves. However, it's worth noting that while pollinators paint the world, in other ways, so can humans, without intending to.

CHAPTER 3

When Bees Are Not Bees and Flowers Are Not Sweet

That Was No Bee

When you see a bumblebee, it's not always a bumblebee. Sometimes it might be a fly. I witnessed one such oddity turn up in a friend's garden. It was stout-bodied and fuzzy, and if it had flown away just then, I would have thought, "Hmm, a bumblebee," and forgotten about it. But since this flower visitor was in no rush to leave, I had time to take in its round, bulging eyes and the akimbo slant of its wings – features that belong to flies, not bees. This six-legged disguise artist was the Narcissus bulb fly (*Merodon equestrisi*), a renowned bumblebee mimic. It uses this type of trickery for self-protection. Bumblebees are feared for their stings, and their bright-coloured bands broadcast that threat. Narcissus bulb flies don't sting, but they can make predators think twice about eating them, if they look like creatures capable of stinging. When harmless species resemble harmful ones to scare off enemies it's called "Batesian mimicry," named for British naturalist Henry Walter Bates. Batesian mimicry happens in different fly families such as robber flies (Asilidae), botflies (Oestridae), and bee flies (Bombyliidae). Six thousand or so species in the family Syrphidae, including the Narcissus bulb fly, use Batesian mimicry.

Syrphid flies are known colloquially as "hoverflies" because these manoeuvrable insects are known to hover in place like helicopters. Syrphid flies often do their hovering act around flowers, which they visit to feed on pollen and nectar. For this reason, they are also called "flower flies." The deceptive powers of syrphid flies range from near-perfect bee (or wasp) mimicry to slightly off-target imitations that aren't great, but probably good enough. Less precise disguise artists are known as "imperfect mimics." For instance, the common drone fly (*Eristalis tenax*) doesn't so

Not a bee: The Narcissus bulb fly (*Merodon equestrisi*) is renowned for its convincing bumblebee mimicry. This brand of deception is called "Batesian mimicry," which is when harmless species resemble harmful ones to scare off predators. Unlike bumble-bees, these flies can't sting; they do, however, pollinate flowers. (Stephen Humphrey)

much resemble a bee as it looks like a fly hand-painted with yellow and black stripes. Less precise mimicry works well enough for smaller flies, since predators overlook them much of the time, anyway.[1] Their imperfect deceptions even fool humans at times. A number of supposed bee photos in newspapers, magazines, and books end up being drone flies. The 2004 cover shot for the science textbook *Bees of the World* features a drone fly, not a bee.[2]

Fly researcher Jeff Skevington keeps a personal collection of these interspecies publishing gaffes. He found one such fail in his son's school-book, where a math problem about bees was illustrated with a hoverfly photo. Errors of this sort sometimes anger bee experts, but Skevington sounds more amused than anything.

"It's always fun," he notes cheerfully.

Close enough: Some species, like this common drone fly (*Eristalis tenax*), are less exact copies of what they imitate. These flies look "sort of" like bees, but their "imperfect mimicry" is probably good enough, since their small size makes predators less interested in them. However, such approximations can sometimes even fool humans. (Stephen Humphrey)

Skevington oversees an impressive number of pinned fly and insect specimens in the Canadian National Collection of Insects, Arachnids, and Nematodes in Ottawa, Ontario. The collection is housed in the K.W. Neatby Building, a heritage structure known for blending classical and modern architecture. Its foundations are sturdy enough to hold metal cabinets filled with the National Collection's 17 million specimens.

"It was used for file storage for a long time," Skevington explains. "I don't know that there are many buildings in Ottawa that could support the weight of the collection."

However, this sturdy building seems a bit space-challenged. Blocky cabinets, filled with dead bugs, spill out of rooms into hallways. In one hallway, Skevington comes to a sudden stop, eyes glued to a section of ceiling, thinking for a moment he saw water dripping. It's a tense few seconds. Water damage can ruin collections.

"It's always a worry," he confirms. "I would say the only thing I lose sleep over with the collection is worrying about fire or water." When Skevington was a graduate student at the University of Guelph, water pipes burst, destroying a roomful of specimens. "They lost everything," he recalls.

The National Collection contains around 230,000 pinned and preserved syrphid flies. They are colourful and prettily patterned, like fashionable pins in a jeweller's display cabinet. If houseflies (*Musca domestica*) are shabbily common, flower flies are artisanal. It often takes a jeweller's eye to tell the difference between insect species. Skevington's work as a taxonomist requires specialized seeing, where small details delineate one species from another. Syrphid flies vary in appearance, but most syrphid species have an extra line, like a pencil mark, through roughly the middle of each wing. This feature, called a "spurious vein," takes viewing under a powerful lens to spot. Taxonomists engage in this fiddly, exacting work because in the life sciences, researchers want to know precisely what they're looking at.

"It's a foundation science, so it serves all the other sciences," Skevington says. "The better the taxonomy is, the better the comparisons can be, and the better those analyses can be."

Even when decorated with similar colours and patterns, bees and flies have striking physical differences. Bees have four diaphanous-looking wings, hooked together in pairs. Their eyes are sleek ellipses that resemble dark sunglasses. Flies have bulging, hemispherical eyes and just two wings, plus two stunted structures called "halteres," which help them stabilize in flight. One thing flies and bees both share is their shape-changing life cycle. Several insect orders, including those of butterflies (Lepidoptera), bees (Hymenoptera), and flies (Diptera), are holometabolous; they undergo complete physical transformation from larval youngsters to winged adults. Bees and flies go through similar stages from egg to adult, but the kinds of lives they lead through these stages are very different.

A bee hatches from a tiny oblong egg that grows into a white-coloured, grub-like larva with one job: to consume carbohydrates from flower nectar and protein from pollen. Bee larvae stay put, sedately feeding until it is time for them to spin cocoons and transform into adults. Flies also begin as eggs, which hatch into larvae (nicknamed "maggots"), and later

Larval predators: While nearly all adult syrphid flies feed on pollen, nectar, and honey-dew, larvae from different syrphid species forage throughout the food chain. Some are scavengers; others feed on sewage. Many are predators. These syrphid larvae (*Parasyrphus melanderi*) prey on leaf beetle grubs. (NCalBeetleGuy via Creative Commons)

morph into adults. But their active lives start right away. They fend, forage, and sometimes hunt for themselves. What these intrepid larvae eat varies hugely from one fly species to another. The diets of syrphid fly larvae especially vary. While adult syrphids eat the same staples of pollen, nectar, and honeydew, the diets of their larvae range all over the food chain.

"They have virtually every ecological role that you can imagine a larva might have," Skevington enthuses. "They're really, really diverse. Syrphids are really weird that way."

Larvae from some syrphid species feed on pollen, others dine on tulip bulbs, and still others scavenge on rotting plants and animals. About a third of syrphid larvae are predators. Larvae from one syrphid species in Indonesia forage in pitcher plants, poaching prey from the insect-devouring plants. Others invade ant nests to devour ant larvae. Some syrphid larvae gang up on beetle grubs, or hunt soft-bodied insects such as aphids. Others filter feed on bacteria while snorkelling through sewage. However, once they become adults, the majority of syrphids feed on pollen and nectar from flowers, spreading pollen as they forage.

Pollination Habits of Flies

The impact of flies as pollinators is not small. In 2016, Australian scientist Romina Rader and several colleagues tried to quantify non-bee contributions to crop pollination. According to their research, flies account for 39 per cent of agricultural pollination by insects.[3]

"No-one's come up with a figure for syrphids, but they must be at least half of that," Skevington thinks. "In the natural world it's probably higher."

Skevington sees advantages in certain un-beelike habits of flies, such as long-distance flying. "On average, flies will go farther between plants and that allows for more genetic diversity in pollination," he says. Also, flies return more times to flowers they visit, he adds. "They may not be as effective on a one-time visit as some bees, but because they go more often, they're more effective."

Frequent pollination trips might especially be good for certain fruits, such as strawberries. Strawberries are technically "aggregate fruits," which makes them several fruits in one. Tiny fruits the size of pinheads, called "achenes," are embedded in bright red, pulpy vessels. With patience, you could count up to five hundred little bumps on a single strawberry. Each one is a seed-bearing fruit. This aggregation of mini-fruits originates from one small flower with a complicated cluster of female organs, or "carpels," at its centre. The carpels are encircled by twenty to thirty-five male organs, or "stamens," topped with pollen-making anthers. In such crowded flowers, anthers sometimes drop pollen on carpels, fertilizing their flower's own stigmas. Little accidents like this still produce fruits, but not the best ones. Better fruits require cross-pollination. For strawberries, that's no small job. To cross-pollinate even just one flower, pollen has to sprinkle dozens of stigmas.

"Each little facet on a strawberry is a pollination event," Skevington says. "To get the full strawberry with all those pieces pollinated, you have to have multiple visits by flies." A UK experiment put flies to the test with strawberry flowers. Scientists at the University of London released two

Many fruits in one: Strawberries are "aggregate fruits," which are several fruits in one. They embed numerous small yellowish fruits the size of pinheads, called "achenes," in a bright red, pulpy vessel. The strawberry's true fruits are produced by up to five hundred ovaries in a small white flower. Each of the flower's female organs needs pollination. (Henry G. Gilbert Nursery and Seed Trade Catalog Collection)

species of syrphid flies into flight cages with flowering strawberry plants. Pollination by the flies bumped up yields by more than 70 per cent and doubled the amount of marketable strawberries.[4]

Skevington found it difficult at first convincing other scientists that flies were good pollinators. Skevington recalls being "grilled" by a grant panel about whether his fly work merited funds for pollination research. Some questioned whether flies actually pollinated, or just appeared to.

"There were comments like, 'You know, well, flies aren't really pollinators. They just go to flowers. And you have no evidence to show that these things are important pollinators.'"

Luckily, Skevington had the opportunity to gather evidence about flies and what they do in flowers as part of a Canada-wide project to study pollination. In 2008, the Natural Sciences and Engineering Research Council (NSERC) of Canada chose to fund a sweeping five-year science project called the Canadian Pollination Initiative, or CANPOLIN. The project's ambition was to research pollination in as many ways as possible. CANPOLIN ultimately decided to bring Skevington, and fellow fly researcher Steve Marshall, on board.

"It was good forethought to not just make it all about bees," he says. "And it really gave us the foothold needed to actually start some work on something other than bee pollination."

Skevington and others in his field have been surprised not just by the pollinating habits of flies, but by which plants they pollinate. For instance, syrphids nicknamed "sedgesitters" pollinate grasses and sedges, which typically spread pollen by wind. Experts also thought pine trees were just wind-pollinated. However, another syrphid species, the yellow-cheeked conifer fly (*Dasysyrphus lotus*), appears to pollinate pines.[5]

"I find them very, very commonly on conifer flowers," says Skevington. He reports seeing these flies "picking up massive quantities of pollen and transferring it around as they're moving, carrying it as well as eating it."

Flower-Like Cones

Pine cones are not strictly flowers. Like other conifers, pines have male cones with pollen and females with ovules, but no floral parts, such as petals. However, one lineage of ancient, tropical conifers has flower-like features. Cycads evolved 280 million years ago. They dodged the Permian extinction, and out-survived dinosaurs. Cycads have long fronds similar to palm leaves, but are not related to palms, which produce flowers and fruit. Cycads have huge upright cones growing from their centres. Their female cones generate large, bright-coloured seeds that contain cycasin, a potent poison.

At first, botanists believed cycads exchanged all their pollen by wind. But cycads turned out to have insect pollinators, and crudely flower-like parts where insects could land.[6] At their bases, cycad cones have petal-like structures called "bracts." These bracts are not colourful or pretty like flower petals, but they're functional landing spots for pollen-eating thrips, weevils, and beetles — which have a long history as pollinators.

Flowers as Beetle Motels

Beetles have existed for almost 300 million years, dating back to the Carboniferous. There is ancient evidence of them pollinating cycads,[7] and they might also have been the first insects to pollinate flowering plants. A "tumbling flower beetle," encased in amber, might be the oldest proof of insect pollination.[8] There are presently more than 400,000 species of beetle in the world. For context, that's 40 per cent of all insects and 25 per cent of all animals. With so many species, beetles occupy numerous niches. Some are predators, others scavengers. Some are pollen-feeders; others are plant predators. Some are notorious tree killers, such as pine beetles and the emerald ash borer. A lot of beetles like flowers, and their reasons for that are various. Once, I peered into a woodland sunflower and saw two black-and-red blister beetles (*Nemognatha nemorensis*) engaged in sexual congress. The coupling beetles were messy with pollen.

"Yeah, they do that a lot," says Peter Bernhardt, a biologist at the University of Missouri. "I refer to beetle-pollinated flowers as 'motel flowers.'"

Bernhardt is curious about unusual plant-pollinator relationships. Pollinators he has studied include wasps, small Hawaiian birds called "honey creepers" which pollinate lobelias, and beetles. Beetles are so widespread as pollinators, says Bernhardt, it's difficult to nail down just one type of "beetle flower."

"You have to realize that there is no such thing as *the* beetle flower," he explains. "Beetle pollination spreads over several families and in fact different superfamilies of beetles. It's very complex."[9]

Beetles adapt to different flowers in various ways. Some species have spongy mouthparts for sipping nectar from bowl-shaped blossoms, while "chewers and crunchers," such as blister beetles, ravage petals and other flower parts while they pollinate. Plants that co-evolved with beetles are built for such punishment. Magnolias have been around long enough to have fossils identical to their contemporary form. These primordial flowers have stamens like pointed sticks and their carpels are massed into shapes like dragon's eggs. Their simple, cream-coloured petals (called "tepals") are thick, leathery, and tough enough to take over-excited beetle chewing.

Bees, on the other hand, show little interest in magnolias. They buzz right past these dull-coloured, nectarless flowers. A magnolia's odour is nothing like the sweet smell of "bee flowers." Some people compare its bouquet to dirty gym socks. Magnolias evolved before there were bees, and never evolved scents or colours to entice them.

"The earliest flowering plant fossils occur during the period where there are no bee fossils, so we can see what's going on there," says Bernhardt. "The flowers of that period are offering things, but they're not in fact attracting bees, because there ain't none."

Early flowers reached out to small, flying creatures already present in the world, such as beetles and flies. They needed sensory triggers that worked for those insects. Bernhardt references *umwelt*, a German word that roughly means "world view" – how living creatures perceive the world.

"*Umwelt* means the range of senses and what an animal perceives," he explains. Beetles "understand" flowers differently from humans, or bees. Their sense of sight is not all that great, and many beetles are nocturnal. They react largely to odours, but they aren't necessarily sniffing for sugar. Magnolias have a subtly "unpleasant" odour, but other flowers produce even nastier smells (according to human noses). Another ancient flower, *Austrobaileya*, is the last species from possibly the oldest flower dynasty. Its yellowish-green petals have bruised-looking purple spots, and it reeks like rotting fish. Instead of smelling sweet, early flowers smelled rotten to entice carrion feeders.[10]

Some flowers still exploit beetles and other carrion insects with morbid trickery, especially in habitats where bees are scarce, such as the understories of Indonesian jungles. The Sumatran corpse plant, one of the largest and arguably worst-smelling flowering plants, has little flowers clustered in the towering, yellowish column known as its "spadix." This structure broadcasts an overpowering, deathly smell, which grows more pungent toward evening, when carrion beetles and flesh flies are out. *Satyrium pumilum*, a desert-blooming orchid in South Africa, has petals with the marbled look of rare meat. The orchid's most outward part, the labellum (or "lip"), is deep red and glistens like blood. Sarcophagid flesh flies are driven by its deathly scent to lay eggs inside it. However, because the flower contains no rotting meat, the fly's larvae starve and die after hatching.[11] Flowers adapt to the senses (and expectations) of their pollinators in many ways, but not always in ways that benefit the pollinators.

The Dishonesty of Orchids

Orchids play an assortment of dirty tricks on pollinators. They are one of the most diverse flower families, and their modes of deceit are strikingly diverse. Close to half the orchid family's (Orchidaceae) 25,000 species are fertilized through some form of subterfuge. Not all their floral trickery relies on corpse appeal. Some orchids deceive with sweeter deceptions, such as promising nectar they don't have.

Many straight-dealing orchid species reward pollinators with nectar. However, many species do not, and pretend they do. Eighteenth-century German botanist Christian Konrad Sprengel branded such flowers *scheinsaftblumen*, or "flowers with sham nectar."[12] These floral cheapskates mimic the colour, scent, and appearance of "honest," rewarding orchids. They even hide in plain sight among similar-looking cousins, so bees have no easy way to tell which orchids have nectar and which ones don't. Other species deceive with difference. They produce multiple "morphs," with different-coloured petals, or give off a range of scents, so pollinators can't figure out which flowers to avoid.

Lady slipper orchids are whimsically beautiful flowers that resemble fancy slippers. Two of their petals dangle like undone straps. When bees enter these enticing but nectar-free flowers, they're blocked from leaving. They are faced with two exits, each one narrow and cramped. Bees too large for these passages must chew through the flower or die trapped and confused. When a bee tries to squeeze through one of these restrictive exits, she is forced into close contact with special, sticky anthers.[13] Once she finally escapes (visibly distressed), she has packets of pollen glued to her, called "pollinia."

One of the strangest orchid deceptions is to lure male bees, wasps, and certain male flies with false sexual invitations. The copper beard orchid (*Calochilus cupreus*), native to southern Australia, imitates the look and pheromone smell of a female scoliid wasp. Excited male scoliids, intoxi-

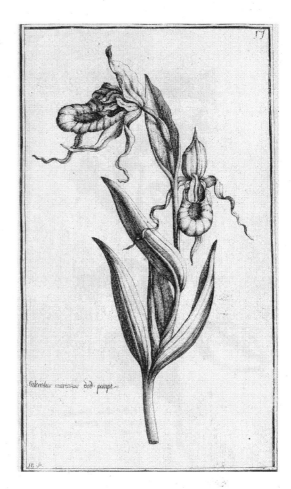

Floral deceiver: Many species of lady slipper orchids deceive their pollinators by promising nectar with sweet smells, when in reality they are empty. Once inside the flower, pollinators must break out through narrow exits, where sticky packets of pollen are pressed onto their bodies. (Pierre Joseph Garidel)

cated by false pheromones, have vigorous sex with the flowers. Researchers have found semen on these orchids where male scoliids climaxed.[14]

Not all is fun and games, though. Floral deceptions come at a cost. One cost is small populations. If too much fakery happens in one place, pollinators catch on, so deceptive orchids can only maintain limited numbers. This works against them when things go wrong, ecologically.

The small white lady's-slipper (*Cypripedium candidum*) grows in North American grasslands. This deceptive orchid is listed as threatened where it hasn't already disappeared. The flower finds it hard to hold on as agriculture, urbanization, and other threats fragment its range. The copper beard orchid, already rare, is critically threatened in Australia, where bushfires increasingly tear through its habitat. Sometimes orchids are threatened by too much human interest. Bernhardt witnessed an assemblage of lady's tress orchids (*Spiranthes spiralis*) over-harvested for traditional medicine in China.

"We lost one of our populations to the herb pickers," he says. "Over a hundred orchids dug up."

When one orchid species disappears, other species potentially follow, especially deceptive orchids, which depend on "magnet" species to augment their deceits with at least occasional truth.[15] Flowers with "sham nectar" have trouble keeping pollinators interested without rewarding neighbours to sweeten the deal once in a while. Pollinators can't survive on promises alone.

"If habitat destruction removes plants that normally feed the bees, even if the orchids are left, they're not going to get pollinated," says Bernhardt. "That is a big problem."

While nature is full of ingenious adaptations, advantages can become liabilities when conditions change, especially when they change quickly.

CHAPTER 4

Floral Darwinisms

Darwin's Orchid Anxiety

In a letter dated 1 October 1861, Charles Darwin wrote to his friend and mentor, geologist Charles Lyell, "I am very poorly today and very stupid and hate everybody and everything. One lives only to make blunders."[1] Darwin was prone to anxious, self-critical thoughts. In 1997, two doctors diagnosed him posthumously with panic disorder in the *Journal of the American Medical Association*.[2] In his letter to Lyell, Darwin described the source of his anxiety as "a little Book I am going to write ... on orchids." He added, "Today I hate them worse than everything."

Although Darwin's orchid opus got less attention and sold fewer copies than his more famous book, *On the Origin of Species by Means of Natural Selection, or the Preservation of Favoured Races in the Struggle for Life*, it has had lasting influence on botanists. Unlike its world-famous predecessor, the orchid book narrowed its focus to one family of flowers – not that its title was any more brief. Darwin entitled his flower-focused opus *On the Various Contrivances by Which British and Foreign Orchids Are Fertilised by Insects, and on the Good Effects of Intercrossing*. The title's Victorian wordiness is not simply florid; it's a granular description of what Darwin fretted over in his orchid research. He wanted to understand the various physical "contrivances" orchids used to achieve "intercrossing," when pollen is shared between two parent flowers.

Darwin performed meticulous experiments, dissecting flowers to see how their living machinery worked. He tried to match up insect and flower shapes like puzzle pieces. He rubbed dead bees across floral parts to see how their bodies made contact. He got in on the act of pollination himself, using pencils and paintbrushes to hand-pollinate flowers. Darwin

Unusual moth for an unusual flower: Predictions made by Charles Darwin and his colleague Alfred Russel Wallace came true in 1903 when a sphinx moth with an exceptionally long proboscis (tongue) was discovered in Madagascar. The moth was a perfect match for the flower it pollinated, the Madagascar star orchid. (Thomas William Wood)

credited orchids with "endless diversities of structure ... for gaining the very same end, namely, the fertilization of one flower by pollen from another plant."[3]

In 1862, an odd-looking white orchid was delivered to Darwin from Madagascar. The plant was a large night-blooming flower that would later be named the Madagascar star orchid (*Angraecum sesquipedale*). The flower had five long, pointed petals, like a Christmas tree star, and an extremely long, tapering tube called a "spur." The spur is the location for nectar in certain flowers, such as orchids. This particular orchid's spur was 11 inches (28 centimetres) long. It was hard to conceive what pollinator could reach it.[4]

Luckily, Darwin's deductive imagination did not fail him. After examining the flower and trying to fertilize it himself, Darwin wrote, "In Madagascar, there must be moths with probosces capable of extension to a length of between ten and eleven inches."[5] By "probosces," Darwin meant the plural of "proboscis," an insect's specialized tongue. The proboscis is a fleshy mouthpart used for licking, but simply calling it a tongue is like just saying an elephant has a nose. The proboscis is part appendage and part drinking straw. The insect Darwin envisioned would have an impressive tongue indeed, able to reach almost thirty centimetres.

In 1903, twenty-one years after Darwin died, a species of sphinx moth, *Xanthopan morganii*, was discovered in Madagascar. As Darwin predicted, the moth had an abnormally long proboscis, capable of reaching the star orchid's deep nectary.[6] However, the insect was nicknamed "Wallace's sphinx moth" after Darwin's fellow naturalist, Alfred Russel Wallace. In fairness, Wallace refined Darwin's prediction with a more specific one about what type of moth pollinated the flower. Nonetheless, this moth's discovery is often cited as powerful proof of Darwin's ideas.

While in some ways Wallace was Darwin's competitor, he was also one of his public champions. In his 1867 essay "Creation by Law," Wallace defended Darwin's theories about "co-adaptations of organic beings," the idea that organisms adjust and change as they adapt to one another.[7] Wallace used the Madagascar star orchid and its still-undiscovered pollinator to illustrate how, through unconscious natural selection, a moth's proboscis can evolve to fit down a flower's spur with such precision its design looks intentional.

Spencer Barrett, a plant biologist at the University of Toronto, is just as adamant about nature's lack of specific plan or purpose, however elegant or purposeful adaptations, or co-adaptations between species, seem to be. Plants in particular have no way to adapt on purpose. They change in small, unconscious ways, over generations. Changes that succeed get passed on, but not through any reasoned process.

"Nothing does it 'because,'" he insists. "It so happens that natural selection favours genetic variants that can do this or that. Unfortunately, even as scientists, we tend to use evolutionary shorthand and we talk about strategies and give the impression plants are somehow figuring this out and predicting the future. They can't. That's not the way evolution by natural selection works."

"It's Complicated, Man, Plant Sex"

Nature's lack of foresight is keenly demonstrated by things that don't work – or do work, but not efficiently. Flowers adapt in surprising ways to pollinators, but they also sometimes get in their own way. This is an oc-cupational hazard for hermaphrodites, which most flowering plants are. Not only do flowers tend to be two-sexed, but they often have multiple male and female organs. This array of sexual parts has advantages, such as increasing a plant's opportunities to mate with more partners, in more combinations. Two-sexed flowers can also fertilize themselves when they lack other partners. However, such advantages come with hassles. For instance, so many sex organs in one flower can physically obstruct one another.

Both male and female parts in flowers have components that make them lengthy. The female organ which receives pollen, the stigma, has a tall section holding it up, called the "style." Each anther has a sort of stem, called its "filament," so the whole unit, called the "stamen," can reach out to pollinators. But all these floral parts standing tall can get in each other's way. A flower's style might accidentally block pollinators from getting to its anthers. Likewise, long stamens might prevent polli-nators from reaching the stigma. Barrett refers to such snarl-ups as "sex-ual interference."[8]

Some flowers evolved a workaround, called "heterostyly." There are "distylous" species, which produce two near-identical versions of their flower, with one key physical difference. Both so-called "morphs" look alike in terms of their petals' colour and shape, but their styles are two different heights. Other species are "tristylous." Their flowers have three morphs with short, medium, and long styles and correspondingly long, short, and mid-height anthers. Different sexual morphs of the same spe-cies bloom side by side. Their differences manifest when pollinators land on the flowers and make contact in different ways with stigmas and an-thers, because of their different positions. One of Darwin's other plant books, *The Different Forms of Flowers on Plants of the Same Species*, discusses these sexually variable flowers at length. He termed their diversity of mating devices a "most complex marriage arrangement."[9]

"About 75 per cent of that book was about heterostyly," says Barrett, who cites it as a major influence on his own research, which he takes more than a little pride in. "I guess I can say this: I'm the world authority on heterostyly."

One of Barrett's study plants is primroses: pleasantly scented, five-petalled flowers with an eclectic community of pollinators that includes bees, butterflies, beetles, flies, and moths. Primrose flowers bloom together in clusters called "inflorescences." Blossoms in the same inflorescence share one kind of sexual "morph." One cluster might have "pin" flowers, where long styles jut out, dwarfing short stamens. Or they might be "thrum" flowers, with long stamens and short styles.

One of Barrett's diagrams shows abstracted bee bodies and their possible points of contact with anthers and stigmas. Those points are marked by little rectangles on the middle segment, the thorax, or the bee's long hind segment, its abdomen.[10] The chart grades the success of different "sexual morphs," from total sexual interference to none.

"What we're looking at is the geometry of flower-insect contact," Barrett elaborates. He investigates this flower-insect geometry and the intricate back-and-forth between plants and pollinators to understand plant "mating systems," which means, in Barrett's words, "who mates with who and how often."

In pollination, the exchange of pollen means the movement of father genes, since pollen is male. Therefore, Barrett wants to know about plant paternity – not just who mates with whom, but who is the father. Or fathers. Plant paternity is not remotely simple.

"Well, you know, it's complicated, man, plant sex," he says. "Plants are highly promiscuous."

Barrett studies the sexually licentious ways of purple loosestrife (*Lythrum salicaria*),[11] a tristylous flower. When he first came to Toronto, he knew about the plant as a problematic weed. "Purple loosestrife was just going crazy and invading wetlands and everywhere." However, Barrett maintains his interest in purple loosestrife was never about weed control. "I'm studying things because I'm curiosity-driven. I'm a basic scientist and there's nothing wrong with that."

What fascinates Barrett is the flower's three differing lengths of style and stamen. Its parts exchange pollen in baffling combinations.[12] A long-styled mother gets pollen from short- and mid-styled fathers. Meanwhile, short-styled flowers receive pollen from the other two morphs, and so on. To work out these complexities of plant parentage, Barrett uses laboratory tools Darwin never dreamed of, such as gene analysis. "They've revolutionized plant reproductive biology," he says.

His investigations of plant paternity start with collecting seeds from mother plants. These "seed families" are analyzed for "genetic markers,"

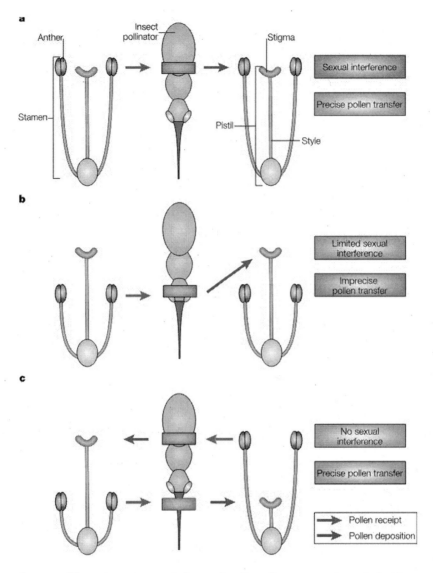

a

Anther

Insect pollinator

Stigma

Stamen

Pistil

Style

Sexual interference

Precise pollen transfer

b

Limited sexual interference

Imprecise pollen transfer

c

No sexual interference

Precise pollen transfer

Pollen receipt

Pollen deposition

Geometry of flower-insect contact: As hermaphrodites, flowers sometimes deal with "sexual interference," during which their own male and female parts get in each other's way. The solution for some flowers is having their sex organs at different heights. In such flowers, the female's style is taller than the male part (the "stamen"), or vice versa. Flowers that are "polystylous" vary these different "morphs" from flower to flower, within their own species. This gives their anthers (which release pollen) and stigmas (which receive pollen) more chances to make contact with pollinator bodies. (Spencer Barrett) which are familiar, recurring gene combinations that stand out like sign-posts on DNA strands. Barrett uses these markers to trace plant parentage and learn how flowers were fertilized.

"With genetic markers, you actually estimate for those seeds, for a given plant, how much of the seed comes from self-fertilization, how much comes from cross-fertilization," Barrett explains. "That's a very different thing than just looking at the way bees forage."

It was Darwin who first noticed that heterostylous flowers are less likely to self-pollinate because their anthers and stigmas are too awkwardly positioned to exchange pollen. In one sense, this is a genetic win, since less self-pollination means more gene-sharing. On the other hand, heterostylous plants have fewer mating opportunities because flowers can't mate with their own morph. Morphs must mate with their opposites, which cuts mating chances in half for distylous flowers. By the same math, tristylous plants lose a third of their mating chances.

Heterostyly isn't the only polysexual solution for plants, though. Other flowers limit self-interference through "enantiostyly." In that system, female parts either swing left or swing right to make room for pollinators. There is also "flexistyly," where flowers switch sexual roles throughout the day — as seen in *Alpinia zerumbet*, a tropical ginger in China. Half its flowers are male in the morning and female by afternoon, while the other half are the opposite. Styles on such flowers stand up for part of the day and then drop down, to let stamens have a turn.

Buzz Pollinators and Floral Burglars

Not all plants necessarily take a more-is-better approach. Some opt for selectiveness. They reduce their pool of pollinators by making themselves harder to pollinate. Blueberry shrubs have bell-shaped, whitish flowers tinted a faint violet blue. These blossoms grow upside-down, but there is limited chance of their pollen dribbling out. Their anthers hold on tight. Most anthers dispense pollen through longish slits, but blueberry flowers have "poricidal anthers," with small, restrictive openings. These anthers only give up their pollen when certain bees (or flies) buzz vigorously to shake it out.

Bumblebees are highly capable at "buzz pollination." They have mastered the trick of buzzing without moving their wings. When a bumblebee encounters a blueberry flower, she executes an impressive upside-down landing, then grasps its stamens with her pincer-like mouthparts, called "mandibles." Her next trick requires the special mechanics of her body. Like all insects, she has three body segments (the word "insect" is a shortening of "in sections"). Her six legs and four wings attach to the middle segment, her thorax. As an invertebrate, she has her skeleton on the outside and her muscles on the inside, the opposite of vertebrates like us, who hook our muscles to internal skeletons. Her exoskeleton is composed of chitin, the same tissue as our fingernails. This tough yet flexible material distends when her muscles pull back and forth, moving incredibly fast. We hear those muscles buzzing inside her thorax when she takes flight. As she clings to a blueberry flower, she makes the same buzzing sound while her wings stay still. When her buzzing hits the right pitch, pollen shakes loose.[13] Smaller bees (or flies) grab onto single anthers when they buzz pollinate.[14]

Some bees aren't capable of buzzing pollen out of flowers, so they resort to breaking and entering. Carpenter bees are visibly similar to bumblebees, but can't buzz pollinate, so they bite their way into blueberry flowers to filch nectar. I once watched a carpenter bee commit such an act of "nectar robbing." I thought I heard an audible snap as the bee bit down. This type of floral smash-and-grab accomplishes little to no pollination, since nectar robbers don't make contact with anthers, and flowers end up with holes in them.

It might not be all bad, though. James Thomson, also at the University of Toronto, found nectar robbing can help plants indirectly. In one instance, he experimented with common toadflax (*Linaria vulgaris*). This time, the nectar thieves were bumblebees, which chewed into the clustered yellow flowers to filch nectar. The bees left holes, which ants then crawled into, to nectar rob, themselves. None of this floral thievery sounds good for the plant, but Thomson wanted to see how things would work out. Without waiting for bumblebees, he and a colleague pulled off their own copycat crime, making holes in flowers with forceps. They watched ants come and go through their makeshift holes. Then they created barriers to stop ants from invading. Instead, beetles broke into ant-free flowers and ate the seeds, an even worse fate for the plants. Ants proved to be a lesser evil for toadflax, since they kept beetles away and at least some seeds survived their attentions.[15]

Bats versus Birds

While Thomson makes regular field trips to observe pollinators in nature, much of his work happens in laboratories. He manipulates and even builds his own flowers to see how plants and pollinators co-adapt, and to learn how relationships between plants and pollinators keep evolving. Some flowers change shape over time, to fit new pollinators. Their new shapes might exclude previous pollinators. One experiment in Thomson's lab, conducted by his postdoctoral student Nathan Muchhala (now a professor at University of Missouri St Louis), followed one such progression. His experiment involved caging bats with flowers. Bats are the second-most-diverse order of mammals after rodents, and many species, such as nectar bats (*Anoura geoffroyi*) in South America, pollinate. Nectar bats forage on flowers similar to those visited by their fellow vertebrate pollinators, hummingbirds. For example, *Aphelandra acanthus*, a fluted yellow blossom in Ecuadoran cloud forests, attracts hummingbirds as well as bats.[16]

When flowers start favouring bat pollination, they widen their openings to better admit bat noses. This makes their corollas, the shapes formed by their petals, less of a snug fit for hummingbird beaks. If star orchids, by their shape, imply that moths will come along with super-long tongues, certain floral forms imply hummingbirds. These flowers have tubular or trumpet-like shapes that look almost like sleeves designed for hummingbird beaks. Such flowers produce copious nectar, which suits the energetic bird's high-sugar diet. In return, hummingbirds transport large quantities of pollen, stuck to their beaks and heads.

But bats, it seems, are even more heroic pollinators. Thomson and Muchhala built floral facsimiles of wood, thermoplastic, and living flower parts, held together by tape. They set bats loose to feed on them, and then hummingbirds for comparison. Bats proved to be more prodigious pollinators by a factor of seven. In nature, a number of flowers have opted for the greater pollinating power of bats. This is not to suggest their "decisions" were consciously reasoned out; things just went that way. Some flowers even became faithful again to hummingbirds, with an equal lack of conscious choice.[17]

Other flowers have switched from bees to hummingbirds, not just once but multiple times. It's happened repeatedly in the flower genus

Beak-friendly flowers: Hummingbird-pollinated plants, such as these scarlet gilia, have tubular, trumpet-shaped flowers that are well-fitted to the beaks of hummingbirds, such as this male broad-tailed hummingbird. (David W. Inouye)

Penstemon — the beardtongues. "Within that genus, there have been many separate evolutionary branches where we've seen a shift from the bee-type flowers to the bird-type flowers," says Thomson. "And it always seems to go in that direction."

When a beardtongue transitions from bees to hummingbirds, its corolla gets narrower and longer. This fits hummingbird beaks better and frustrates bumblebees when they try to climb inside. Thomson and some of his students tinkered with the shape of a bee-adapted flower, the Rocky Mountain beardtongue (*Penstemon strictus*), to see what bumblebees would do with the altered bloom. When Thomson and his students experimentally constricted the flower's corolla, they saw bumblebees get progressively more discouraged.[18]

While such experiments taught him and his colleagues the mechanics of floral transitions, Thomson finds it strange that flowers would switch pollinators at all. "It would seem to be an onerous requirement to fire that one and to hire a new one because your flowers are not adapted to the new one," he says. "We need some kind of rationalization, some kind of explanation that would make this doable."

The answer Thomson settled on was "floral fidelity." Bumblebees are flexible, adventurous, "generalist" foragers. They visit many different flowers, collecting pollen and nectar. This open-ended approach is great for the bees, but faithful flower specialists may suit plants better. Hummingbirds stake claims on particular flower patches, and fiercely defend them from competitors. They also schlep more pollen than bees.

"Birds are fundamentally more efficient pollinators," Thomson says. "We did some modelling to suggest that if bird visits are frequent enough, then you cross a threshold where the bee visits actually start becoming detrimental. The bees become pollen parasites."

How Flowers Hurt Bees

Flowers that don't switch to birds and instead stay open for bee pollination are not necessarily "bee-safe" in all respects. Ralph Cartar at the University of Calgary studies the damage flower petals do to bumblebee wings. Wings are a body part that no bee can do without. They're not able to forage unless they're able to fly. But then, some folk suggest bumblebees shouldn't be able to fly at all. Flight engineers have even disputed their aerodynamic readiness. Of course, bumblebees can and do fly, and do it very well. A bumblebee's top speed is around fifteen metres per second, so a racing bumblebee could clear a football field in six seconds. Cartar says the bumblebee flight mechanism makes no sense for birds or airplanes, but perfect sense for bees.

"Birds shouldn't be able to fly too, when you look at fixed-wing aircraft," he points out. Bumblebee flight works less like an airplane and more like a helicopter, through rapid wing motion, not gliding. "Bumblebees are moving their wings at almost two hundred times a second. They're constantly generating lift, mainly on both upstroke and downstroke. They never soar. They're always moving."

This constant wing movement has a terrific energy cost, and keeps bees hungry for nectar. Bees also risk striking their fast-moving wings against flower petals and leaves. "Petal" comes from the Latin word *petalum*, which means "blade." Over time, leaves and petals chop bits out of bee wings, wearing them down. A bee's wings can get quite ragged over its short life, yet apparently never so bad it can't fly. Even severe damage doesn't ground a bee. Cartar and his students discovered that even when they got scissors and clipped most of a bee's wing off, it still flew.

"It can fly as well as a bee that has the same amount on both sides," says Cartar. "How can it be that a bee's performance is insensitive to having one wing that looks like normal and another wing that's just a little stub?" Equal wing size doesn't matter as much as average wing surface, he thinks. "Shouldn't that just be crazy? I would have thought asymmetry of wing would be the worst thing to have. I just don't get it."

There are performance costs, though. Wing-damaged bees lose lift. They can't carry as much pollen – or nectar, which is especially heavy.

"For each relatively small increment in average wing loss, you have a big cost in terms of what you can carry," says Cartar. "Every 1 per cent wing loss results in about a 4 per cent loss in carrying load. And that's huge."[19]

One thing bumblebees and hummingbirds have in common is the high energy cost of fast-moving wings. Yet the only way they can pursue high-energy food is through their costly mode of flying. When they take flight to forage, failure is not an option for very long. The trope about busy bees starts to make sense.

"I think many bees, but particularly bumblebees, are working all the time," says Cartar. "They're very high energy use per individual. So, if you choose that lifestyle, it can only be subsidized by having a world in which resources are abundant."

Nectar is not zero-cost for plants either. Producing nectar uses up to 37 per cent of a plant's energy budget.[20] The high costs constantly paid by plants and pollinators highlight nature's inefficiency, Cartar thinks. Flowers and bees both work harder than they would need to if their system were better designed.

"I think it's interesting how nature ends up with these solutions that are not necessarily the most efficient way of doing things," he muses. "If you were a planner, you wouldn't allow for bees."

But nature doesn't plan. Nature simply does.

CHAPTER 5

Casting Pollen to the Wind

Windy with Chance of Pollen

The Weather Network's pollen report for Monday, 26 April 2021, announces high amounts of airborne pollen from birch, ash, and boxelder maple. The same is expected for Tuesday and much the same for Wednesday, but with more prevalence of oak pollen. According to Asthma Canada's website, tree pollen should likely peak around late April or May. Pollen from grasses will pick up between May and mid-July. Just when we think pollen season is over, count on another blitz between mid-August and October.

The World Allergy Organization estimates that up to a third of humanity suffers allergic rhinitis (or hay fever), an allergy response to little airborne particles including innumerable spores and pollen grains. Things are even worse for an estimated 300 million people around the world who are stricken with asthma.[1] How allergies function is a large area of study. Immune systems react with inflammation and other unpleasant bodily responses to antigens. Antigens are proteins, peptides, and other normally benign living particles that our bodies mistake for pathogens. Allergic episodes can range from mildly irritating to medically extreme, even deadly in some rare cases.

For allergy season sufferers, the Weather Network adds airborne pollen forecasts to its reports. The network sources its data from Aerobiology Research Laboratories, which has sampling stations across Canada that capture pollen and spores in small metal boxes. These are shipped for analysis to an office space converted to a biology lab in Ottawa. Instead of desk cubicles, there are tables with microscopes. Staff wash up lab equipment along with coffee cups.

"We have a machine which is what jewellers use to clean rings and stuff like that," says Frances Coates, head researcher and chief executive. "It's in the bathroom. That's what we use to clean the rods."

Coates shows me the sampling rods used to collect airborne pollen and spores. The rods are about the size of matchsticks. They are coated with a clear silicon-based gel that particles adhere to. I mentally compare the rods to flower carpels, which make their own sticky substance called "stigma exudate" to trap pollen when it falls on them. Around 12 per cent of plants are wind-pollinated.[2] They don't depend on direct contact with animal pollinators, at least not exclusively. Instead, they are fertilized by airborne pollen.

Not Pretty, but Plenty of Pollen

Pollen grains from pines are easy to spot on a laboratory slide (stained pinkish purple for better viewing). They're on the large side for pollen, and have bulbous protrusions on each side. The two bulges are hollow bladders, which keep the big grains aloft as they surf air currents. Pine pollen travels well. It has been found hundreds of kilometres from its starting point and been collected 600 metres up, by helicopter.

Leafy, deciduous trees such as birch, beech, and oak don't have pollen with elaborate bladders. Their pollen grains are small and light, so they don't need extra features to keep them aloft. Birch pollen, a lumpy sphere with three protruding pores, is a mere twenty-four micrometres across. It is released from catkins – bedraggled-looking, yellowish-green formations that dangle from branches. These are flowers, just not alluring ones. Male catkins hang downward in pollen-spewing clusters. Female catkins stand up, unlike the dangling males, but they are no more attractive.

"[Birch] doesn't have pretty flowers," Coates agrees. "People don't think much of them."

Since these unpretty flowers don't rely on animal pollinators, they dispense with attractive displays. Instead, they count on strong winds blowing through high branches to move their pollen. Male and female birch catkins occupy the same tree, but birches can't fertilize themselves, so they need to trade pollen with other birches. And since birch trees have no animal pollinators making flower-to-flower deliveries, they send out large amounts of airborne pollen. A single birch releases up to five

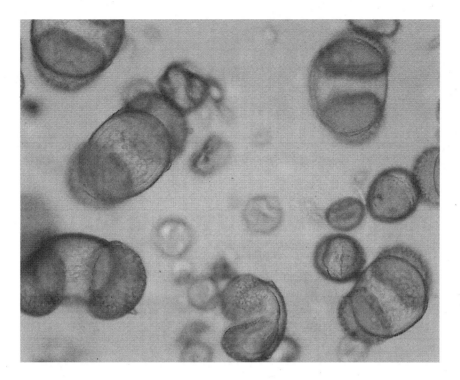

Pine pollen: Pine pollen grains are relatively large for pollen, so they have hollow bladders to help keep them airborne as wind carries them between male and female cones. (Aerobiology Research Laboratories)

million pollen grains. Most of that pollen doesn't reach female catkins. A lot of it gets inhaled by allergy sufferers. Many people's inflamed sinuses are pollinated by birch trees.

Coates clarifies that pollen itself isn't specifically what makes people allergic. "A misconception that a lot of people have is that the pollen is the thing that contains the antigen that people react to," she says. "That's the smallest particle that people inhale, that's what they're most subjected to. All parts of the tree carry the antigen."

People have different pollen (and spore) allergies, so it's helpful to keep tabs on when specific plant particles become airborne. Pollen flow doesn't keep to strict timelines. Changeable weather factors such as El Niño years impact when pollen release is triggered, so no allergy season has a fixed start date. Birch pollen that caused sneezing this May might be blowing around in April if next year is warmer.

"It varies so much," says Coates. "And people need to start their meds two weeks prior to the season, because the antigen is in the air before we see the pollen." There is demand, therefore, to make pollen data predictive. Coates feels that after a couple of decades, her lab has a decent track record of allergen trendspotting.

"We will come very close to being able to tell allergy sufferers/allergists, 'Okay, we think that this is going to be the start of the season.'"

She opens a binder filled with records of nothing but birch pollen, dating back to 1993. There are tables of data, plus summaries for her customer base of allergists, pharmacists, and media.

"We try to forecast a week ahead," says Coates.

Longer, Hotter Pollen Seasons

Her lab's data contributes to scientific papers as well. Coates is listed as co-author on research by Lewis Ziska, a plant physiologist and climate researcher at Columbia University in New York City. One of his studies uses pollen records from across three continents to find out whether climate change makes allergy seasons longer. That paper, published in the *Lancet* medical journal's climate change offshoot, *Lancet Planetary Health*, suggests that as the atmosphere warms, pollen remains airborne longer. Twelve of seventeen locations surveyed showed higher pollen levels, while eleven of these had "significantly extended pollen seasons."[3]

Still, the study cautions, it has only twenty-six years of pollen data to base its predictions on, which is not very much time in the long, slow lives of trees. It is especially tricky to figure out how trees will react to weather changes. Coates, versed in long, patient tree lives, explains how hard it is to find patterns in their years-long cycles, which include sudden spikes in fertility called "mast years."

"They produce a lot of nuts, they produce a lot of pollen," she says about these mysterious bonanza times. "And then they will have a low year."

The reason for mast years and how they work is still largely unknown. So is their frequency, up to a dozen years apart. With such long cycles, two or three decades of data might be too short to decide how climate change affects trees.

"It changes every year, depending on if you have El Niño, La Niña, what kind of winter we had, what kind of spring we had, how much rain there was, temperature, all of that stuff. The trees aren't listening to climate change yet."

But other plants might be. In 2019, Coates's lab provided data to the Canadian Broadcasting Corporation (CBC) for an investigative piece about pollen levels rising year by year in Canadian cities due to climate change. Longer warm periods mean longer growing times and potentially longer pollen seasons.[4] In a recent statement, the World Allergy Organization raised concerns about "climate-related health impacts," including "allergic respiratory conditions" such as asthma.[5]

Some of Ziska's other research suggests pollen seasons for ragweed (*Ambrosia artemisiifolia*), a common allergy culprit, are lengthening by two to four weeks.[6] As a weedy plant, ragweed has a knack for rapid adaptation, and warmer seasons seem to egg it on. Researchers in Europe found ragweed can evolve in response to climate change "within a single generation," growing faster and bigger each year.[7]

Flowers That Forgot Pollinators

Ragweed is part of the aster family, a grouping of plants large enough to break down into numerous subfamilies. Ragweed shares one of these subfamilies with sunflowers. Pollen grains from sunflowers are much too large and heavy for wind to pick up, but a modest summer breeze is enough to trigger the release of ragweed pollen. The plant's flowers are more stunted than showy, but its features are still flowery enough for people to confuse it with goldenrods, another aster relative. Goldenrods are pollinated by insects, which flock to them in fall. Ragweed's shared history with so many insect-pollinated plants points to a past where its predecessors had animal pollinators. At some point, ragweed gave up the relative directness of animal pollination for the chancy inefficiency of wind. This kind of evolutionary backtracking is actually not that unusual. Flowering plants have transitioned to wind pollination an estimated sixty-five times.

Grasses are one group of plants that made this transition. We seldom see grass as a flower. Yet all 12,000 identified grass species are flowering plants. Grasses hail from a lineage of plants that formerly had pollinators. Their plant order, Poales, has species in it with striking flowers, including the bright-red blossoms of summer torch, and others with

Secret flowers: Grasses are
not normally seen as flowering plants, but their seed
heads are actually clusters
of wind-pollinated flowers.
Many food crops, including
wheat, are wind-pollinated.
(Arthur and Fritz Kahn
Collection)

sumptuous fruits, such as pineapples. Yet flowers in the grass family Poaceae are generally so small and unassuming, we notice their leaves more
than their flowers. Grass leaves join their stems underground, so it's
simple to mistake single leaves for whole plants. These leaves are usually called "blades," and they do have glassy teeth to cut with. Tiny silicate
structures called "phytoliths," in grass leaves and other tissues, may have
evolved to discourage plant eaters. Nature answered this cutting defence
with herbivores whose stomachs digest grasses. Even some dinosaurs
were grass grazers. The oldest fossil traces of grass are remnants of their
special silicates found in coprolites, fossilized dung from dinosaurs.[8]
Humans relegate eating grass leaves to ruminants such as cows and goats.
But we heartily feast on the seeds of grasses: corn, rice, and grain species such as oats, barley, and wheat. Half our calories come from these
so-called "cereal grasses."[9] Like those of other plants, grass seeds form in
their flowers, or "seed heads," the feathery parts atop their stems.

The seed head is an inflorescence, a cluster of several small flowers. The flowers are not bright blossoms, but if you look close enough, you can pick out petal-like shapes, yellow anthers (white or purple in some species), and up to three carpels. Some grasses are separately male and female, while others (including wheat) are hermaphrodites with sexually crowded interiors. In Canada, grass pollen is airborne roughly May through June. Commonly allergenic grasses include ryegrass, Johnsongrass, and the familiar lawn variety, Kentucky bluegrass.

Being wind-pollinated may seem like a passive way for plants to mate – just waiting for pollen to blow into them – but grasses may take a more "active" role in catching pollen. Biologist Josef Ackerman and his student Dori McCombe observed how Timothy grasses moved in the wind. They noticed seed heads had a kind of "collector motion" as they swayed back and forth. This action scooped pollen from the air four times more effectively than when they stayed still.[10]

The On-Again/Off-Again Flower

Even if plants have techniques to make wind pollination work for them, why do it in the first place? Why do more than 10 per cent of flowering plants retreat from animal-assisted pollination and let wind do the job? Unless scientists get big enough research grants to build time machines and visit the past, no-one will see first-hand how or why present-day plants transitioned to wind pollination. However, one researcher, David Timerman, found a flower that regularly transitions between wind and insect pollination. *Thalictrum pubescens* is majestically nicknamed "king of the meadow." This white flower in the buttercup family has a crown-like appearance, which perhaps explains its naming. *Thalictrum* flowers are bejewelled with reproductive parts, which stick out in several directions. While it makes no nectar, this flower receives enthusiastic visits from bees and other pollen-seeking insects.

"If you go out into a population when it's in peak bloom, they're absolutely inundated with bees," says Timerman. "The flowers are very, very perfumed. It's incredible how perfumed they are, for what is ostensibly a wind-pollinated species."

Perfumed or not, *Thalictrum* flowers are well-equipped for wind pollination. Their stamens, which jut out like needles from pincushions, are

Flower in transition: King of the meadow (*Thalictrum pubescens*) is a flowering plant that's pollinated by insects and by wind. In technical language, plants such as this are "ambophilous." (Alpsdake via Wikimedia Commons)

easily triggered by wind to release pollen. In technical language, plants like this are "ambophilous." They are potentially both wind-pollinated ("anemophilous") and insect-pollinated ("entomophilous"). There are 190 identified species in the genus *Thalictrum*. Some of them depend more on insect pollinators, while others are more wind-reliant.

"It's a genus in flux, for whatever reason," says Timerman. "There have been independent transitions from animal pollination to wind pollination. And now there's the potential that there are reversions back to animal pollination."

Timerman studies the "biomechanics" of flowers. He investigates their pollination from an engineering perspective. Mostly he's concerned with stamens — anthers and the slim filaments supporting them.

"I study the structure of stamens," he elaborates, "how flexible they are, how thin and long they are, and how they vibrate physically in the wind. That's my shill."

Timerman observed *Thalictrum* closely, both in wind tunnels and outdoors in natural wind, to see how their stamens quivered when moving air hit them. Wind-induced vibrations were what seemed to shake pollen loose. He compares this action to a musician plucking strings.

"There's definitely a music analogy there," he says. "They need to be tuned to specific frequencies. The frequency has to be within a very specific range in order for this mechanism to operate."

For wind to strike the right tune, it has to make stamens vibrate at their "natural frequency," which sets off oscillations powerful enough to shake pollen from anthers.[11] This takes a fair amount of force. When pollen sits on an anther, it's held there by a "boundary layer," an invisible sleeve of air that flows over a surface and slows the velocity of particles to zero. The same physics makes dust stay on tabletops. Because boundary layers flow around anthers, wind alone can't blow pollen off of them.

"If you're a really small pollen grain, you're deeply embedded in the boundary layer because you're so small," he says. "This sets up a challenge for a plant."

Thalictrum's shaking stamens cause pollen grains to breach their anther's boundary layer. In his experiments, Timerman found *Thalictrum* species with stamens that vibrate more easily are most likely to wind-pollinate. While a tendency to quiver makes flowers more inclined to cast pollen to the wind, environmental pressures also nudge them toward wind pollination. When habitats run short on pollinators, plants start to rely more on wind.[12]

Presumably, when pollinators return, variable plants such as *Thalictrum* reach out to them again, but frequent switching takes its toll. Some *Thalictrum* species seem caught between two states – wind-pollinated but still strongly scented, or pollinated by insects but missing features to attract them. When plants transition to wind and away from insects, they stop investing in such qualities as showy petals and nectar rewards. When they transition back, not all their tools for attraction necessarily return.

"It might not be possible to regain all of the characteristics that the lineage had previously," says Timerman. "That would perhaps be my explanation for why you have flowers that appear to be wind-pollinated but don't necessarily function as wind-pollinated flowers ought."

Thalictrum plants seem to be coping with their variable existence for now. But they are a floral oddity.

"There's very few genera like *Thalictrum*," says Timerman. "There are maybe, like two or three others that I can think of where you have all of this variation."

There are not many plants as "evolutionarily labile" as those in the genus *Thalictrum*. While numerous flowering plants have transitioned to wind pollination, not nearly so many have beckoned pollinators back. But in nature, never say never. Certain "pretty" flowers, currently serviced by pollinators, give signs their predecessors were wind-pollinated. Plants in the mulberry family (Moraceae) have transitioned from wind to insect pollination at least twice.[13] Other plants show the potential to transition, especially members of the sedge family (Cyperaceae). In experiments, sedges showed they could develop more flowery features.[14] Even certain wild sedges are showier and more scented than their grassy cousins. Some have even picked up insect pollinators, such as sedgesitting flies (see chapter 3). However, most plants that leave animal pollinators behind seem to have cast their fates, indefinitely, to the wind.

CHAPTER 6

Bee Flowers and Earth Mothers

"Tongues Out" in the Atacama Desert

Laurence Packer, a scientist at York University, shows me the specimen of a bee with a distended-looking head that he collected from the Atacama Desert in Chile. The bee's elongated body stretches the popular notion of what a bee should look like. Also, its origin extends common perceptions of where bees can survive. The Atacama Desert is one of the driest places on Earth. NASA has made use of its near-alien barrenness to simulate Mars in astronaut training. For Packer, the Atacama Desert is a good place to search for undiscovered bees.

"Because I go to deserts, I often find oddball things," he says. "You get more species per square kilometre in semi-arid habitats. You'll get stuff that nobody's ever seen before."

Packer is a "melittologist," which, according to Merriam-Webster, is "an entomologist specializing in the study of bees."[1] Finding and identifying new kinds of bees is not only his profession but his passion. When he can't get research grants, he sometimes funds bee-finding trips himself, for his own enjoyment.

"It's fun," he says. "I get to go to weird places. I get to drive by the Taj Mahal without seeing it, except in the distance, because I'm collecting."

Packer has personally discovered or taken part in describing more than one hundred new bee species. Prominent in his lab is a huge lens on a jointed arm to minutely examine bee bodies. He describes his work like an artistic pursuit.

"I got into this line of business for reasons of aesthetics," he says. "It was the physical beauty of the things that got me into it." Not that he dismisses scientific necessity. "There's a purpose to it. If you want to understand how life has evolved, both through evolutionary time and space, then you've got to know what things are where."

These days a lot of species are identified using gene-mapping techniques such as genetic barcoding. This streamlined method for gene analysis was developed by Paul Hebert at the University of Guelph. It focuses on certain lines of mitochondrial DNA instead of the whole genome. Packer has used this method himself, but a lot of taxonomy still relies on looking carefully for small visible differences under a lens.

"In general, a species is what a good taxonomist says it is," he says. "And then it's up to other people to say, 'No, you're wrong.'"

Each weekday, Packer's lab shares bee pictures on social media, which showcase some of the more exotic-looking species. Photos are assigned to five visually impactful categories: Metallic Monday (shiny bees), Tropical Tuesday (bees from the tropics), Weird Wednesday (like it sounds), Thirsty Thursday (desert-dwelling bees), and Furry Friday (hairy bees). To switch things up, his lab posted a desert bee picture one Tuesday, with the hashtag #TongueOutTuesday, a tag usually attached to tweets with funny pictures of cats and dogs.

"*Xeromelissa rozeni* is a Chilean #bee whose #tongue is over 2X its own body length!" the post enthuses.

The bee's lengthy proboscis is too long to retract, so it folds up and notches into a groove on the underside of her head. Unfolded, the tongue is longer than the rest of the bee. Its exceptional length helps her reach the deep nectaries of desert flowers in the genus *Nolana*.[2] The bee's proportionally long, squished-looking head is adapted for crawling inside these tubular flowers.[3]

"The nectar is really deep," says Packer. "The bees have got to have long tongues to get to it and/or they've got to have long faces to be able to get there."

Even then, it's a tight squeeze for these narrow-bodied bees to reach the flower's nectar. They are forced into close contact with the flower's anthers, first while going in and again when backing out. Both male and female bees from the genus *Xeromelissa* make this cramped flower dive. Females also collect the flower's pollen, which they ferry back to their lairs. The nests of these slim-bodied bees are tight spaces themselves. They're mostly located in hollow twigs and abandoned beetle burrows.

Strange bee: This oddly long-faced bee is *Xeromelissa rozeni*, a solitary bee in Chile's Atacama Desert. This bee uses its lengthy, folding proboscis (tongue) to feed on deep-down nectar from flowers in the genus *Nolana*. (Sheila Dumesh)

Inside her nest, the bee rolls pollen into a ball, lays an egg on top of it, and flies off to collect more. Her eggs will eventually hatch and mature into full-grown bees that will, in turn, forage by themselves in desert flowers to feed their own offspring.[4] Until then, this hard-working single mom is the only adult bee in her tunnel. Her austere, solitary existence paints a different picture from the oft-repeated image of hives buzzing with innumerable bees. Living alone is the rule more than the exception for most kinds of bee. Out of more than 20,000 known species, three-quarters are solitary.

Spreading Cellophane in Dark Tunnels

The genus *Xeromelissa* belongs to the bee family Colletidae, which includes some two thousand species, from all over the world. Colletidae derives from "collectus," which means "concentrated" or "gathered together." Bees from this family are known in plain language as "plasterer bees," "cellophane bees," or "polyester bees." They make their own kind

Ground dweller: This ground-nesting cellophane bee (*Colletes inaequalis*) pokes her head out of the hole she nests in at Toronto's High Park. Three-quarters of all bees are solitary. Many are ground-nesters. (Stephen Humphrey)

of cellophane with secretions from an organ in their abdomens called the Dufour's gland.[5] Using her brush-like tongue tip, called a "glossa," a plasterer bee paints this gauzy substance onto the wall of her tunnel. This cellophane lining keeps moisture, fungus, and pathogens away from her larvae, as they quietly mature in pitch darkness.[6] Species from this group live in twigs or cavities, or nest in the ground. All of them are solitary. None live in hives.

In spring 2019, the first sign of bees I see in my city is not actually bees, but a hole in the ground. I'm with a group of nature enthusiasts on a chilly spring morning in High Park, a 161-hectare green space in Toronto's west end. We're out looking for wild bees, but the bees seem to have stayed in. Undaunted, our guide, graduate student Susan Frye, points out small, circular holes in the ground, a pencil's diameter wide, ringed with dirt. These unassuming burrows are nests for bees from *Colletes*, a genus of Colletidae.

Later that spring, we catch and temporarily detain one of these "miner bees," cooling her down with an ice pack to make the cold-blooded insect too drowsy to fly off for a few minutes. The bee is not exotic, colourful, or very large. Her body length, from head to stinger, is about a dime's diameter.

Some other drizzly Saturday, we find males, likely also from that species. They're smaller than the females, with doll-like proportions. They are torpid, indifferent to rain droplets beading their heads, backs, and eyes. They cling to flowers where they spent the night, since they don't have holes to live in. Male bees don't excavate tunnels, gather pollen, or do work of any kind. They mate when they're able to and shelter where they can. Frye confesses to finding them cute.

Sizing Up Solitary Bees

Bees range in size quite a lot from species to species. *Megachile pluto*, or Wallace's giant bees, are nearly big enough to be small birds, while the very tiny *Perdita minima* measure just two millimetres. But whatever a species' general size, females are usually bigger than males. How much bigger depends. A honeybee queen can be twice as large as honeybee males, or "drones." This queen among bees is certainly not solitary. She is surrounded by 20,000–80,000 much smaller females, called "workers," since around beehives, these little females do all the work. They collect pollen, harvest nectar, build honeycomb, feed larvae, defend the hive, and make sure the queen is groomed and fed. With these jobs covered, the queen concentrates on one task: laying eggs. Each day she deposits over 3,000 eggs in hexagonal wax cells.

I mention all this to help you visualize a solitary bee's life, which no doubt sounds counter-intuitive. But now that you have this picture of a honeybee queen in her teeming hive, I'll ask you to mentally remove all the workers. Now the queen is alone, left to do every job herself. This is a solitary bee's life. She is both queen and worker. The solitary "queen" gathers pollen, builds her nest, and defends it all alone, and she still has to lay eggs. How does this six-legged supermom manage? For starters, less gets done. She will not lay thousands of eggs a day. In her lifetime, she might lay twenty or thirty eggs. Her lifespan is too brief for one-on-one parental care. By the time her young chew out of their cocoons, she will have died. These new bees have no queen and no hivemates, so they, in turn, fend for themselves. The mother bee's parental task is to provision enough food for her family's long, cloistered months as larvae. It's important to find a cozy hole or a warm, dry tunnel for this purpose.

Solitary Living in Bee Condos

Solitary bees sometimes nest in human-made structures: slabs of concrete, gaps in walls, old cars, telephone poles, broken doorbells, even keyholes.[7] Some people build dedicated structures to study solitary bees or just to appreciate them. Sarah Peebles, a musician and installation artist in Toronto, works with artisans to design structures she calls "bee condos." The structure's main part, where bees live, is a panel of wood with tunnels for nesting, and Plexiglas on one side, so observers can look at bees. Sarah's partner, sound designer Rob Cruikshank, invented microphones sensitive enough to pick up the clickings and scratchings of solitary bees as they work. Peebles oversees the making of decorative wooden cabinets (and sometimes elaborate cob structures), which she places in city parks, in conservation areas, and on green roofs, throughout Canada and the United States. These are like solitary bee zoos, except the animals are not confined. They fly in and out as they please. When you open a cabinet's doors, you see solitary bees, or wasps (and hear them, if you put on the headphones provided). If you read the doors' instructions, you will kindly close them again. Nesting bees prefer the dark.

I've filmed and photographed residents of these cabinets while they fashioned found materials into cells and packed them with pollen. Different bees use different materials. I've seen leafcutting bees assemble circular pieces cut from leaves into layered mâché like hand-rolled cigars. Mason bees use mud, tiny pebbles, even chewed-up leaves like cement. These tunnel-nesting bees work without any seeming sense of down or up, casually turning somersaults or hanging upside-down while they work. Bee bodies are specially built for pollen collection. Like the rest of their genus, *Megachile*, leafcutting bees pack pollen under their abdomens, the hindmost of their three segments. There, they have a mass of stiff hairs called a "scopa," which pollen sticks to. When a leafcutting bee returns from foraging, her underside is gilded with pollen. After several foraging trips, she rolls the pollen into a ball, lays an egg on top,

Bee watching: Biologist Susan Frye takes a close look at tiny residents of the "Sonic Solitaries sensory bee cabinet," an observation habitat for solitary bees and wasps that nest in tunnels. Specially built microphones also let viewers listen to the cabinet's dwellers as they work. (Sarah Peebles)

and closes off the cell. Then she heads out to gather more pollen and leaf parts. She repeats this for another few weeks, the rest of her adult life.

From Bug Hunters to Pollen Collectors

Hylaeus or "masked" bees are frequent visitors to Sarah's cabinets. These tiny, tunnel-dwelling cousins of *Colletes* make cellophane to line their webby-looking, diaphanous cells. They look suspiciously like ants that have had their faces daubed with white or pale yellow paint. The

Bees not ants: These nearly hairless solitary bees emerging from their cocoons in a bamboo pole are "masked" (*Hylaeus*) bees. Their ant-like appearance is no coincidence: bees, ants, and wasps are all relatives, in the insect order Hymenoptera. (Rob Cruikshank)

comparison isn't unreasonable, since bees share the insect order Hymenoptera with ants and wasps. It is believed that ants, bees, and wasps diverged from their common ancestor around 120 million years ago. The resemblance between masked bees and ants is easy to spot because their dark bodies are almost hairless – though not completely. One defining trait of bees is "plumose" or "branched" hairs, which look like twiggy branches under microscopes. Masked bees have small quantities of such hairs around their middle segment, the thorax, but not enough to stick a lot of pollen to. They carry pollen in their foregut, or "crop," like the non-digesting stomachs honeybees use to carry nectar.

Wasp bodies have no branched hairs, but they share a number of other traits with bees. For instance, most wasp species are solitary. Out of over 100,000 species of wasp, only sixty-seven have queens with workers.[8] The rest of wasp-kind forage alone, like solitary bees, but instead of pollen, they harvest live insects. Some take prey back to homes in Sarah's bee cabinets. Dried grass spills out of one tunnel in the bee condo at

High Park. A leggy, black-bodied grass-collecting wasp keeps her cache of bright green grasshoppers there. While I watch, she arrives with another victim, impressively larger than herself, paralyzed with her venom. Her intent is not to kill the grasshopper, at least not right away. Though immobilized, it still lives. Being alive keeps it fresh (and helpless) for wasp larvae to feed on. This might sound gruesome, but young wasps need protein and that's how they get it. Bee larvae need protein too, but their protein source is pollen. This pollen diet is another way bees diverge from wasps – other than the wasp subfamily Masarinae, known as "pollen wasps."

No-one can pin down exactly when bees started being bees, but there are clues, such as a 100-million-year-old insect body, preserved in amber, from an extinct hymenopteran species. This ancient insect had pollen grains on its body and some of the branched hairs found on bees, but still exhibited wasp-like physical traits.[9] Some biologists argue the insect was a "stem" species, a missing link between bee and wasp, or perhaps a wasp with a pollen habit. Some scholars even say all bees are just hairy wasps. Bees share their branch of the hymenopteran family tree with many wasp species. They are part of the "superfamily" Apoidea, which includes wasp families such as Crabronidae, the digger wasps.[10]

In one High Park outing, we encounter sand wasps (*Bembix pruinosa*), a species of digger wasp. They're oddly beautiful, with ovular, candy-green eyes. Their spearmint-tinted abdomens are banded with wavy black lines. Like their burrowing bee neighbours, sand wasps are hole-diggers. They burrow into sand, rebury their holes, and somehow find them again after hunting trips. They throw impressive quantities of sand around on a sandy park path. One wasp drags the denuded thorax, legs still attached, of some prey insect from her nest, after her larvae consumed all its soft parts. Female sand wasps are attentive mothers. They lay relatively few eggs and keep bringing home fresh prey, which they've lovingly stung into paralysis.[11]

While wasps don't drag paralyzed humans to their lairs, people still fear the temporary pain of bee and wasp stings (which mostly come from social species, not solitary ones). It's a powerful asymmetric attack, which causes us to live in terror of creatures hundreds of thousands of times smaller than ourselves. While smarting from stings (and hopefully not suffering allergic shock), we may not consider the stinger's original

Mother wasp cleans house: This solitary sand wasp (*Bembix pruinosa*) cleans out her nest, a hole in the sand under an acorn. She removes the denuded thorax of an insect consumed by her larvae. This gruesome provisioning of prey transitioned to pollen provisioning by ground-nesting bees. (Stephen Humphrey)

purpose, which is motherhood. Only female bees, wasps, and some ants have stingers. That appendage started as an egg-laying tool and is still used for that way by many hymenopterans.

Consider Hymenoptera's fourth and most primitive branch, sawflies. As relatives of bees and wasps, they're not flies, but they do have a saw. Sawflies have a curved, spiky part on their abdomens, where other Hymenopterans have stingers. This appendage slices into plant tissues and deposits eggs. That invasive motherly act is called "oviposition." The most primitive wasps, Ichneumonid wasps, oviposit as well, through syringe-like parts, creepily longer than stingers. They lay eggs not inside leaves, but in the bodies of living insects. These insect hosts later die as Ichneumonid larvae eat their way out. Not nature at its prettiest, but the mother wasp is just doing what's necessary, and her hunting keeps at least some pest insects from getting too populous. The hydraulics used to push eggs through a slim tube on the abdomen were later repurposed by stingers to inject venom. Stinging wasps now oviposit from another opening, and they lay eggs on top of prey, not inside it. When wasps started stinging – and hunting – they needed places to cache their prey and shelter their young, so they started to dwell in tunnels and holes. This way of living was kept up by bees, which now provision with pollen instead of insects.[12]

When Bees and Flowers Flirted with Extinction

The transition from bug-hunting to pollen-gathering closely follows the origin of flowers, which the wasps that became bees quickly adapted to. In return, flowers adapted to bees. Bees have had a long, fruitful partnership with the largest flower lineage, eudicots, which comprises three-quarters of all flowering plants. The smallest eudicot grows just a centimetre tall, with one-millimetre blossoms. The largest eudicot, Tasmania's mountain ash (*Eucalyptus regnans*), stands up to 100 metres. Yet eudicots look much the same when they burst from their seeds. Each one sprouts two tiny leaves, its seed leaves. This sets eudicots apart from the rest of the flowering plants, the monocots, which have one seed leaf. Grains of eudicot pollen share common features. They typically have three apertures for pollen tubes, instead of monocot pollen's single aperture. Once eudicots entered the world, bees spread tremendous quantities of "tricolpate" pollen from these plants – which radiated, along with bees, through much of the world.[13]

This all seemed to go well, until a point when bees and eudicots both faced extinction. Much life on Earth was wiped out when an asteroid ten kilometres across struck what is now the Gulf of Mexico, 65 million years ago. The asteroid left a crater 150 kilometres across and 20 kilometres deep. An estimated 15 billion tonnes of debris hung in the atmosphere for a year and a half, shrouding the world in continuous night. When the debris came back down, it settled across the globe, leaving a layer of soot, fractured quartz, and tiny, polished-looking spheres, condensed from vaporized rock. This debris layer has a name: the K-T boundary, a.k.a. the Cretaceous-Tertiary boundary. (The "K" is for Kreide, "Cretaceous" in German.) Those who consider "Tertiary" too non-specific call it the KPg boundary, to signify when the Cretaceous lurched into the Paleogene. An estimated three-quarters of all plant and animal species were wiped out by this event.

Seed leaves: Eudicots are the most diverse dynasty of flowering plants, but they all start off looking more or less the same, with two "seed leaves." Bee pollination helped these plants diversify. (Stephen Humphrey)

According to Sandra Rehan at York University, this mass extinction was nearly the end of all bees. One bee family's genetic history strongly hints at this. In 2013, Rehan and two other scientists found gene-based evidence that carpenter bees declined massively following the K-T (or KPg) cataclysm.[14] As with many discoveries, it happened while people were researching something else. Rehan and colleagues wanted to analyze and compare gene fragments from a couple hundred species of carpenter bee (*Xylocopa* spp.) to fill in genetic blanks of their evolutionary history. The scientists did not expect to stumble upon an ancient population crash.

"We didn't set out to find this," says Rehan. "We just happened to be studying a bee group that spanned this timespan. And that showed just a remarkable loss of diversity."

Carpenter bees, tunnel-making cousins of honeybees and bumblebees, emerged during the Cretaceous Period, while eudicots busily expanded their family tree. As eudicots diversified, so did carpenter bees. Then, suddenly, they did not. Rehan's data reveals a precipitous drop in carpenter bee diversity, as much as 95 per cent, following the K-T aster-oid's impact.

"There was just a dramatic bottleneck of genetics," she says. "Very few individuals persisted to the other side of that mass extinction event."

Around when carpenter bees crashed, the expansion of eudicots stalled. According to plant and pollen fossils, this flower lineage prac-tically dropped out of existence.[15] Rehan qualifies that her study was just focused on carpenter bees, and it would take more research to find out what happened to other bee families. Still, Rehan's work suggests how closely bees and flowers shared the K-T impact's devastation.

"Bee-flower coevolution is remarkably strong," she says.

Present and Future Histories

Rehan keeps an eye on more than the distant past. She's also curious how bees fare in their relationships with present-day flowers. A meteor hasn't hit the Earth recently, but there are slower-moving threats, such as cli-mate change and the rapid expansion of human habitations. In 2020, Rehan checked bee population trends over the past century or so. In col-laboration with Minnae Mathiasson at the University of New Hampshire, she combed through museum records spanning the past 125 years. Out of 119 bee species native to New Hampshire, Mathiasson and Rehan found fourteen were in serious trouble. Most of these were solitary bees; almost all were ground-nesters. As with Rehan's survey of Cretaceous records, she and Mathiasson found evidence of plants suffering fates similar to bees. The hardest-hit species were specialists – bees that specialize on one type of flower, or plants that depend on one type of bee.

"The more specialist a pollinator, having one, or few plant species that it'll visit, the more sensitive it is to changes in the environment," says Rehan. "So we see specialists are very sensitive and typically more apt to decline."

Rehan and Mathiasson also tested the strength of pollination networks. They tried to estimate the number of missed interactions between flow-ers and pollinators over the past century and a quarter. Their findings indicated 94 per cent fewer interactions between pollinators and plants. Almost a third of these pollination networks no longer existed.

"We were able to show that bee species which were formerly abundant and common also used to have a lot of host plants in the area," says Rehan. "And as those host plants are locally endangered species in the last fifty years, not surprisingly, the bee species that used to specialize or be strongly associated with those plants are also declining or locally extinct. So yeah, there is that tight relationship, there."[16]

After opening windows on the past and present, Rehan is trying to peek at the future, through the science of population genetics. By analyzing genes, she and her lab are scanning whole bee populations for drops in diversity. They're keeping an eye out for red flags that signal which bees might be vulnerable, going forward.

"A lot of the work ongoing in my lab is really examining these questions in populations," she says. "The tools of genetics allow us to ask those questions for particular species or across species. It's really at the cutting edge of research right now."

Unlike her work with fossils, Rehan is not looking forward one hundred million years. Not even a hundred.

"It's a different scale of data," she admits. Reading ahead is hard; it often ends up being a catch-up game. "We're always behind in studying this. We don't study things until they're declining, unfortunately. The power of hindsight is always a little bit stronger."

It is easier, she says, to uncover mass extinctions in the past than to tell whether we're close to one now. One problem with predicting mass die-offs is no two past events happened exactly alike.

"They're all unique in their own way. And you can't predict what species may or may not survive."

It's also hard to anticipate which species will adapt or recover from calamities, yet some always do. Bees and flowers arose from the K-T asteroid's carnage and diversified again. Like each previous mass extinction, there were survivors.

"Yeah, it's just like any evolutionary process," says Rehan. "What's devastating opens niches for others to colonize and proliferate. So if something survives — life's pretty resilient that way. But *something* needs to survive."

CHAPTER 7

Mutual Exploitation

Pollen's Deadly Side

Can pollen kill? We know a pollen grain carries a plant's male genes, and that for bee larvae, pollen is food. It nourishes them with protein, fats, minerals, and vitamins. But is it potentially poisonous? In some cases, perhaps. Plants that depend on specialist pollinators might discourage or eliminate non-specialists by making their pollen poisonous, or at least lethally non-nutritious for the "wrong" bee. In 2008, Swiss scientist Cristof Praz swapped pollen from different plants between larvae from four bee species considered pollen specialists, meaning they only consumed pollen from certain flowers. The larvae did not react well to these substitutions. Larvae failed to develop, remaining unnaturally small. Some turned green, others orange. Many died. Whether the larvae were poisoned or simply couldn't nourish themselves, they were clearly sickened by what Praz described as "protective properties that hamper digestion."[1]

Not all pollen nourishes equally. Protein content alone ranges from 2.5 per cent to 61 per cent in different pollens.[2] But some larvae in Praz's experiment died feeding on high-protein pollen. This prompted him to suggest that pollen from certain flowers has compounds harmful to non-specialists. Known plant toxins, such as protoanemonin and pyrrolizidine alkaloids, have been found in pollenkitt, the sticky substance that coats pollen grains. Perhaps specialist bees have resistance to these substances that other bees lack. Some scientists propose that certain "defence compounds" in pollen might protect bees against viruses[3] and other harmful microbes.[4]

Microbes: Medicine or Meat?

However, not all microbes on pollen are life forms that bees need protecting from. Pollen grains have numerous microbial passengers: bacteria, fungi, and other tiny travellers that trek their way into bee guts. They are not all necessarily harmful. Microbes can be healthy, even necessary. Health-promoting microbes in human guts are a popular field of study. Research shows a person's "microbiome" can aid good digestion, boost immunity, and possibly regulate mental health. It should come as no surprise that other animals, including insects, have gut flora.

Plants, on the other hand, don't have guts, but they have no shortage of resident microbes. Some microbial residents help plants attract pollinators. For instance, there are odd-smelling lilies that bloom close to the ground in South Africa. Single-celled yeasts inhabit these flowers and ferment their nectar, producing smells comparable to beer or wine gone bad. These rank-smelling flowers attract rats, mice, and gerbils that sip their nectar, and spread their pollen.[5]

Pollen-borne microbes can also count as food. In 2019, Shawn Steffan, a researcher with the United States Department of Agriculture (USDA), was surprised at one experiment's results, when fourteen species of bee were subjected to high-tech analysis to find out their "trophic signature," a molecular profile of what they eat. Steffan and his fellow researchers were astonished when the bees' dietary profiles looked closer to those of omnivores than strict vegetarians. This meant the bees had fed on non-plant protein, which they apparently got from microscopic fungi and other tiny things on pollen. Steffan and his colleagues branded these microscopic foodstuffs "microbial meat."[6]

Quinn McFrederick at the University of California, Davis, finds Steffan's hypothesis compelling but takes it with a grain or two of scientific caution.

"I don't think the story is a hundred per cent sewn up," he says. "I wouldn't be surprised if Shawn was 100 per cent right. I also wouldn't be surprised if that's true for certain bees and for other bees it's not very true."

Pollen-Borne "Meta-Communities"

McFrederick studies how microbial life ships back and forth between bees and plants. He describes these networks of pollen-borne microbes as "meta-communities."

"Inside of a pollen provision there's one [microbe] community and that community can get connected to other pollen provisions," he explains. "All of the pollen provisions and bees and flowers kind of connect these bee nests to each other."

Meta-communities vary from bee to bee and from one batch of pollen to the next. Some communities are large and diverse, others minimal. When McFrederick examined pollen collected by *Anthophora neglecta*, a furry ground-nesting bee in the western United States, he didn't find much in the way of microbes.

"I was not able to isolate that many microbes from their pollen provisions," he says. "For each ten pollen grains, there might be one microbial cell. That's a pretty low microbial biomass." Meanwhile, other bees collect pollen that literally bubbles with microbes, comparable to fermented foods such as cheese or kimchi. "I think we have a lot to learn, still."

There are different ways to study microbes. One method involves microscopes. Another uses gene sequencing. Researchers view lines of colour or strings of letters on computer screens that represent the molecular "alphabet" of DNA and RNA molecule chains. While more abstract than viewing cultured microbes, reading genes can help scientists identify whole microbial communities or to pick out specific traits. This method is valuable for learning which microbes bees and plants exchange during pollination. In one molecular foray, McFrederick's lab discovered that a microbe taken from pollen had genes for making fibronectin, a "binding protein" that bacteria normally secrete when they glue themselves to gut walls in animals.

"Fibronectin is not found in plants," says McFrederick. "So, this kind of suggests there is at least a couple of genes specifically adapted to the bee gut in these bacteria."[7]

Much bacterial sharing seems to be environmental. Another study by McFrederick tested whether bees that specialized on one type of flower had different gut microbes than generalist bees, which collect pollen from various plants. He studied gut microbes from two closely related solitary bees: one a pollen specialist, the other a generalist. In human guts, microbes eat what we eat, so the make-up of our gut communities varies depending on our diet choices. Perhaps, he thought, this held true for bees with different pollen diets. Instead, one of McFrederick's students found microbial communities in bee guts depended more on where bees lived than what exactly they fed on. As pollen spread through habitats, so did microbes. Pollinators inhabiting the same locale were hosting more or less the same gut microbes, no matter which flowers they frequented.[8]

"My guess would be that everything's just all mixed up," says McFrederick. "Generalists are introducing the same microbes into the plants that the specialists are visiting, so everybody kind of has similar microbes."

McFrederick's lab explored this idea further by embedding blue orchard bees (*Osmia lignaria*), which are pollen generalists, in seventeen urban gardens. What kind of microbial communities the bees hosted in their guts seemed to depend on habitat features, including which plants were abundant, how much bare soil there was, and what other insects were foraging.[9] What microbes lived inside them depended on the microbial world around them – in other words, their meta-communities.

Yet there are bees of a certain genus that have more or less the same gut microbes, wherever they inhabit. Those bees are extreme pollen generalists, and they live all over the world. McFrederick collaborated with an expert on these super-generalists, Sandra Rehan at York University. *Ceratina*, or small carpenter bees, look like rotund, shiny ants with a dark green metallic sheen. They make their tunnels in stems, not hunks of wood like larger carpenter bees. Their stem nests are found on every continent besides Antarctica.

A peculiar social life goes on in these stem tunnels between a mother bee and her small band of willful daughters, which Rehan describes as "a bunch of future queens." Relations between mother and daughters are fraught and frequently combative. Rehan has personally witnessed a number of their battles (for research purposes). A *Ceratina* mother seems especially hard on her firstborn. That unfortunate offspring is the "dwarf eldest daughter" or "Cinderella daughter." Her overbearing mother keeps her deliberately small by feeding her less and saddles her with much of the work. The parent bee's mothering style may not sound kindly, but nonetheless this small-scale queen cares for her feisty family from egg to adult, which many bees don't. To keep everyone fed, the mother (and

Small carpenter bee: Ceratina, or small carpenter bees, nest in stems, where they live in small social groups. These bees are extremely generalist in their diet choices. They collect pollen from a wide variety of sources, even "trashy" invasive plants. (Stephen Humphrey)

eldest daughter, whom she coerces into foraging) is flexible about what kind of pollen she brings home. She does not even mind getting "into the weeds."

"They really are opportunistic," says Rehan. "They'll actually gladly occupy invasive plants."

"I like to call them 'trash bees' because they like really trashy environments," says McFrederick.

Their innate appreciation for trashy plants made small carpenter bees excellent subjects to study bee microbiomes. Rehan provided McFrederick's lab with pollen samples from *Ceratina* nests in the United States and Australia. Regardless of where the bees lived or what flowers they foraged in, their core bacteria stayed largely consistent. Very little differed, besides local microbial fungi.[10] McFrederick suspects the bee's gut microbes make defence compounds. He thinks bacteria from the genus *Lactobacillus* might change pH balance, effectively pickling gut parasites. This kind of chemistry is familiar in food science.

"The bacteria are pretty closely related to the bacteria that are in sourdough starter," McFrederick says. "People have shown that *Lactobacillus* that are in sourdough starter actually extend the shelf life of the bread. And we kind of think maybe the *Lactobacillus* that are in these pollen provisions do the same kind of thing. Maybe they also help the bee digest the pollen."

"Balanced Mutual Exploitation"

By mixing their pollen diet, generalist bees might also be hedging their bets nutritionally. Jessica Forrest's lab at the University of Ottawa tested this principle with bumblebees, which are pollen generalists. Since not all pollen is equally nutritious, one type alone may not be enough for bumblebee larvae. Pollen from sunflowers is plentiful, but it's not always the heartiest. When Forrest and her lab-mates fed nothing but sunflower pollen to bumblebee larvae, they lived markedly shorter lives than those fed mixtures of flower pollen from broad beans, rapeseed, and squashes. Pollen mixing seemed to compensate for the nutritional shortfalls of sunflower pollen.[11]

Forrest eclectically studies the multimillion-year relationship between flowering plants and pollinators. Her explanations of plant-pollinator relations make the give-and-take between pollinators and plants sound as complex and involved as any long-term relationship. Relations between flowers and their pollinators are not necessarily elegant, poetic, harmonious, or tidy.

"Nature is messy, in part because things are not as reciprocally specialized as we might think," says Forrest. "Everything is being selected to maximize its own fitness and not the fitness of other species." She admits she took a long time becoming a relationship realist about plants and pollinators. "To a large extent, I started my PhD with that idea there's this perfect harmony, but I've gradually become disillusioned," she says. "Sort of the happy, glowing Gaia idea is, I think, not really a realistic portrayal of the world."

As in many relationships, self-interest complicates mutual goals. Two parties have different needs and expectations. Mutual satisfaction is not necessarily guaranteed. Nor is mutual faithfulness. It is hard to find flowers and pollinators with complete fidelity to one another.

"Specialization is rarely reciprocal," says Forrest. Some bees might specialize in one flower, or one group of related plants, but that doesn't mean plants won't keep their options open. "Those plants are almost never solely dependent on those specialist bees." Likewise, some plants may depend on one or two pollinators, but their pollinators still forage on other flowers. "There's always other options out there that may be more or less attractive, depending on environmental circumstances."

The German/Brazilian pollination biologist Christian Westerkamp typified plant-pollinator relationships as "balanced mutual exploitation."[12] Westerkamp observed that flowers evolved for bee pollination succeed in part through their ability to hide pollen from bees. For example, some flowers have different stamen lengths and offer "fodder pollen" to bees while keeping half their anthers out of sight. Some of those hidden anthers brush sneakily against bees, to make them carry off pollen they're not aware of. Pollen secretly sprinkled on a bee's body is more likely to fertilize flowers than pollen she puts away in her nest.

"For the plant, it's better if all of that pollen actually doesn't get fed to bees and gets transported to other plants," says Forrest. Bees returning again and again to flowers are not trying to pollinate. They are taking care of their own needs and the needs of their offspring. "They're super-efficient at harvesting pollen from that plant because they bring that pollen back and feed it to their young."

So-called "bee flowers" tend to overproduce pollen, but even then, just a fraction of what they produce reaches the next flower's stigma. An experiment in Forrest's lab looked closely at flower stigmas, using close-up macro photos and analytical software to count pollen grains in them.[13]

"A pollinator might visit one plant and pick up a few thousand pollen grains," says Forrest. "Then it visits another plant. It might only deposit a few hundred pollen grains on the stigma, or even fewer. Some of those pollen grains might not be viable, some might get brushed off by a subsequent visitor, or whatever."

Considering the resource cost to a plant, which spends a lot to get very little, it's maybe not surprising that plants use various methods to deceive, discourage, even kill pollinators that don't pollinate them efficiently. Sometimes an okay job is just not good enough.

"Visitors that are not effective pollinators can be worse than ineffective," Forrest says. "They can be parasites, in the sense that they're removing pollen from the system or removing nectar that would otherwise be available to a more effective pollinator."

Sex and the Single Flower

Furthermore, a flower's stigmas don't necessarily treat each grain of pollen that lands on them equally. The reason relates to female priorities, which can clash with male concerns, even for hermaphroditic plants. When pollen fertilizes a flower, a complicated dance of male and female cells ensues. A pollen grain carries two types of male cells, the vegetative cell and generative cell. The vegetative cell forms a hair-like pollen tube, which exits the pollen grain and penetrates the stigma. The tube then tunnels through the style, and proceeds to the flower's ovary, where it enters an ovule, the organ that becomes a seed. The other cell in pollen, the generative cell, divides, becoming two sperm cells, which travel down the pollen tube to fertilize female cells in the ovule. One sperm cell merges with the egg inside the ovule, making a plant embryo, while the second sperm fuses with another cell, the ovule's "central cell." This sets off the formation of endosperm to nourish the embryo. The flower's ovary ripens and swells, forming fruit around the seed. This process sounds harmonious, but throughout it the plant sexes quietly compete. The priority of a flower's female self is to obtain the best male genes and produce the best fruit. Its stigmas are receptive to pollen from multiple "partners," to receive the widest selection, but the flower can be picky about quality. It's sometimes able to "decide" which ovules will germinate after they're fertilized.

"To some extent, the plant, from the female perspective, can 'choose' to allow her ovules to be fertilized by one pollen grain or another," says

Forrest. "The female definitely has the capacity to allocate resources to one fruit or another. Even within a flower, resources could be allocated to one ovule or another." In response, anthers produce pollen with faster-growing pollen tubes, so sperm can reach plant ovaries sooner. "If you want to sort of view it from the male perspective, the pollen grains are competing to reach the ovules. And some might be more vigorous and grow more quickly down the style than others. So again, having a diversity of mates means there's the potential for the most vigorous ones to father progeny."

The botanical battle of the sexes even extends to competing male and female interests on the same plant. Male organs are "motivated" to release pollen before stigmas on the same flower become receptive. This might be why two-sexed flowers are most often "protandrous," where male organs mature sexually before female organs; instead of "protogynous," where female parts mature first.[14]

"There's a tug of war, basically, with selection on the males to do more siring and selection on the females to be selective, same as with animals," says Forrest.

Competition, even self-competition, is business as usual for plants. Pollen, itself, is more than just a passive traveller. Chemically, physically, and even genetically, plants and pollen assert their own sort of agency.

CHAPTER 8

No Bee Is an Island

Sable Island's Special Bees

Sable Island is a slim, sandy strip of land three hundred kilometres off of Canada's Atlantic coast. It is forty-four kilometres long and at no point more than two kilometres wide. Ten thousand years ago, glaciers pushed masses of sand there, which now form the island ("sable" means "sand" in French). Winds and currents converge on the island and keep its sands in place. Gusts and tides once drove many unfortunate vessels onto Sable Island's shores. Even worse for sailors was fog that formed when warm air from the Gulf Stream hit the cool Labrador current. Since 1583, more than three hundred and fifty shipwrecks were recorded there. Thanks to radar, there have been no wrecks since 1947, but Atlantic winds still periodically unbury weathered masts and other wreckage from nautical mishaps.

There are those who think the island itself might eventually sink. As the climate warms and glaciers melt, the Atlantic Ocean's sea level is rising. This raises the prospect that Sable Island might one day be submerged.[1] This could mean an uncertain future for Sable Island's small, isolated ecosystem. Upwards of four hundred thousand grey seals use its beaches to spawn. Around five hundred wild horses run and graze on its modest community of plants, which has one single tree. The island's six hundred or so insect species include *Lasioglossum sablense*, a dark, delicate-looking bee, five to six millimetres long, called the "Sable Island sweat bee."[2]

Until title claims are settled with Nova Scotia's Mi'kmaq people, Sable Island won't have official national park status, so it is currently a national park reserve. All living things on the island are protected, including Sable Island's eponymous bee. Miriam Richards from Brock University is one of a very few scholars that has had an opportunity to study the Sable Island sweat bee, which ekes out its living on the remote, windblown island. The little bees seem to struggle with the high winds of their island home. Richards, who had to bundle up in midsummer to brave the island's gustiness, watched them repeatedly blown back, attempting to reach their millimetre-wide nest holes.

"They clearly have a tough time flying in the wind," says Richards. "They'll be coming along into their nest entrance and a gust of wind will pick them up. Then they have to come again."

Sometimes it takes them two or three attempts to reach their holes. It is unknown how this little bee, which so visibly struggles with north Atlantic winds, ended up on the island.

"The Sable Island bees are a mystery," says Richards. "How do you get a species there, in an island system that's only ten thousand years old? Because we normally think it takes a lot longer to create a separate species."

Like Sable Island's other fauna, the bees might have been displaced from somewhere else. More than a third of the island's plants were introduced from elsewhere. Sable Island's beloved horses have only been there a few centuries. Perhaps they survived a shipwreck or were deliberately beached by horse traders. Like the pony-sized horses, the Sable Island sweat bee exists nowhere else. Should Sable Island's sands erode to nothing or be submerged beneath rising seas, the bees' sole habitat will disappear, and so will they.

"I don't think anything on Sable is going to be okay in the long run, because the ocean levels are rising," says Richards. "Sable and a whole lot of other islands are going to go under. So yeah, they're doomed. This little sweat bee is going to disappear unless we remove it." Nor does Richards see any point in relocating the bee. "Its specialness was the fact that it somehow got onto Sable and evolved into something different that belongs on Sable. So, removing it won't really be useful."[3]

A few other bee species live on Sable Island, including another sweat bee, *Lasioglossum novascotiae*, which, unlike its island neighbour, also occupies the mainland. The two species are difficult to distinguish. Sharp-eyed scientists can just barely manage.

"They differ in a characteristic that you can actually see with a magnifying glass," says Richards. It also helps that there are no other sweat bees on Sable Island. "If there were more than two, it would be hopeless."

CANADA, Nova Scotia
Sable Island, on *Achillea*
43.9319 N, -59.9985 W
2008-08-08, *P.M. Catling*

Island bee: The Sable Island sweat bee (*Lasioglossum sablense*) is native only to Sable Island, which is three hundred kilometres off of Canada's Atlantic coast. This ground-nesting bee was found to be social. (Packer Lab, York University)

Lasioglossum is the largest bee genus, with around 1,700 species. Within that vast assemblage, the subgenus *Dialictus* has 630 species, including Sable Island's resident bee. *Dialictus* bees are small, dark, and maddeningly hard to tell apart. One entomologist complained the group was "morphologically monotonous."[4]

Richards agrees. "They're terrible," she says. "Absolutely ghastly."

It took a *Dialictus* authority to identify the Sable Island bee as a separate species. Jason Gibbs, from the University of Manitoba, has rare expertise on these stressfully similar bees.[5] But even for Gibbs, it was far from a picnic when he took up the task to scientifically prove the bee's uniqueness.

"Jason says he's had nightmares after he described it as a separate species," says Richards about her colleague. "'What if it isn't?'"

"You're trying to figure out where to draw the lines," explains Gibbs, at his laboratory in Winnipeg. "Sometimes the distinctions are very clear and then sometimes they blur. That's where you spend long days and long nights thinking, was I right or was I wrong?"

"Social" versus "Truly Social"

Why go to all that trouble? One reason is because even when species look practically alike, their behaviours might differ profoundly. For example, while many *Dialictus* bees are solitary, the Sable Island bee is social. After Richards left Sable Island, one of her students reported seeing multiple bees come and go from one single nest. This meant Sable Island sweat bees lived in groups. The bees were not only social, it turned out, but eusocial. In other words, they had colonies with queens.

The term "eusocial" means "truly social" in Latin. It describes a type of social behaviour rare in the animal kingdom. There is one eusocial crustacean: snapping shrimp. One mammal is eusocial – and no, it's not humans. Even though we humans live in vastly complex societies, zoologists do not define us as "truly social." Naked mole rats, on the other hand, are eusocial mammals. Their society has workers and a queen, who is the only female that mates and bears young.

Beyond these interesting exceptions, most eusocial species are insects. All termites, some thrips and aphids, about fifty "true bugs" (insects classified biologically as "bugs"), and one species of beetle are eusocial. However, most eusocial insects belong to Hymenoptera. Eusocial hymenopterans include all ant species, one wasp family, and 300–400 species of bee. Bees are fascinating social organisms because their behaviours cover the gamut from solitary to eusocial, and many stages in between.

"Bees, as a group, are arguably the most socially variable of all animals," says Richards. "Not just insects, but of all animals."

Even eusocial bees range widely. Some sweat bee colonies have just a few workers and a queen, whereas honeybee colonies have tens of thousands. However populous they are, colonies of eusocial hymenopterans are family units. They have one egg-laying mother (the queen) and sexually non-active daughters (called "workers") that collectively feed and protect the queen's children, their siblings. The fact that squads of females care for young that are not their own is an ongoing riddle for evolutionary scholars.

Entomologist Edward O. Wilson, who chiefly studied ants, researched and wrote extensively about eusocial behaviour. Over his long career, Wilson proposed two possible reasons why workers would care for offspring that are not theirs. For years, he said the cause was shared genes. Among ants, bees, and wasps, workers are more related to their sisters than their mother – because, to put it plainly, hymenopteran genetics are weird. Males are fatherless. They hatch from unfertilized eggs, and have one set of chromosomes, just from their mother. In biological terms they are "haploid." Females are "diploid," with DNA from both parents. Each worker has half her mother's genes, and all her father's. According to hereditary arithmetic, sisters are three-quarters related to one other, but only 50 per cent related to their mother. Therefore, they feel such strong affinity for their little sisters, they raise them without complaint. This idea, of "kin selection," is widely embraced.[6]

Wilson promoted this hypothesis for years, but around 2010 he retreated from that position. Instead, he started to assert that eusocial traits, such as cooperative behaviour and altruism (putting the colony's needs ahead of self), evolved, over time, in stages. For example, a mother bee provides well for her young, so her well-fed offspring stay close to home and help defend the nest. Cooperation becomes habitual, then permanent over generations.[7] Interestingly, Wilson used sweat bees to illustrate his hypothesis. According to Richards, the term "eusocial" first referred to sweat bees. Richards is a vocal advocate for the scientist that coined the term, American biologist Suzanne Batra, who's been overshadowed by male scientists, including Wilson.[8]

"Wilson was very influential, but he didn't invent it," Richards explains. "Partly because she [Batra] studied sweat bees, partly because she was a woman in the male-dominated entomological world of the 1960s and 1970s, she was completely overlooked. And basically, for decades, Wilson and then other males have been given credit for things that she did. Those of us who study sweat bees always knew." Some scholars, Richards adds, went so far as to claim sweat bees were *not* really eusocial. "How disrespectful is that? Good story about sexism in science. Or a bad story, depending how you look at it."

Stages of Sociality

Richards finds sweat bees intriguing for what they reveal about social evolution. If bees are the most socially variable animals, sweat bees are the most socially variable bees. Richards sees in them a chance to view different social stages, from "primitive," intermittent sociality to full-blown eusociality.[9]

"You're actually looking at this process in real time," she says.

Unlike some of its cousins, the metallic green sweat bee (*Agapostemon virescens*) is easy to recognize, even by non-experts. It is striking enough to have been named Toronto's official bee. This bee's social style is egalitarian. Its queenless colonies consist of several mother bees sharing one set of tunnels. Each female stores pollen and lays eggs in her own tunnel. Their only shared task is nest-guarding. Other sweat bees have eusocial colonies that range from just a few workers to hundreds. Queens are sometimes so close in size to workers, they're hard to recognize. Even workers can't tell, at times. They lay their own eggs and even try to usurp the queen, so there are fights. A honeybee queen is impressively large, and attended at all times, but she is passive and fearful. If you're looking for warrior queens, consider sweat bees. Their queens constantly battle to stay in charge.

"Workers are cooperative because their queen is beating them," Richards explains. "They come out into the world and the first thing that happens is this great big female comes and bites them on the head and picks them up by the neck and pushes them into the side of the tunnel. They say, 'Oh, okay. I am clearly the worker and she's clearly the queen.' But you take away the queen and that little worker isn't going to act like a worker. She's going to act like a queen."

Some primitive social groups might even revert to solitary living. Richards sees this happen frequently with carpenter bees. Carpenter bees are largeish like bumblebees and easily confused with their eusocial relatives. What sets them apart is their black, shiny, practically hairless abdomens. Carpenter bees nest in tunnels they bore into wood, like living power tools, with their powerful mandibles. Evolved to live in stumps and logs, they've come to prefer milled wood, to the chagrin of homeowners. "They really love pine and spruce," says Richards, who's had them in her deck. In retaliation, she catches them as lab specimens, claiming scientist's privilege. "We're kind of allowed to do that."

For a long time, carpenter bees were thought to dwell alone in their tunnels. Sometimes they do, but not always. They often live in small groups – not more than five, and not necessarily relatives. They unite around real estate. Drilling tunnels is hard work, so carpenter bees hold onto their

Home makers: Carpenter bees bore into wood to create their tunnels. Evolved to live in tree stumps and other natural structures, they prefer milled wood. Carpenter bees are considered primitively social. Some of them reside alone in their tunnels, while others live in small groups with one dominant female. (Internet Archive Book Images)

tunnels and keep living there. They continue to renovate, adding more chambers. As the nest expands, more bees move in. As a group they overwinter, huddling close for warmth. Come spring, things are less harmonious. Battles ensue over who runs the nest. Whichever bee wins the title of matriarch does not inherit workers so much as adult dependents. The dominant bee collects all the pollen and nectar, not just for her offspring, but for everyone. Her needy nestmates harass her for food, acting more like baby birds than self-sufficient grown-ups. When they are not fed, they bite their benefactor, and try to eat her eggs. When they're not begging or trouble-making, they laze around, awaiting their moment to be boss.

"It's not the classic division of labour," Richards concedes. "The dominant bee does everything and the other ones do nothing while they wait for their chance to do something. So that's a kind of division of labour."

Some bees get sick of waiting and strike out on their own. Disgruntled daughters may join other groups, start their own households, or revert to solitary living. In carpenter bee groups, subordinates are not sterile workers. They are capable of reproducing and founding their own dynasties.

"When you've got daughters, three of whom are capable of running their own colonies, they should really go and each run their own colony," says Richards. "We've seen that."

Rogue daughters may not necessarily start colonies. Instead, they might live alone, especially if flowers are plentiful. When times are leaner, they're more likely to seek nestmates. Similar things happen with socially flexible sweat bees. They're more often solitary in times of abundance, but when flowers run short they'll band together. Scarcity impacts more than colony size. It can also affect bee body size. When a sweat bee colony has less pollen, larvae get less food, so they grow into smaller adults. The queen, once similar in size to her workers, becomes visibly larger. Her nest starts looking more like a bumblebee or honeybee colony, where queens are always huge and workers are always small.

Too Big to Fail? "Hyper-Social" Honeybees

More "advanced" social bees habitually control food portions to keep workers small. Honeybee larvae destined to become workers receive "royal jelly," a nutritious mélange of water, nectar, and predigested pollen, but only for three days. Larvae raised to be queens are fed royal jelly constantly, even as adults. Queens grow to twice the size of workers and become incredibly fertile. Ovaries and eggs in a queen's long abdomen account for much of her extra size.

Nonetheless, celibate daughters run things around the hive, not the queen. Despite their reputation for having hierarchies, honeybee colonies are self-organizing, with no single leader. Yet their collectively run colonies are hyper-organized. Everything has its place. Stores of pollen, nectar (which becomes honey), and brood cells with larvae are arranged much the same in every hive. Labour divides along specific lines. Some bees build, others clean, some nurse, others guard, some care for the queen, others forage. Foragers specialize further in collecting pollen, nectar, water, or propolis (plant resin that serves as antibacterial caulking). Richards balks at calling these complex colonies eusocial. She classes honeybees as "hyper-social."

"They're quite a special case," she says. "We think of them as typical, and they aren't. They're not typical of bees in ecology."

One of the honeybee's atypical talents is language. After humans, honeybees have the most complex symbolic language. In 1973, Karl von Frisch won the Nobel Prize, with his collaborators Konrad Lorenz and Nikolaas Tinbergen, for discovering this language, which uses dance, not speech.[10] The topic of most honeybee discussions is where to find rewarding flowers. The direction a bee dances maps the direction to flower patches, relative to the sun's position.[11] The number of turns in her dance denotes distance. During her performance, a dancing bee "waggles" her body to express her opinion of nectar quality. In Asia and Africa[12] honeybees dance in the open and fellow bees watch. European honeybees, the kind imported to North America, dance inside dark hives, where they waggle audibly. There is give-and-take in these exchanges. Some bees head-butt other dancers to interrupt.[13]

Stingless honey-producing bees, native to Africa, South America, and other southern continents, have their own communication style. Bees that make honey but don't sting might sound wonderful, but stingless bees have other nasty defences, such as biting. Some species secrete formic acid when they bite, and raise painful blisters. Stingless bees point the way to flower patches with odour trails, like ants. They get nestmates to follow them by running around in excited circles, jostling and grabbing them, and making short "zig-zag" demonstration flights.[14]

Complex communication has great value in warm climates, where flowers bloom in huge clumps, practically year round. Recruiting many bees to patches bursting with flowers makes sense. However, on cooler continents, too much talk can be counterproductive. North America's forty-six species of bumblebees are all eusocial. Their colonies range in size from a hundred to a few hundred workers. Getting food is a group effort, but bumblebees have no language to compare notes about flowers. In his influential book, *Bumblebee Economics*, bee scientist Bernd Heinrich explains why it's better bumblebees don't get chatty. North American flowers are farther apart and fewer. Bumblebees take long solo flights searching for them, alert to sudden finds. It would be worse if they waited around for news of flowers when they could be out searching.[15]

Groups can become too organized for their own good, says Richards. "One problem with working together is that individuals do interfere with each other." She points to human corporations as an example. "A company with 30,000 workers doesn't produce 30,000 times as much as a company with one worker," she says. "A colony with, say, twenty workers doesn't bring twenty times as much pollen in as a colony with two workers or one worker, but it does bring so much more. In that, they overall are doing better."

At times, solitary bees have proven more efficient than social bees. Blue orchard bees, a solitary species, can pollinate cherry trees faster than honeybees, one study in Utah demonstrated.[16] In California, hundreds of blue orchard bees did a job equal to thousands of honeybees, when they were employed to pollinate almond groves. But less efficient or not, honeybees possess advantages, such as reproducing quickly in large numbers. In 2018, one of California's largest almond orchards abandoned its pilot program with blue orchard bees. The bees might have been good pollinators, but the orchard claimed it wasn't cost-effective to breed them.[17]

Where honeybees fall short is in too-big-to-fail scenarios. They constantly need flowers to feed their thousands of workers.

"They need to be collecting pollen all summer long," says Richards.

This is no problem in lush places with lots of flowers. But honeybees would utterly fail in deep desert, where plants grow sparsely and flowers may bloom years apart.[18] Bees adapted to deserts are often flower specialists that keep in sync with specific plants. Bee larvae stay in their cocoons, waiting for moisture, like their reticent "host" flowers. The ground-dwelling desert bee *Perdita portalis* nests in colonies without queens in the Chihuahuan desert, which straddles the American southwest and northern Mexico. These tiny, egalitarian bees are small enough to crawl inside globemallows, the flowers they pollinate. Bryan Danforth, at Cornell University, discovered these bees delay their adult emergence until rainfall, which also prompts globemallows to bloom. *Perdita portalis* practise a kind of "bet-hedging." Only half the bees in a brood come out of their cocoons, even when globemallows are blooming. The other half stay dormant, in case conditions are not favourable after all.[19]

Honeybees are not capable of such austerity. Researchers found real-life proof of this in north Africa, one place honeybees are native. Until ten thousand years ago, the Sahara Desert was lush and verdant, with many flowers, and bees to pollinate them. Honeybees died out locally wherever desert replaced vegetation, but native honeybee colonies still persist

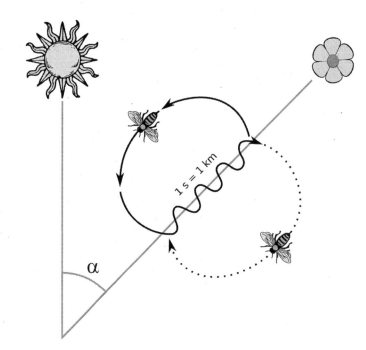

Dance language: The most complex animal language (after human languages) operates through dance. The honeybee's dance language communicates direction and distance to flower patches, plus the quality of nectar. When honeybees swarm to relocate their colonies, the dance communicates possible new hive locations. (Jüppsche commonswiki via Creative Commons)

in spots with green oases, such as Libya's Kufra district. Yet there are no honeybees at all where these oases end. The desert draws a clear line in the sand.[20]

Nor are honeybees adapted to North America's shorter summers, colder winters, and intermittent flower patches. They flourish on that colder continent because of human intervention. They depend on care and maintenance by beekeepers and on farmers requesting, even paying for, honeybees to come pollinate their crops.

"We've made them into domesticated farm animals, basically," says Richards.

Honeybees Gone Wild in Upstate New York

Some honeybees have returned to wilder ways on their adopted continent, at least as far north as upstate New York. Honeybees live ferally in the Arnot Teaching and Research Forest, owned by Cornell University. For decades, their wild hives have interested Thomas Seeley, an expert on honeybee social behaviour. He has written books on the subject, such as *Wisdom of the Hive*[21] and *Honeybee Democracy*,[22] to explain and demystify the honeybee's elaborate social system, which operates through surprisingly simple mechanisms. For instance, their coordinated flower foraging is not centrally organized.

"Each bee only has to know about her particular patch of flowers and report on it in the appropriate way," he says. "There doesn't have to be any central control and no bee has to really have any broad knowledge of the whole process."

How several thousand honeybees decide to decamp *en masse* from wooden hive boxes into the hollows of tree trunks involves "swarming," one of their most complex social behaviours. When hives begin to overcrowd, around 70 per cent of their workers leave, taking the queen with them. While picking where to live next, a clump of bees hangs from a tree limb or other temporary perch, such as the overhang of some startled citizen's roof. That roiling mass of bees might look ominous, but in this state, they are actually quite docile. On the surface of a swarm, bees are too busy watching their sisters dance to pick fights with strangers. In swarms, "scout bees" use dance language to report on possible hive locations. Unless a swarm is recaptured before the bees in it reach consensus, it might relocate to some hollow space inside a tree or some other cavity. Seeley first went looking for tree-dwelling, formerly domestic honeybees in Arnot Forest during the 1970s.

"I and everybody else knew there was this population of wild colonies living out in the woods," he says. "I just wanted to find out how abundant are they? How many of these wild colonies are there?"

Three decades later, Seeley's attention returned to Cornell's wild hives, which he found alive and well — once he found them at all. Locating such hives is not easy. It requires "beelining," a test of human intelligence and patience. Seeley temporarily traps bees at a baited feeding station and then re-releases them after daubing them with paint to identify later. Then he tries to chase them home. It takes several outings to find one hive. Beelining involves careful note-taking, educated guesses, and a lot of bee-watching. In the process he gets to know bees by their individual tics.

"Each worker bee has her own, you might even say, personality," he says. "Some are very bold, some are shy. Some get up and go start working early in the morning and others kind of linger for a while. They're certainly not clones of each other."

Seeley has seen naïve honeybees get lost trying to follow dance directions, and old honeybees on the last flight of their six-week lives, loaded with nectar they are finally too weak to carry. "You see this bee that's been coming and going. She gets slower and slower and finally she's too weak to fly home. That's the kind of thing you see."

When at last Seeley locates wild hives in trees, he finds them very different from managed hives in boxes. Group size is one key difference. While commercial hives contain around 60,000 bees, wild colonies have closer to 10,000 or 20,000 residents.[23]

"The colonies are smaller in the wild," says Seeley. "They haven't been put in huge spacious hives. They've chosen a nest cavity that is quite modest."

He says wild beehives are also less densely spaced than those in commercial bee yards. He estimates no more than one colony per square kilometre. "In contrast, where there are beekeepers, there might be twenty or thirty or forty or fifty colonies in the same location."

A number of naturalists worry that beehives in such densities threaten food sources for native bees. Highly concentrated colonies make short work of wildflowers. Small, feral hives are less greedy, says Seeley.

"[Managed] colonies are going to hoover up lots, if not the majority, of the nectar and pollen in the area," he says. "Humans are selecting them for honey production, whereas in nature they're being selected for survival and reproduction. I make that distinction because the selection pressures on those two populations are very different."

Feral honeybees in upstate New York might reside in local forests, but they are still not native to North America. Yet Seeley considers them naturalized. "Historically, they are an introduced species, but they've had lots of time to become locally adapted to the various places in which they live. They're not freshly introduced. They've adapted very well." Like other bees in nature, they respond to pressures from their local environment and resources available to them. "I've always been very respectful of the honeybee as it lives in the wild," says Seeley. Wild hives, he thinks, have their own sort of wisdom.

CHAPTER 9

Honeybees Aren't Good at Everything

Beehives by the Truckload

I slide into the cab of the grimy white pickup truck and snap open the wax-caked flip phone in the cup holder. I quickly answer, thinking it's a call from Elmer, my mother's husband and the head beekeeper at Kamisak Apiary, near Beaverlodge, Alberta. I pull back the bee suit's netting over my face and say a breathless, "Hello?" An automated voice from some sales robocall hits my right ear, just as a bee flies up and stings me in the mouth. Half my bottom lip swells up like a botched Restylane treatment and stays like that for two days.

I've been stung in other places – once in the back of my head when a bee got snarled in my hair, on my right bicep when another bee crawled inside my coveralls. While photographing a beehive (with no bee gear on) I felt something prick my right temple like a suture needle. The sting gave me an instant headache and then swelling under my right eye, which made me see rainbows for part of a day. At some point I lost track of the total number of times I'd been stung. Enough times to find the sensation familiar. The pain subsides after a few seconds, followed by a demoralized moment or two. You get used to that.

Over two summers in the early 2010s, my days were spent driving from one bee yard to another in the vicinity of Beaverlodge, Alberta. The yards were spread across two rural counties, a couple just inside the provincial bounds of British Columbia. Each yard had around twenty hives. This was far from the largest bee business in Western Canada, but there was plenty to do – more than enough to keep three people on the move. I enjoyed the changing scenery: ruins of old wooden farmhouses, huge cylindrical haybales, and fields of yellow canola in flower, rippling like waves out to the horizon.

Throughout midsummer, we worked twelve-hour days, racing to stack enough honey "supers" to keep up with honey flow. The supers were wooden boxes we piled on top of hive boxes to collect honey. A metal grate called a "queen excluder" prevented the queen from climbing into the supers and laying eggs in them. Workers were small enough to climb through the grate and make honey, as intended. When the supers were full and heavy, we loaded them in the rear of a pickup and drove them back to the apiary. The work was sticky, gruelling, and satisfyingly physical.

Long days sometimes got longer, with extra trips around dusk or just before sunup. Those late and early trips were for moving hives between bee yards. At predawn, the sky was shades of grey, tinged with ochre. The morning chill penetrated my grubby white coveralls as we stealthily loaded the truck with drowsy hives. This early (or late), bees were too torpid to get riled about us hauling them around. We moved hives to populate new bee yards, to balance hive counts in existing yards, or to put bees close to nectar sources, such as wildflowers or crops in bloom. Elmer had informal, barter-based arrangements with farmers, who let him keep bee yards next to their fields. His bees got nectar for honey and farmers got free pollination.

Some beekeepers charge a lot of money for crop pollination. As a billable service, "pollination services" costs around US$45–200 per hive in the United States and CAD$90–150 per hive in Canada.[1] One survey estimates the world honey market will be around US$10 billion by 2026,[2] but pollination for agriculture is also a booming industry. The United Nations Food and Agriculture Organization (FAO) calculates the global value of crop pollination at around US$235–577 billion a year.[3] Some apiaries specialize in commercial pollination. Such operations do more than drive around a few dozen hives in pickups. They load up semitrailers with three to four thousand boxes of honeybees. Beekeepers become freight operators. They haul their bees cross-country to pollinate cash crops, such as apples, blueberries, and canola.[4]

What Pollinates Canola?

Canada was the first nation to grow canola and remains its largest producer. There, around 20 million acres of the oilseed crop require pollination. Samuel Robinson, at the University of Calgary, shares an aerial image of one vast yellow field, someplace in Alberta. Clumps of coloured rectangles huddle along its outskirts. These are boxes of bees, one for each acre.

"A quarter section like you see in this picture here is about 160 acres, and so they'll use about 160 hives," says Robinson.

Canola (*Brassica napus*) was developed as a crop in the 1970s by cross-breeding different species of oilseed rape. Growers now combine traditional crossbreeding with genetic modification to optimize the plants for pollination. As members of the mustard family, canola flowers are prone to pollinating themselves. Habitual self-pollination is not a trait desired by breeders who want to make hybrid strains; they need different breeds to cross-pollinate each other. Gene hacks are to limit self-sexing in these four-petalled hermaphrodites. The flowers, in factory-perfect rows on Robinson's computer screen, were modified to be male and female. Sort of.

"I guess 'males' and 'females' wouldn't quite be the right term," he clarifies. Robinson explains that half the rows are "female bays," constrained to be female-only flowers. The "male bays" are actually hermaphrodites. Male bays have to be mown down periodically so they too don't self-pollinate. When 15–20 per cent of the crop is blooming, beekeepers place hives among rows at some dim, chilly hour when bees are sleepy.

"One night they'll come there, and they'll plonk the honeybee hives down," Robinson says.

At CAD$150 per hive, the service is on the expensive side. In part, this is because honeybees are not well-nourished by the work. Canola pollen offers decent nutrition, but the bees don't get enough of it, necessarily.

"They don't have a huge yield off canola fields because of the density of honeybee hives," Robinson explains. "Often, the hives will lose weight. The amount of honey and stuff inside the hives will go down because there's just so much competition. They don't get enough food. Beekeepers get compensated for that."

But do results merit the expense? Robinson and graduate student Riley Waytes wanted to know how effective honeybees were at cross-pollinating canola. Their findings made them doubt how much honeybees help create canola hybrids.

"Between Riley and I, we kind of figured out that the honeybees aren't actually doing a whole lot."[5]

Bee on canola: Commercial honeybees are rented by farmers to pollinate hybrid canola—but they may not be its most prolific pollinator. (Ivar Leidus)

Not to say the honeybees slacked off. They moved plenty of pollen around. They just weren't cross-pollinating. The reason was their complex division of labour. As units, honeybee hives are generalist. Collectively, foragers bring home pollen from a variety of plants. But individual honeybees develop specialties. Once an individual bee learns the workings of a given flower, she sticks with it.

"If you learn the morph of one flower, then you can very quickly find where the nectaries are and get the energy that you want and then move on," says Robinson. "Whereas if you're stuck with the problem of learning a new flower each time, then that could be quite inefficient."

Beekeepers know this tendency of honeybees to specialize, so they wait until canola's in bloom to put hives out. If they place hives too early, foragers specialize in wildflowers and become indifferent to canola. What no-one knew, Waytes and Robinson found, is that honeybees treat male and female bays as separate flowers and specialize in one or the other. They don't fly back and forth between them, so cross-pollination doesn't occur. Nonetheless, cross-pollination must be happening, since hybrids are getting produced. Another kind of bee does it, says Robinson: alfalfa leafcutting bees.

There are several species of leafcutting bees native to North America, but a European species, *Megachile rotundata*, is imported for commercial pollination. The bee has a particular knack for pollinating alfalfa (*Medicago sativa*), which farmers grow for silage and hay. Alfalfa is part of the pea family, and like other legume plants, its flowers are "papilionaceous." The root word "*papillon*" means "butterfly" in French, and in that respect, two of the flower's five petals are called "wings." The names of its other three petals take a nautical turn. The top petal, unfurled like a sail, is called the "banner." The bottom two petals, fused together, are the flower's "keel." The alfalfa flower's keel encloses a bundle of stamens fused into a foot-like shape. These remain hidden until a bee lands on the keel, which sets off a trip mechanism and sends anthers swinging upward to wallop the bee with pollen. After getting sucker-punched by anthers, honeybees avoid landing on the keel. They might still do some vengeful nectar robbing by biting flowers from underneath.[6] Alfalfa leafcutters don't seem to mind taking the punch, because they keep coming back, so they are bred to pollinate alfalfa's purple flowers.

I once dropped in on a leafcutter breeding operation, situated not far from Kamisak Apiary. Its proprietor was Sterling Smith, a former beekeeper. His operation took up less space than one of Kamisak apiary's sheds. Inside a sort of high-tech hut for bee breeding, little black leafcutters hatched from cocoons. The bees were so docile I was able to lie down to look at them in a dim, narrow room where the brightest light came from heating elements. The leafcutters crawled around, looking unhurried – except young males, already anxious to mate with females.

In nature, leafcutters nest in tunnels. Commercially bred leafcutters make their nests in holes punched out of Styrofoam blocks. Those blocks are installed in crop rows. Some are visible in Robinson's photo of a canola field. The blocks are sheltered by structures like miniature A-frame roofs. Robinson calls these "leafcutter shelters."

"It's basically just made out of tarpaulins and two-by-fours," he says. "And then inside they have these boards made out of Styrofoam."

Leafcutting bees don't have to worry about canola flowers punching them in the face. They also don't seem to care which canola flowers they

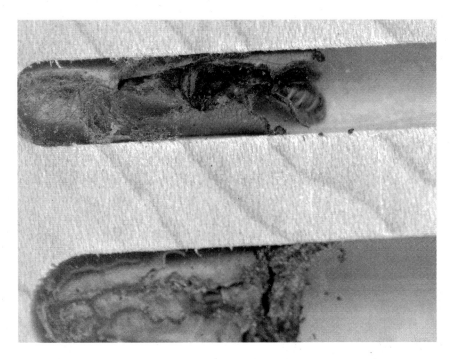

Leaf collector: Leafcutting bees use their serrated mandibles to scissor circular pieces out of leaves to build single-occupant cells for their offspring. Here a bee stuffs pollen into a nearly completed leaf cell. Next she will lay an egg, cap off the cell, and start the next one. (Stephen Humphrey)

visit. They zig-zag between male and female bays without settling for either type.

"They're really only interested in getting enough food for provisioning their kids," says Robinson. "They're constantly looking for more pollen more quickly, so they're more willing to switch around. That would be my sort of running hypothesis."[7]

To Buzz or Not to Buzz

Honeybees outright shun the flowers of certain other profitable crops. They ignore the small yellow flowers of tomato plants, which make no nectar and demand buzz pollination. Honeybees can't vibrate their flight muscles to buzz pollinate like bumblebees can. For that reason, bumblebees are raised commercially to pollinate greenhouse tomatoes.

In 1985, Belgian veterinarian Dr Roland De Jonghe discovered that European buff-tailed bumblebees were exceptional greenhouse pollinators. He founded the company BioBest in 1987 to breed bumblebees for this purpose. A Dutch company, Koppert Biological Systems, started up a year later, followed by Bunting Brinkman Bees in 1989. Canadian tomato growers started using commercially bred bumblebees in 1990, ahead of the United States, Israel, and other countries. Greenhouses in the Ontario town of Leamington were early adopters of bumblebee pollination. Many are now renowned for their tomato growing. Tomatoes from Leamington supply North America's big ketchup companies, including French's and Heinz.[8]

A commercial bumblebee colony comes in a white cardboard box, helpfully labelled with directional arrows and bee graphics. The box holds a plastic container with dozens of bumblebees inside. The bees enter and leave through small openings in the box and go about their business in tomato rows. Growers who purchase them place three colonies per quarter acre in greenhouses that might be as large as thirty, fifty, or even sixty acres. In total, Leamington has nearly three thousand acres of greenhouse space to pollinate.

Bumblebees naturally buzz pollinate blueberries, which are native North American plants. Blueberries are also valuable commercially. In Canada, they are the top-marketed fruit crop, with an estimated annual worth of CAD$400 million. Despite their inability to buzz pollinate, honeybees are rented to pollinate blueberries.[9] Cranberry plantations also hire honeybees, yet these floral relatives of blueberries also need buzz pollination. However, while honeybees can't buzz pollen loose by vibrating their thoraxes, they find workarounds, such as brute force. They stick their legs and heads into the flowers and simply pry them open.[10]

Hum of the Wild

Not that brand-name bumblebees languish unused. Growers purchase them to pollinate blueberries and cranberries, along with melons, peppers, and other crops. Some bee experts wish commercially bred bumblebees were not used so widely. They warn against utilizing them for "open-pollinated" crops, which are not enclosed in greenhouses. They worry that artificially reared bumblebees spread pathogens and interbreed with local wild colonies. Some scientists are unnerved at how managed bumblebees behave in comparison to their free-roaming counterparts. Jason Gibbs, at the University of Manitoba, sees concerning differences between how managed and native bumblebees act around blueberry plants.

"They do not behave the same way," he says of managed bumblebees. "They're sluggish." In comparison, he says, wild bumblebees are "big" and "robust," and look like they have "a job to do."

Gibbs suspects blueberry growers could benefit from tapping into the robust, purposeful, and cost-free contribution of wild pollinators. In 2016, Gibbs and other scientists from the United States and Canada investigated unpaid, largely unnoticed "pollination services" by wild bees among highbush blueberries to see whether native species improved on commercial pollination in any measurable way. They surveyed blueberry fields in the state of Michigan and the province of British Columbia with "pollination deficits" that adding more honeybee hives didn't seem to solve.

"They weren't getting enough pollination," he says. "Some of the growers were exceeding the honeybee stocking rates by a factor of ten and they still weren't getting [the] pollination services that they'd wanted. So just throwing more honeybees at the problem doesn't always solve it. Whereas a lot of the native bees, they're often more tied to blueberries, at least in parts of North America."

In 2013, Gibbs and his colleagues researched whether they could enhance the benefit of native pollinators. However, the idea of "native" seemed to be blurred in some instances, because agriculture had shifted the historical ranges of blueberry plants. This was less the case in Michigan, where blueberries still grew more or less within their old ranges. As a result, Michigan's berry bushes retained their hometown edge with local, native bees, which showed up to pollinate them. However, in British Columbia, blueberry crops were stationed well beyond where they used to grow wild. The list of local bees pollinating them had resultingly shrunk. One upside of British Columbia's shorter list was that it included four species of bumblebee, which together had more pollinating power than Michigan's diverse but smaller bees. Not to dismiss them, though; Michigan's less sizeable bees were faithful pollinators – but having more of them around would be better. Gibbs and his team of pollination doctors gave diagnoses for each locale. They prescribed more efforts around bumblebee conservation in British Columbia and suggested planting native flowers around field edges in Michigan to build up wild bee numbers.[11]

Gibbs isn't the only researcher interested in strategically planting wildflowers to increase crop pollination. Many scientists support this eco-friendly answer to pollination shortfalls. In 2020, twenty-seven scientists jointly submitted a piece to the journal *Ecology Letters*. Their article strongly supported growing wildflowers and native hedges around farm fields to increase native pollination. It also surmised that the presence of more pollinators would leave less space for crop pests.[12] The article acknowledged that it takes patience for this method to succeed. The presence of wild pollinators builds up over time and doesn't peak until three years after planting wildflowers. How readily farmers will try this approach may depend on whether they're willing to wait three years for results, when they could immediately hire commercial pollinators. Some experts suggest trying the two strategies at once with "integrated crop pollination." In this scenario, farmers plant flowers around field margins, while also renting beehives, so as to benefit from both strategies.[13] Some researchers claim wild pollinators could as much as double the output of managed bees.[14]

As a billable service, commercial pollination has a definite dollar value. But it's hard to calculate a total financial figure for "pollination services" by wild species, since native pollinators don't generate receipts. Even so, people have tried to theoretically monetize their input. One model estimates dollar value by replacing unpaid services from wild pollinators with comparable amounts of invoiced work by managed bees. Another metric matches lost revenues from crop production with data on pollinator declines.[15] Using this type of math, a paper out of Germany valued "global pollination services" at around USD$1 trillion.[16] Focusing on economic losses in agriculture between 2016 and 2018, the study estimated services lost from wild pollinator die-offs impacted global GDP in the short term by 1–2 per cent. Long-term economic harms from losing pollinators still remain to be seen.

Some academics wonder what consumers think native pollination is worth in terms of food costs. In Maine, scholars did a survey asking people if they would pay more for food that contributes to wild bee ecology. They tested people's reactions to customer-targeted efforts such as

Bee Better Certified, an initiative sponsored by the Xerces Society for Insect and Invertebrate Conservation, the world's largest NGO for insect preservation.[17] The American researchers found shoppers are five times more willing to pay higher prices for products labelled "native bee pollinated" or "bee friendly." This survey suggests there may in fact be a public appetite for wild bee preservation, even a dollar value.

CHAPTER 10

The Curious Case of the Vanishing Bees

"A Mystery Worthy of Agatha Christie"

In 2007, all of a sudden, honeybees were at the top of the news cycle. Reports had them dying en masse – or worse, just vanishing. Beekeepers in the US and Europe opened hive boxes and found no worker bees inside them, just untended larvae and abandoned queens. A *New York Times* article called the situation "a mystery worthy of Agatha Christie." The mysterious new calamity had a suitably ominous name: "colony collapse disorder."[1]

American beekeeper David Hackenberg was one of the drama's early players. Hackenberg is a "migratory beekeeper," with an apiary that is also a licensed trucking and shipping company. His business is driving his bees literally coast to coast to pollinate crops. In 2006, Hackenberg returned to check on hives he'd left at a bee yard in Florida to feed on Spanish needles after they had been pollinating pumpkins in Pennsylvania. He was shocked to find most of the worker bees gone. By Hackenberg's tally, just nine of four hundred hives were still intact. The bee yard felt like a "ghost town," he told reporters.[2]

Hackenberg got in in touch with Diana Cox-Foster at Penn State University, who brought samples from his hives to Dennis van Engelsdorp, acting state apiarist for Pennsylvania. Van Engelsdorp and other scientists got to work investigating the problem. Similar samples started flooding in from other beekeepers. At first, researchers called the mystery blight "fall dwindle disease," but the name that stuck was "colony collapse disorder" (CCD). Van Engelsdorp defined colony collapse as "a condition that leaves few, if any, dead bees in the collapsed hive or in the apiary."[3] That spring, one-quarter of US beekeepers lost hives to CCD.

In 2008, Hackenberg took his concerns to Washington. He is pictured making that trip in the 2010 documentary *The Disappearance of the Bees*, voiced by Elliot Page. In Washington, Hackenberg was joined by fellow beekeeper David Mendes, then vice-president of the American Beekeeping Federation. In his address to a congressional panel, Mendes acknowledged that the cause of CCD was unknown, but that many beekeepers had "a pretty good idea of what is hurting their bees." He went on to discuss systemic pesticides, used on crops such as corn. "You bring your bees to an area where these products are being used, several months later they're collapsing."[4]

The doc premiered for a small audience of mostly beekeepers at the 2010 North American Beekeeping Conference and Tradeshow in Orlando, Florida, which had chosen the theme "Keeping the Hive Alive." Hackenberg and Mendes were both at the screening. Beforehand, Mendes chatted with beekeepers and showed off his hives, which were bound for almond fields in California, then back to Florida, next up north to pollinate blueberries in Maine, followed by apple groves and cranberry bushes near the Canadian border. Mendes echoed remarks from the film on his distrust of systemic pesticides. He planned to keep his hives away from corn, soy, and cotton crops, to not risk exposing them to Imidacloprid, a neonicotinoid insecticide ("neonic" for short). Neonicotinoids simulate the properties of nicotine, a natural plant defence of nightshades such as tomatoes, petunias, potatoes, and tobacco.

For humans, nicotine is a mild intoxicant, but for an animal the size of a bee, it's dangerous — even fatal. It overstimulates their nervous systems to the point of paralysis or death. Neonicotinoids possess similar chemical structures to natural nicotine. "Systemic" refers to how they're applied. Seeds coated with a systemic pesticide spread the chemical throughout a growing plant. The compound is taken up by roots and leaves, where it becomes deadly to plant-chewing insects.[5] Systemic pesticides are meant to limit heavy spraying and make food safer for humans. But despite these advantages, there is pushback from conservation groups, such as the Sierra Club and the David Suzuki Foundation. Hackenberg remains a vocal critic of neonicotinoids. He devotes space on his apiary's website to warning about them.

History Strewn with Bee Bodies

It is understandable for beekeepers to be suspicious of pesticides; they have a long history of bad luck with insect-killing poisons. The history of insecticides is strewn with bee bodies. In 1889, the *American Bee Journal* reported dead bees up to three miles from an apple orchard in New Canton, Illinois, after its owner treated his trees with copper acetoarsenite, an emerald-coloured powder better known as Paris green. This copper-based arsenic was first concocted as a pigment. It gave a wonderful green hue to impressionist paintings, women's outfits, and other decorative items – but it could be deadly. In 1861, a worker reportedly died in horrible convulsions while putting the pigment on artificial flowers. Women became cautious of wearing outfits dyed with Paris green as its harmful reputation grew.

The green powder had renewed success in more intentionally lethal products. It worked very well killing rats in sewers and striking down insects such as codling moths, canker worms, and caterpillars in apple orchards. Fruit growers knew little about the dangers posed to bees from putting lethal compounds on fruit trees in full bloom. In fact, most of them knew nothing about bee pollination. In 1891, the Ontario Beekeepers Association joined forces with Canadian entomologists and beekeepers to educate the public and campaign for pesticide laws, such as only treating crops after they're finished blooming.[6]

Over the next century, new pesticides emerged, such as dichlorodiphenyltrichloroethane (DDT). During the Second World War, DDT was used in soldiers' barracks to combat bedbugs, malaria-causing mosquitoes, and lice. After the war, the use of DDT became even more widespread. It was sprayed from airplanes on crops such as cotton. These crops flourished from the reduction in pests, but as the pesticide's aerosols drifted into flower patches, there was collateral damage to unintended targets.[7] DDT, which attacks nerve function, absorbs through insect exoskeletons and vertebrate skins alike. In her 1962 book *Silent Spring*, renowned nature writer Rachel Carson laid out the cumulative harms to human beings as use of DDT became widespread. For the first time in history, she wrote, every person was now "subjected to contact with dangerous chemicals, from the moment of conception until death."[8] Carson's book was a call to action, raising a public outcry and prompting then president John

F. Kennedy to form a science advisory panel. In 1972 the federal Environmental Protection Agency enacted a near-complete ban on DDT.

Carson's book warned about other pesticide compounds, including organophosphates, which remained in use after DDT. She specifically mentioned off-target effects these pesticides had on bees. So did a court case in the 1970s against the forest protection agency for the Canadian province of New Brunswick, about use of the organophosphate Fenitrothion. Blueberry growers wanted to know why visits from honeybees and wild bees had dwindled. They reached out to scientists from Memorial University in Newfoundland, led by pollination biologist Peter Kevan. Kevan carefully sampled blueberry fields next to forests aerially sprayed with Fenitrothion to combat spruce budworm, a forest pest. Kevan's data proved there were fewer pollinators alive wherever Fenitrothion was sprayed. He also found the chemical present in dead bees collected near blueberry fields.[9]

While this case set precedents for environmental law, organophosphates never completely went out of use. However, they have been largely superseded by neonicotinoids.

Europe's "Mad Bee" Problem

First introduced in the 1990s, neonics are now the most widely used insecticides. But they haven't been popular with everyone. In 1994, after placing their hives in sunflower fields, beekeepers in central France reported bees acting strangely. Honeybees that suffered from "mad bee disease" were strangely slow in their foraging. They groomed themselves an unusual amount. Some were struck with "a sort of paralysis" when they tried to take off or land. These unusual behaviours by honeybees coincided with "brutal" colony losses. French beekeepers turned their suspicions to Gaucho®, a pesticide manufactured by Bayer to coat sunflower seeds. The active ingredient in Gaucho® was Imidacloprid, patented by Bayer as the first commercial neonicotinoid. Responding to complaints, Bayer argued the pesticide was not fatal to bees in the amounts put on seeds. French researchers argued back that there were "sub-lethal" effects which didn't kill bees, but still produced "clinical signs of impairment," such as confusion, disrupted motor activity, and paralysis.[10] Confused honeybees had trouble finding their way home and communicating in dance language.

In 1998, when France's government seemed to drag its heels, beekeepers took to the streets of Paris. The pressure worked. In 1999, French lawmakers suspended the use of Imidacloprid on sunflowers until it was proven not harmful to bees. Citing the "Principle of Precaution," France's government chose to err on the side of caution, in lieu of absolute proof.[11] In 2004, the chemical was also banned on France's corn crops. When colony collapse, or something like it, hit Europe a decade later, the UK dubbed the bee crisis "Mary Celeste Syndrome," after a sailing ship found mysteriously adrift without crew in the nineteenth century. In 2008, seven hundred beekeepers along the Upper Rhine in Germany blamed another neonicotinoid, Clothianidin, for their hive losses. The beekeepers reached a settlement with Bayer for two million euros.[12]

Multiple Suspects

Europe's pesticide problems were not lost on van Engelsdorp, but as he and his colleagues worked to uncover reasons for vanishing bees in the United States, they happened upon other probable causes. He noted that while pesticides had affected French beehives, three-quarters of France's collapsing colonies were also beset by honeybee diseases. His sleuthing dredged up other past episodes of "unusually high colony mortality." Accounts from Colorado in the 1890s spoke of "May disease," where "large clusters of bees" vanished or rapidly declined. Those die-offs were tied to fungal infestations.[13] A spate of losses hit Australia in 1975, called "disappearing syndrome." Australian experts cited excessive dampness, poor nutrition, and a possible virus. Elsewhere during the seventies, Mexican hives succumbed to a blight called "disappearing disease," with no clear trigger, but most likely environmental.[14] These historical examples suggested colony collapse might not be so unique. They also suggested die-offs and disappearances of honeybees might not have just one singular cause.

There was no Canadian version of colony collapse in the early 2000s. Still, the spectre of vanishing bees to the immediate south helped highlight higher-than-average "winter losses." Canadian hives were not found ominously void of workers, but in spring, many were full of dead bees. Honeybees did not evolve to deal with Canadian cold, so winter losses always happen to some extent. Overwintering honeybees keep each other warm through a kind of convection process. In winter, they all cluster in one large group, around the queen. As bees at the cluster's centre get hot, they move outward, while the ones feeling cold move inward. However, in Canada, this behaviour is not enough on its own. Beekeepers wrap their hives with insulating materials and maybe move them into sheds. Even then, it's not unusual for bees to die over long winters.

Still, spooked by the news of colony collapse, Canadian apiarists spoke up to say they were losing too many bees.[15] Ernesto Guzman at the University of Guelph tried to get to the bottom of these losses. He led a team that monitored over four hundred colonies, through three honey seasons, across the province of Ontario. When the team brought forth their findings in 2010, news stories had a "mystery solved" sort of tone to them. But Guzman's team of hive detectives had not collared a single obvious culprit. They produced more of an itemized list citing multiple "stressors," all likely acting at once.

"We don't really know what's causing all this mortality," Guzman said. "But we all agree this is a multifactorial problem."

Pathogens and parasites are definite stressors on honeybees. Like all farm animals, they are vulnerable to pests and disease. Their most troublesome pest is *Varroa destructor*, an invasive mite. These parasitic mites found their way from Asia to Europe, then into North American beehives, where they attach to bees and their larvae, sapping hemolymph, the bee version of blood. Varroa mites don't kill honeybees outright but weaken their bodies, making them vulnerable to other hazards, including viruses – and, yes, pesticides. Guzman's team linked Varroa mites to 85 per cent of colony losses they studied.

In 2012, Agriculture Canada's northernmost research station in Beaverlodge, Alberta, opened its National Bee Diagnostic Centre to investigate pests and pathogens. Scientists proudly announced this facility was the first of its kind. Some lab rooms were still unfinished by the time of an introductory tour for the research centre's Annual Beekeepers Field Day. Guests had to imagine what the microbiology lab would look like when microbes were finally cultured there. One lab, already up and running, had live test subjects – honeybees so new to adulthood their wings were too damp to fly with. Researchers had deliberately infected the bees with mites to study Varroa infestations.

Mite versus bee: *Varroa destructor*, an invasive parasitic mite, was accidentally imported to Western Europe and North America during the 1980s. Since then, it has become a debilitating pest for honeybees. The mites find their way into brood cells, where they attach to bee larvae and pupae (above in photo), sapping hemolymph, the insect version of blood. (Gilles San Martin)

Varroa mites recurred several times as a topic throughout the day-long conference. Presenters showed beekeepers how to test for mites and how to treat hives with formic acid pads and miticides. Worried beekeepers seemed eager to learn, which was promising. The second highest honeybee stressor on Guzman's list was beekeeping practices. Pest treatments are important, but so is leaving adequate food reserves for winter. Honey is more than a popular human confection; it's a beehive's winter food supply. Hives might freeze out during cold snaps, but overwintering honeybees most often die of starvation. One extra honey draw, late in the season, may deplete needed provisions for over-wintering hives.[16]

Efforts by researchers and beekeepers to be proactive largely paid off. The latest news about honeybees sounds significantly less dire. In 2021, the Canadian Association of Professional Apiculturists (CAPA) claimed colony numbers were up 26.7 per cent since it started reporting losses in 2007.[17] Worldwide, it seems like honeybees are *not* going extinct. *The Washington Post*, which ran headlines in 2007 along the lines of "Honeybee Die-Off Threatens Food Supply," printed an op-ed in 2015 titled "Call Off the Bee-pocalypse: U.S. Honeybee Colonies Hit a 20-Year High."[18]

Wrong Bee Apocalypse?

However, it's possible that this whole time we were following the wrong bee apocalypse. In 2006, while colony collapse grabbed headlines, the National Academy of Sciences (NAS) in the United States issued a harrowing and highly influential report titled "Status of Pollinators in North America." This report addressed more than disappearing honeybees. It announced "demonstrably downward" trends in wild pollinator populations, from bumblebees to bats, in Canada, the United States, and Mexico. The NAS warned that some declining species could be vulnerable to "an extinction vortex," a vicious spiral that ends in a species' collective doom.[19]

Honeybees are well ahead of many other bees, population-wise. According to data from the UN's Food and Agriculture organization, the number of beehives around the world was more than 90 million in 2020.[20] Against conservative estimates of how many bees are in a hive (30,000), there are more than 2 trillion managed honeybees on Earth. Meanwhile, there are wild bee species so threatened they number no more than a few hundred individuals. The ongoing presence of honeybees may not improve chances too much for these species. In 2016, researchers in Utah estimated that all the flower foraging done by one forty-hive apiary over just three months took away pollen from around four million wild bees.[21] Managed bees also share pests with wild species. The fungal parasite *Nosema*, which does enormous damage to bee guts, reportedly jumped from honeybees to a species of special concern, the yellow-banded bumblebee (*Bombus terricola*).[22] Canadian scientists who found this infestation also saw signs the threatened bees were exposed to neonicotinoids, along with Fipronil, another type of systemic insecticide.

Susan Chan at the University of Guelph worries systemic pesticides might be harming the solitary, ground-nesting bees she studies. Her

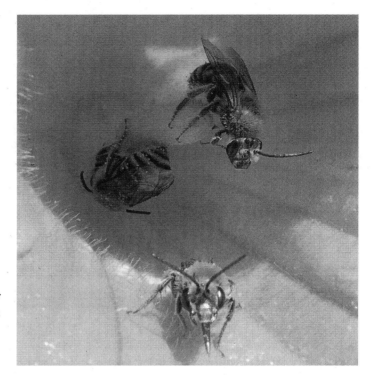

Squash specialists: Hoary squash bees are specialist pollinators of squashes, pumpkins, and other edible gourds, which might be humanity's oldest cultivated crops. (Ilona Loser)

research focuses almost entirely on one species, the hoary squash bee (*Peponapis pruinosa*).

"I always say I'm a one-bee woman," she jokes.

Chan finds these fuzzy, mild-natured bees pleasant to work with. They are gentle enough for her to pick up and she enjoys the simplicity of their pollination system. They only visit plants in the genus *Cucurbita*, which includes squashes, pumpkins, and other edible gourds such as zucchinis. Squash bees seek out the big, bright-coloured flowers of these plants, which bloom as separate males and females on the same vines. While most bees enjoy the copious nectar of *Cucurbita* flowers, they find the pollen difficult to feed on, or even to pick up. Honeybees and bumblebees, distant relatives in the bee "superfamily" Apidae, have corbiculae, or "pollen baskets," concave parts of their back legs fringed with stiff hairs, which they pack pollen into. These "corbiculate" bees have such trouble stuffing *Cucurbita* pollen into their pollen baskets, they give up trying. Instead, they brush it off their bodies. Chan describes "garbage heaps" of pollen, discarded by unimpressed bees. On the other hand, squash bees have no problem with these unwieldy pollen grains, which Chan calls "weird stuff."

"It's very oily, it's very large and it's very spiny," she says. "The key here is that they can handle *Cucurbita* pollen."

Chan finds the squash bee's close connection with human agriculture fascinating. Over 7,000 years ago, people domesticated squashes and other gourds in what is now Mexico. These plants might be the earliest cultivated crops on Earth. In Ontario, the Huron Wendat first farmed these plants around 1400 CE. Over centuries, as squashes and their relatives were planted farther north, squash bees followed. They are now the most widespread bee native to North America.

"Because this bee is a strict specialist, it has expanded in relationship to human cultivation," says Chan. "I would say it's just as interesting as the honeybee-human relationship. Humans are part of this ecosystem, in a sense."

Their close dependence on one type of plant and its human growers puts squash bees at risk when people plant fewer squashes and pumpkins. In 2020, when the COVID-19 pandemic imposed limits on social gatherings around Halloween and Thanksgiving, growers thought of skipping that year's pumpkin season.

"Pumpkin and squash farmers said to themselves, 'Are we going to be allowed to have pumpkin festivals?'" Chan recalls. "And many of them thought, 'We're not going to plant pumpkins because we have no-one to sell them to.'" Chan got in touch with farmers, urging them to keep planting. "If they didn't plant those pumpkins and squash, the squash bees would emerge and there would be nothing for them to eat. They're totally dependent upon human beings across most of their range."

The squash bee's intimacy with human agriculture exposes them to farm practices that include spraying crops for pests such as striped cucumber beetles, which carry bacterial wilt, a destructive and costly blight. "Bacterial wilt will just wipe out a crop in a day," says Chan.

Neonicotinoids are the weapon of choice against cucumber beetles. What worries Chan is planters spraying these pesticides on soil, where squash bees dig nest tunnels. Ground-nesting means more than just hunkering down in holes. Squash bees make vigorous contact with soil to excavate their branching tunnels. First, the bee digs a vertical shaft, up to forty-five centimetres straight down. She makes three to five lateral tunnels adjoining this shaft, each of those twelve or more centimetres. After depositing pollen and eggs in those tunnels, she heaps soil back in to cap them off. Throughout this process one bee, weighing just a tenth of a gram, moves thirty-three and a half grams of dirt.

"It's three hundred times her own weight in soil," says Chan. "It's a huge exposure." Chan sampled soil from a farm after ground-spraying was done, to see how toxic it was. "The picture is not pretty." According to her math, squash bees come in contact with pesticides in excess of the "acceptable risk threshold" for bees.[23] Chan admits her model needs data more specific to squash bees. She's needed to rely on figures from toxicity studies with honeybees, one of the most-researched insects and by far the most-studied bee.

"We don't actually know how much of the pesticide translocates from the soil into the bee," she says. "Honeybees have no exposure to soil because they don't dig in soil."

Chan followed up with field experiments where squash bees were exposed to neonicotinoids and anthranilic diamides, another family of systemic pesticides. She found reproduction dropped drastically for the bees, by 89 per cent.[24]

"It just means that their populations are going to decline," she says. "Eighty-nine per cent fewer offspring is a huge, huge impact."

Chan expects similar results to play out with other ground-nesters. "If you're going to try to protect bees, 70 per cent of which are ground-nesting, then you have to consider soil as a route of exposure."

Chan would like a ban on spraying neonicotinoids directly on soil. She calls that practice "a brutal system." She elaborates: "What you do is you plant seed and then you cover over the seed, and you spray Imidacloprid on the soil. I just don't understand why these are in use. Soil is supposed to be a living ecosystem itself."

Chemical-Free Pest Control

Chan considers herself a realist about pesticide use. She finds it unlikely that the use of chemical pest-killers will ever completely stop. Nor does she necessarily support a total ban on neonicotinoids, because other options are worse. "They're just awful — organophosphates and the pyrethroids. They're highly toxic to humans, highly toxic to every living thing. These are not nice things."

Chan is looking into non-pesticide options. With fellow researcher Peter Kevan, she's looked into "apivectoring," which uses bees to transmit "biocontrol" agents. Biocontrol means using natural enemies of pest organisms to attack them, like living pesticides. Chan has been working with honeybees for a change, to experimentally distribute spores of the fungus agent *Gliocladium catenulatum*, which goes by the product name Prestop. The method used to deliver the fungus duplicates flower behaviour by dusting bees with spores, similar to how flowers sprinkle them with pollen. Bees then drop the spores on flowers, to attack grey mold, which is ruinous for strawberries.[25]

"We're doing what flowers do," says Chan. "We're trying to take advantage of the innate behaviour of something to our advantage and also to the crop's advantage. A lot of insects attack the fruit or the flower. We can get to the fruit via the flower because the fruit develops from the flower."

Chan hopes apivectoring may one day reduce the need for chemical pesticides, which she likens to "using a sledgehammer to kill a flea." Still, she recognizes limits in the system and tempers her optimism with caution.

"I'm not promising the moon, let's put it that way," she says. "It's not a panacea. It's for very specific circumstances." Chan feels a little cautious because, like any agent of pest control, these fungal weapons could reach the wrong targets. "If they attack the pest, they can also attack the bee. They're generalists. They don't care who they're attacking, so we have to figure out systems that keep the dose low enough that they don't actually cause death in the vector."

One recurring theme in the history of bees and humans is the need to better understand how bees behave, whether those who need to know are nineteenth-century fruit growers getting schooled on pollination basics, or a scientist full of questions about the habits and vulnerabilities of bees.

"It actually is hard, hard work," says Chan. "Because human beings don't think like bees. We think like human beings. And so, we always make that mistake. Always."

As a career bee scholar, Chan admits that successfully thinking like a bee is one trick she still has yet to master, herself.

CHAPTER 11

Desperately Seeking Bumblebees

Lost on a Bee Search

Sometimes I tell people I'm a "gentleman naturalist." It's my private little joke, and I guess it's private enough that I don't recall anyone else laughing. It's how I make my nature hobby sound more grandiose than walking around parks with a camera. I can't claim I did anything so grand as stepping aboard the *Beagle* like Darwin, to make staggering discoveries that resonate through all of history. However, I did manage to get lost on the Bruce Trail looking for bumblebee nests.

In 2019, a graduate student at York University, Amanda Liczner, announced she was recruiting "citizen scientists" to join her search for bumblebee nests around a couple of conservation areas in Southern Ontario. If that project is anything to go by, field studies involve a lot of walking. One afternoon on the trail, an undergraduate named Camilla told me that, according to her phone app, we'd walked eight thousand steps and climbed the equivalent of nine flights of stairs. Phones weren't just for fitness stats in the project. Volunteers used them to call up trail maps and check GPS data. We hiked along Canada's longest footpath, gazing at screens as if we were in downtown Toronto. Unfortunately, navigating forest trails is nothing like urban walkabouts. There are no street signs or intersections, just twisting paths and trees. I managed to go astray, even with red pins on my phone flagging the spot I was sent to.

Lurching off the path, I stumbled upon two women in camo-coloured outfits, with insect netting over their faces and a panoply of gadgets. It turns out they were scientists conducting a totally different field study, unrelated to bumblebees. "Do you have a compass?" one of them asked, in a reasonable tone. She produced an orderly batch of papers and thumbed through map printouts to help me reorient. Despite her kind assistance, I never got where I was going. I at least found my way back to our group's meet-up point before anyone had to organize a search party. I suppose I took away the lesson that field science takes preparation, and maybe rudimentary wayfinding skills.

However, a couple of weeks later, even the team's best trackers hadn't found bumblebee nests. Bumblebees hide their homes well enough to flummox both experts and amateurs. One day, Sheila Colla, the professor overseeing Liczner's research, addressed volunteers. She tried to make clear why finding bumblebee nests is important. It's about habitat. When the law protects wildlife, its home is what's protected. You can't preserve a species if you don't know where it lives.

"Only, it's almost impossible to find their nests," she added.

Missing Bumblebees

Colla knows very well about missing bumblebees. Years ago, during her own graduate studies, she noticed an entire species of bumblebee seemed to be gone. The rusty-patched bumblebee (*Bombus affinis*) was once a common sight across North America. Queens of this species are unique among North American bumblebees for looking different from their workers. They are nearly all yellow except for bands of black toward the stinger, whereas males and workers have a distinctive rust-coloured band on their abdomens. This "rusty patch" is their namesake. Wherever Colla went looking, rusty-patched bumblebees were absent.

"Historical information said that we should have seen them," she tells me. "They were quite common in the seventies and eighties."

She found other species were scarce as well. Colla's surveys in Ontario, Quebec, and fourteen American states revealed that three out of fourteen bumblebee species were not where records said they should be. Four other species were declining where they had been plentiful thirty years earlier.[1] The public reacted with shocked interest and Colla became an instant media figure. Suddenly, she was speaking to major news outlets about her graduate work. In 2008, while the press circulated stories about colony collapse, environmental writer Adrian Higgins quoted Colla for a

Absent bumblebee: The rusty-patched bumblebee (*Bombus affinis*) was once a common sight in Eastern North America; but this bee has not been seen in Canada at all since 2009, and fewer than five hundred of them have been recently counted in the United States. (US Fish and Wildlife Service Midwest Region)

piece in the *Washington Post* titled "Signs of Decline: First Honeybees, Now Bumblebees."[2]

"I was doing all that stuff as a first/second year PhD student, which was pretty unusual," says Colla. "So, I ended up having to be the science communicator, because I was one of the only people studying bee declines in Canada at the time and everyone wanted to talk about it."

In 2010, Colla filed a status report for the rusty-patched bumblebee with the Committee on the Status of Endangered Wildlife in Canada (COSEWIC), a necessary first step toward declaring species endangered in Canada.[3] In 2015, Colla collaborated with scientists outside Canada to have the bee declared "critically endangered" on the International Union for Conservation of Nature's (IUCN) Red List.[4] The rusty-patched bumblebee has virtually disappeared from Canada. Colla was the last person to spot one in 2009. In the United States, the only nation anyone still sees it, the bee's historical range has shrunk by an estimated 87 per cent.

The rusty-patched bumblebee is now something of a symbol for insect and bee declines; but it's not the only bumblebee in trouble. According to the Xerces Society, more than one-quarter of bumblebee species in North America face some sort of extinction risk. Colla has collaborated on threatened species reports for other bees, including the American bumblebee (*Bombus pensylvanicus*) and the gypsy cuckoo bumblebee

(*Bombus bohemicus*). It is not clear why so many North American bumble-bees are disappearing.

One hypothesis that's gained traction suggests the cause was patho-gens imported from Europe. In the 1990s, agricultural researchers shut-tled North American bumblebees across the Atlantic, and then back, on a research trip to learn more about breeding them for crop pollination. After the bees returned from Europe, numbers began crashing for the western bumblebee (*Bombus occidentalis*), the yellow-banded bumblebee (*Bombus terricola*), the rusty-patched bumblebee, and Franklin's bumble-bee (*Bombus franklini*), now feared extinct. Perhaps a European virus in-vaded these species, but that may never be verified.

Colla fears more declines are to come. Six of the eight bees listed on Canada's species at risk registry are bumblebees, and the list may get longer. Many more bees still need assessing. The backlog frustrates Colla.

"There are, like, 200 species waiting to be to be dealt with," she says. Her patience with progress sounds frayed. "Yeah, working with govern-ment has got us nowhere so far." Colla laments that the rusty-patched bumblebee, despite its media presence, has not seen much progress, conservation-wise. "It still doesn't have a recovery strategy ten years later. And after the recovery strategy, there's supposed to be a management plan. That's not written, either. So, ten years later, they've done nothing to try to conserve the species. And in the meantime, it's disappeared."

Wild Nest Chase

During her field study, Liczner does not expect to see rusty-patched bum-blebees along the Bruce Trail, but she hopes to encounter more species than she ultimately finds. Most of the time, we sight common eastern bumblebees (*Bombus impatiens*), a species that's actually doing all right. These bees have bright yellow thoraxes and black abdomens, except for one yellow band. We see several of these buzzing around tufted cow vetch, an invasive plant. Farmers dislike cow vetch because the plant chokes out their crops, but bees find their purple flowers irresistible.

"They love it," says Liczner. "It's a really good nectar source. What forage are they going to have if you get rid of that?"

A paper Liczner co-authored with fellow bee scientist Shelby Gibson is titled "Conservation Conundrum." It delves into the quandary between controlling invasive plants and conserving bumblebees.⁵ Such dilemmas aside, the scientists urge volunteers to keep an eye on cow vetch for bumblebees – especially workers, much smaller than queens, but large in importance. Workers mean nests could be nearby.

Each year, young queens (called "gynes") start spring with no nests and no workers. These fuzzy females mated with males the summer before, before going to sleep for the winter. The males died in the fall, when the old queen and her colony's workers also passed away. In the tropics, bumblebee colonies might persist a few years, but in North America, they only survive one season. Young queens, born in summer, are sole survivors. Each gyne wakes from hibernation with an epic solo task: to start a new colony from scratch. She cobbles together a jumbled-looking mound of wax, which she provisions with pollen and nectar and populates with eggs. Once her offspring emerge as workers, she'll have help. But before she can lay down her first wax, she needs a suitable nesting spot, perhaps an abandoned rodent burrow. Some bumblebee colonies nest above ground, and cover their homes with dead grass. Others dwell in trees. There are a daunting number of places to search for bumblebee nests, which take up little more space than a grapefruit, usually. Still, Liczner thought she would try, sensing an ecological need.

"A lot of what we know about bumblebee habitat is just focused on flowers and their foraging needs," she says. "But if we're missing nesting, we're missing a huge chunk of their habitat that they need. If they can't make the nest, you're not going to have bumblebees that year. It's a lot harder to study. But it's important to study."

Finding nests doesn't look all that easy for bumblebees, either. The gynes we saw seemed to be on futile searches. For several minutes, I watched a queen scratch and toil furiously under a pile of leaves. She kicked up a bee-sized quantity of dirt but made nothing close to a hole. Another queen found a hole and disappeared into it, only to emerge minutes later and leave the spot altogether. Liczner has no explanation for such behaviour.

"I don't know," she says. "Sometimes they went in a hole for fifteen minutes and they came back out. I don't know the things that they're looking at. Sometimes they'd go into the dirt and start digging and then they'd just decide to get up and fly away. Why now? Why would you fly away, now? Sometimes they'll search really slow, really detailed. And then other times they're just, zip-zip-zip through the whole place. I was left with more questions than I had answers."

At one point, a perplexed Liczner voiced her exasperation at a searching queen, which seemed to be getting nowhere. "Find a nest," she scolded. "Why haven't you found a nest yet?"

Liczner had cause for frustration. The study was her doctoral project. Pressure further compounded when she got sick and had to power through a tough cold. Meanwhile, queens faced their own deadlines. They were still nest-searching as spring turned into summer. I asked Liczner whether some bees were just destined to fail.

"It could be," she said. "It's like, what are you doing? Were you the sleepy one? Are you just bad at finding nesting habitat? Are these ones that we're still seeing the losers? They're just searching this habitat because there's nothing left? See, more questions than answers."

It became clear that at least some queens had founded colonies when workers started appearing, looking like furry miniatures of queens. During one outing, a group of two scientists and two volunteers, including me, tried to stealthily surround a worker. The bee suddenly flew straight up, swiftly shrinking to a small fuzzy dot, before anyone saw which way she went. Liczner's enthusiasm gradually started to wane for nest-finding false alarms.

"I got more jaded," she admits. "But volunteers are excited, and they're new at it. 'Yeah, it's a nest, it's a nest.' But it was never a nest."

Liczner tried her luck with search dogs, to see whether they could sniff out nests. She spent early mornings training three detection dogs. She brought the dogs nest samples from laboratories and led them to active nests, reported at people's residences, to help give them the scent. The dogs located no nests along the Bruce Trail, but Liczner gathered plenty of data on the challenges of training dogs to find bee domiciles. Detection dogs are renowned for sniffing out drugs, explosive chemicals, and other hidden things. But in wilderness, dogs don't know where to sniff for nests any better than humans know where to look for them.[6]

"There are certain research questions that you wouldn't be able to answer with the dogs," says Liczner. "Like, what's the density of bumblebee nests at this site? Because the dog would have to search every square inch of a given area."

Liczner's efforts with dog detection followed the example of UK bumblebee scientist Dave Goulson. Goulson and his students made use of search dogs trained by the British military, to see if they could sniff out bumblebee nests. The dogs successfully found over a hundred nests in UK search areas. They did not, however, do significantly better than human volunteers, who got equally skilled at nest-finding while training the dogs.[7]

A lot can be said for painstaking human effort. During the summer months of 2018 and 2019 (when Liczner's crew was searching in Ontario), Genevieve Pugesek and Elizabeth Crone from Tufts University, in Medford, Massachusetts, spent 160 gruelling hours conducting systematic surveys that covered six hectares of hayfields, meadows, and forests. These searches were supplemented by many more hours of wide-ranging "free searches" involving four investigators that wandered "haphazardly" through study sites. In all, they located 51 bumblebee nests, belonging to various species. In their paper, published in 2021, the scientists noted the intensity of their searching "may seem prohibitive to ecologists," but added the effort involved was "similar to or less than the amount of labor required to locate nests of cavity- and ground-nesting birds."[8]

Recruiting Citizen Searchers

In counterpoint to Pugesek and Crone's small-staffed, concentrated searches, Elaine Evans at the University of Minnesota relies on widespread efforts from a steady stream of volunteers. Her academic title, "extension professor and researcher," encompasses her dual role as scientist and public educator. She helps people learn about bee conservation while they gather data for the Minnesota Bee Atlas, a volunteer-driven effort to map bee diversity. Evans is well-acquainted with the power of public concern to motivate data-gathering on bumblebees, especially in Minnesota, where the rusty-patched bumblebee is still sighted.[9] Educating people about the threatened bee helps recruit observers, especially those she's able to talk to. Two of the four nests she's found for the rusty-patched bee were reported to her by people she personally met.

"One of them, she's actually on the board of directors of a nature centre where we had done bumblebee surveys and we had found rusty-patched

Elusive bee nest: Wax cells from a nest that once belonged to a colony of rusty-patched bumblebees. This abandoned nest was found by researchers from the University of Minnesota in 2020. The threatened bee is a rare sight, even in Minnesota, where it is still seen. (Elaine Evans)

bees there," says Evans. "The other one was actually a good friend of mine who just moved into a house that year and he was seeing these bumble-bees come out by his back step."

Another nest turned up in the foundations of someone's house. "There was a big open crawlspace," she says. Luckily, the nest was in a spot accessible to researchers and not deeper into the house's structure. "They can be actually inside of walls that are enclosed, and then you'd have to take the house apart to get to them."

Another two nests were found in old rodent burrows, and didn't look like much from the surface. "From outside, it's not distinguishable at all," she relates. "It's just a tiny hole in the ground and you just notice it from the activity of bees going in and out."

Evans welcomes such opportunistic finds but thinks the best way to spot bees and their nests is through regular searches, so she organizes search groups.

"I've had a number of volunteers that have found nests when they're out looking for bees just by walking around on the prairie or in the woods and just stumbling on them."

The internet has proven a valuable tool for recruiting bee hunters. Bumble Bee Watch, a website that Evans took part in creating, solicits bumblebee photos and posts them with virtual pins in maps to show where sightings took place. Evans has coordinated in-person searches using data from these digital maps.

"I was able to home in on locations where I would be more likely to find rusty-patched bumblebees," she says.

In 2006, before Evans had a network of virtual volunteers, she was struggling to gather data for the Xerces Society about rusty-patched bumblebees and their endangered cousins, the yellow-banded and western bumblebees. This information was badly needed by the Xerces Society for its petition to declare the bee endangered. Evans hit on the notion of crowdsourcing the data.

"There were a lot of gaps in records, and we just started a public awareness campaign," she says. "So, we made posters asking people to take pictures and send them in to the Xerces Society."

In response to her call for photos, the Xerces Society inbox was bombarded with images of bumblebees – not just species Evans asked about, but every kind. In an effort to channel the flood of responses, the Xerces Society founded Bumble Bee Watch, which formally launched in 2014.[10] To date, the website has posted more than 98,000 sightings of individual bumblebees and nearly 800 nests. Bee scholars who run the site try to help citizen scientists improve their ID skills with visual guides. Then, like proper teachers, they check the work of their online students.

Victoria MacPhail, from York University, is one of the website's hosts. MacPhail got curious about the accuracy of Bumble Bee Watch's citizen-sourced data. She analyzed it to see how well people learned to recognize bees from the website's guides and prompts. MacPhail's study used a statistical system called "Cohen's kappa coefficient" to estimate whether people made educated choices based on what they had learned, or just random guesses. By MacPhail's estimation, citizen scientists did pretty well. Submitters to the site were 70 per cent accurate, on average. This success rate merits "substantial agreement," or much better than mere chance, in the Cohen's kappa system. MacPhail uncovered biases, though, such as a well-meaning tendency to misidentify species as the rusty-patched bumblebee. The number of people making this error would jump in response to public awareness campaigns about the bee's plight.[11]

"We have these campaigns: 'Find the rusty-patched bumblebee,'" says MacPhail. "And so often I have people go, 'Oh, I've got those bees in my back yard. I see those bees all the time when I go to my cottage.'

"I'm like, 'Are you sure?'

"'Oh yes, I'm sure. I'm sure. That's the bee I have.' But it's not. It's another species. They've heard of the rusty-patched bumblebee. They know it's rare. And so, they're kind of predisposed to find it or they think they have it."

MacPhail hopes this statistical learning helps improve the site's instructional tools, and not just to increase its research value, but to better teach volunteers.

"We don't just want data to come in to us, we want people to develop a passion about bees and conservation," she says. "A lot of them are joining Bumble Bee Watch to learn about bees."

Bartering free naturalist learning for citizen-sourced data seems to work, going by the number of websites like Bumble Bee Watch. There is a litany of sites devoted to bird observations, from hummingbirds to condors. Pl@ntNet is for botany lovers. BugGuide, founded by entomologists at Iowa State University, asks for observations of "insects, spiders, and their kin" from the United States and Canada. iNaturalist, a joint initiative by the California Academy of Sciences and the National Geographic Society, is the largest and most far-reaching. It asks for photos of any species, from anyplace in the world. Scientists volunteer their time to curate the site, which has interactive algorithms to help submitters identify species. It has more than one million registered observers and curates close to 70 million sightings of more than 300,000 species – a sixth of all named organisms.[12]

Every summer, iNaturalist holds its yearly "Backyard Bumble Bee Count," a scheduled blitz of bumblebee observations. In 2021, the site tallied 4,250 sightings of 41 bumblebee species by 356 citizen naturalists.[13]

Photos submitted by people ranged from basic cell phone snaps to lovingly composed art shots.

Bumblebees, while popular, are not the most sighted insects on iNaturalist. According to a 2019 survey, monarch butterflies are the most observed species, followed by honeybees.[14] While not at the very top, bumblebees have their own kind of charisma. The rusty-patched bumblebee itself is a poster child of sorts, a threatened beluga or polar bear among insects. In 2017, an editorial in *Smithsonian Magazine* dubbed it "the bee that breaks your heart."[15] MacPhail muses on the importance of "flagship species" in ecology campaigns.

"Bumblebees are big; they're visible, people like them," she says. "They're nice, big colourful things that are easy to see and easy to picture, versus, 'There's a tiny little black thing that's a couple of millimetres long, crawling on the ground.' There's a lot of public perception, a lot of bias towards a cute bumblebee versus that cute cockroach or something like that. That's why you need to mix social science with natural science."

Good intentions potentially lead to good science. Hopefully, without losing any citizen scientists in the woods, on the hunt for bee nests.

CHAPTER 12

Insect Noses and Night Flowers

Urban Moth Watchers

A group of insect lovers proceeds with a coordinated effort to rescue one small moth that fell off a lighted bedsheet. Mercury vapour lamps illuminate sepia stains on the fabric, which is draped across ropes. An assortment of night insects perch there, indifferent to all the fuss. The fallen moth is trapped somewhere beneath a length of deadwood holding down the sheet. People softly consult with one another, assessing how to remove the wood without injuring the moth. They position themselves around the log, then gently raise it together, finally releasing the moth from a bunched-up section of sheet where it was caught. The small, fluttering creature they liberate is a yellow-spotted webworm (*Anageshna primordialis*). In moth lore, there are "webworms," "cloverworms," "bagworms," and "cankerworms." These wormy nicknames reference their caterpillar phase, before their transition to reproductive adults. Webworm caterpillars spin gauzy nests of silk between tree branches and nest there throughout their voracious, leaf-eating larval stage. In their adult form, yellow-spotted webworms have patterned brown-and-gold wings. They spend three months of maturity, which is the rest of their lives, trying to mate and lay eggs.

The people who showed such touching concern for this little creature take part in the High Park Moth Study, a citizen naturalist effort to observe and identify moths and other night insects. They leaf through much-thumbed copies of the *Peterson Field Guide to Moths of Northeastern North America*, reciting strange names from its pages: "toadflax brocade," "banded tussock moth," "great oak dagger," and "small-eyed sphinx." The pace they work at, rattling off these names, looks impressive to newcomers. But according to the humble moth fans, they're just getting good at it.[1] Formed in 2016, the High Park moth group reached its stated milestone of identifying one thousand species by 2020. Some members pursue their own personal bests with competitive fervour. One moth seeker speaks excitedly of his high standing in iNaturalist's Moth Week Bioblitz. Richard Aaron, one of the group's founders, is proud of its progress but feels it has further to go before its data is meaningful.

"I would say that we don't have enough years of data to make any generalizations about population trends," he informs me. "We've only been doing the study for five years."

Moon Flowers by Many Names

Scientists definitely want more moth data. An estimated half of all insects are nocturnal, and since their lives are lived unheard and unseen in darkness, they're much harder to study. There are plenty of unknowns around these insects, such as their pollination role. There are certainly some flowers that open their petals after dusk. Several plants share the nickname "moonflower," such as tropical white morning glory (a.k.a. "moonflower" or "moon vine"), a trumpet-shaped flower indigenous to Central and South America. Gardeners admire its pearly white petals and intoxicating scent.

Queen of the night (*Epiphyllum oxypetalum*), native to Mexico and much of South America, opens its many petals just one night each year. Hawkmoths come and sip the flower's nectar, hovering in mid-air, and then fly off, pollen stuck to their tongues. Bats that feed on nectar, such as the Mexican long-tongued bat, shove their snouts into these ephemeral blossoms and depart with pollen stuck to their fur. Things can get interesting after dark, when the queen of the night opens for business.

"There's a lot that goes on at night," says Robert Raguso, a biologist at Cornell University.

Raguso has long held an interest in hawkmoths and plants they pollinate, such as *Oenothera caespitosa*, a desert flower called by many names: tufted evening primrose, desert evening primrose, rock-rose evening primrose, and fragrant evening primrose. What fascinates Raguso about these white-petalled flowers is their many distinguishable scents. He encountered desert evening primroses one night early in his career, while taking an evening stroll. He was struck not only by the flower's strong fragrance, but the variety of smells one patch of flowers, just of that species, produced.

"I could smell, on the side of the road, different chemistry in different individuals," he recalls. "Their individual variation was off the chart. It would be like entering a population of buttercups and finding red, blue, green, and yellow buttercups of the same species." This olfactory epiphany sent Raguso down a unique research path. His focus became floral scent. "From the beginning of my career, my feeling was, 'Whoah, it's not just colour.' The world is full of really different fragrances."

Uncorking the Science of Smells

One of Raguso's lectures is tantalizingly titled "When Flowers Smell Like Wine." It introduces the intriguing chemistry of "floral volatiles," molecules that make flowers smell like flowers. In part, the talk's title plays on evening primrose's genus, *Oenothera*, which means "wine-seeker" in Greek. As he unpacks the science of smells, Raguso sounds like a wine connoisseur, making picturesque comparisons of floral odours to redolent things like "Earl Grey tea" and "very sweet bergamot oil."

"I have to," he tells me. Raguso felt he needed compelling language to win over skeptical colleagues, reluctant at first to give grants to a young scientist who wanted to sniff primroses. "The pushback I got at meetings was, 'We're not convinced that flower scent matters in generalized pollination.'"

While expanding his connoisseur's vocabulary, Raguso enlarged his knowledge of organic chemistry to get better at finding extraordinary proof for what others thought of as offbeat claims. "Almost like a cook, I wanted to smell something and say, 'I know what that is. I smell clove oil. I smell vanilla. I smell grape.' And then I wanted to know, in terms of biochemistry, what that means. The smell of a grape involves an amino acid, tryptophan, and benzene, an 'aromatic' compound frequently found in perfumes. That's a very powerful thing, to be able to smell a note and say, 'Ah, that has a citrus nose to it.' But I know the chemistry now."

A chemist's kitchen features different appliances from that of a master chef. Instead of oven ranges, it has mechanisms to pump and collect scent-laden air, in a process called "dynamic headspace sampling." Contraptions called gas chromatographs analyze compounds in air samples, down to their smallest chemical components.[2] We can think of plants as sophisticated chemical factories. Botanists estimate that plants manufacture anywhere between one hundred thousand and one million different chemicals.[3] All of these are fabricated through photosynthesis. With the building blocks of water, CO_2, and sunlight, plants manufacture sugars, fats, proteins, enzymes, and other "metabolites" to help them grow and flourish. They also make sweet-smelling benzenes; pungent terpenes, which produce the "skunky" smell in cannabis; and jasmone, the odorous component of both jasmine and freshly mown grass.

"What they all have in common is that they're small molecules with vapour pressure," says Raguso. "That's what makes them odours."

If plants are natural chemical factories, animals are living chemical detectors, with instruments to sense with, or rather to smell with, since smell is a chemical sense. Olfactory equipment ranges from Robert Raguso's well-trained nose to a moth's multiple intakes for smells on its abdomen, thorax, legs, antennae, and wings. Scent is a crucial part of floral attraction because insects are better at smelling than seeing, even in the daytime. Primroses are a large and varied family, with 2,600 species. Many of them are day-bloomers, with sunny-sounding nicknames such as "suncup" and "sundrop." When diurnal primroses flash their yellow petals in daytime, Raguso believes their scent, not their hue, is what first alerts sun-loving pollinators.

"Insects are generally very near-sighted," Raguso says. "They can't really change their focal depth. If you're in a field full of yellow or blue flowers, you can see all that from a distance because it fills your visual space, but you can't resolve individual shapes."

Sensory Studies of Hawkmoths

Hawkmoths are lured by the striking scents and moon-reflecting petals of desert evening primroses. Pollen dangles from primrose flowers on wispy threads of sap-based material called "viscin," which stick to pollinators like crazy string. As long-distance flyers, hawkmoths carry these sticky strands, bejewelled with pollen, several kilometres at times. The large moths, comparable in size to small birds, have been tracked winging their way between islands in the Caribbean.

Primrose pollen: Primrose pollen grains dangle on wispy strands of sap-based material called viscin, which sticks to pollinators like crazy string. (Djpmapleferryman via Creative Commons)

"Hawkmoths are wayfarers," says Raguso. "They're vagrants. They don't defend territories like bees or hummingbirds. So, if they get loaded up with pollen, they could fly twelve kilometres with that pollen and visit another *Oenothera* (evening primrose). Hawkmoths are famous for this."

Raguso has measured the long-distance smelling power of hawkmoths by hooking electrodes to their antennae. Working with fellow scientist Jeff Riffell, Raguso mapped which parts of their brains lit up when they smelled chemicals such as methyl benzoate, found in essential oils including ylang-ylang and linalool. Raguso sees hawkmoths as a "model system" for insect olfaction. Still, he realizes scent does not replace vision, which evokes different notions of spatial reality. "The problem with olfaction is it's not three-dimensional," he says. "It's hyperdimensional. It's a lot harder to visualize olfactory space."

Raguso compared the workings of sight and smell in moths with help from Mark Willis, a biologist in Tucson who studies moth pheromones in wind tunnels. In return, Raguso cajoled Willis out of his lab into a flower patch.

"I said to Mark, 'Hey let's go out in the desert and study these moths in real life.'"

Raguso took Willis just outside Tucson to the Sonoran Desert Museum, which has a night-blooming garden. The two hunkered down among evening primroses and trumpet-shaped jimsonweeds (*Datura stramonium*), another white-petalled species known as "moonflowers."

"These night-blooming flowers are white against the dark background," he recalls. "They glow as the sun is setting. It's an amazing visual effect that they have. It was perfect. We could film them, we could watch them, we could manipulate flowers. We did experiments."

One night, Martina Wicklein, a colleague of bee vision maestro Lars Chittka, joined Raguso and Willis. Wicklein studies the different visual neurons hummingbirds and hawkmoths possess, which fire when they recognize flowers.

"In the car, we're having a playful argument about whether olfaction or vision would be more important to moths," says Raguso. "Then, during the first ten minutes of watching them visit the flowers, that argument was popped like a balloon." Sitting motionless, in dark clothing, Raguso and company crouched at flower level and waited. Approaching moths were first summoned by the scent, which Raguso and Willis tried, with difficulty, to visualize.

"What we started to imagine was, you perceive odour from a distance as a cloud or as a trail. And you [the moth] orient yourself into that cloud." But then the three lurking scientists watched a subtle shift happen within about one metre of the flower. "Their velocity of flight changes and their tongue comes out. And from that point forward, it's visual. It was so obviously a multi-channel, multi-modal behaviour. That was amazing for us to see. I mean, we didn't cure cancer, right? But we saw it again and again."[4]

Another dimension follows in that sensory progression: touch. Moths feel their way by sensing tiny textures in flower petals. Research by one of Raguso's students, Joaquín Goyret, from Uruguay, zeroed in on these floral microtextures. Through high-speed video, Raguso and Goyret watched moth after moth tap its proboscis "like a blind man's stick."[5] Again, one sense didn't act in isolation. Before tapping its tongue on a petal's surface, a moth would work out visually where to place its proboscis according to

Aerial pollination: Airborne hawkmoth feeding on the desert flower jimsonweed. Multiple senses are successively triggered in hawkmoths as they pollinate: scent, sight, touch, and finally, taste. (Mike Lewinski)

light and dark contrasts. It then felt around to find the flower's nectary. "There are these rules: there's olfaction, then it's vision, then it's touch. And then the last rule is taste. The tip of the proboscis is studded with sugar receptors, and it just goes, 'Boom! Hey, there – target, we got it.' So that's four sensory channels in a second and a half."

Super Scented Flowers with Live-In Pollinators

Blooming at night is a good adaptation for desert flowers such as jimson-weed and desert primroses because deserts are dry places and flowers lose less moisture at night.[6] Some nocturnal desert flowers specialize on certain pollinators and scent can be a powerful prompt for specializing. Another plant group Raguso studies is yucca flowers. These powerfully scented flowers are so closely linked with moths that pollinate them, the moths share their host flower's name. The small, whitish yucca moth is considered a case study in "obligate mutualism," because of its evolved codependence with yucca flowers. Yucca moths don't simply sprinkle pollen on their night-blooming namesake. With great care, a female yucca moth stuffs pollen into the flower's bulky female part, its pistil, which has a cup-shaped vessel for pollen to go in. When the moth's larvae hatch, they consume some of the flower's seeds, but leave enough of them uneaten to sprout new yucca plants.

The yucca moth's one-flower lifestyle includes mating in yucca flowers, which give off an aphrodisiac smell.[7] In 2021, Raguso took part in research which examined how the yucca flower's bouquet sets off amorous impulses in its resident moths. He and fellow scientists proved the powerful influence of the flower's odour by removing its floral parts until nothing remained but its smelly centre. Yucca moths still wanted to mate in dismembered flowers with no petals at all.[8]

Throwing Light on Nocturnal Pollinators

While nocturnal pollinators are clearly important to desert wildflowers, UK researchers wanted to see whether night pollination had any benefits for agriculture. Scientists at University College London set out to see whether moths pollinated in or around farm fields. The British scientists took nighttime trips across Norfolk County, on the eastern tip of England. Between 2016 and 2017, they went to flower fields next to crops of sugar beet, oilseed rape, cereal grains, and beans.

They caught moths around the margins of ponds, where wildflowers were diverse, and swabbed pollen off of their bodies. For comparison, they collected bees, hoverflies, wasps, and butterflies from the same flower patches during daytime. Half the moths they caught had zero pollen on them, but the rest had picked up pollen from forty-seven plant species. This gave the moths a slight edge over their daytime competitors, which altogether pollinated forty-six flowering species. The researchers were fascinated to find pollen on moth thoraxes, not just their tongues as expected. This implied that moths pick up more pollen than previously thought.[9]

Fascinating though their findings were, the researchers did not witness moths pollinating crops. But moth activity in flower patches might help crop plants indirectly. By competing for flowers with bees, flies, and other insects, moths may drive these pollinators to forage more often in farm fields. The scientists suggested making competition more intense, by planting moth favourites such as bull thistles (*Cirsium vulgare*), gypsywort (*Lycopus europaeus*), and water mint (*Mentha aquatica*), so more moths would visit.[10]

Authors of another UK study urged people to turn off lights, especially in cities, to increase moth pollination. The British scientists compared pollination in dark places to that in areas flooded with artificial light. They recorded up to 25 per cent fewer moth visits in brightly lit locations. They also saw pollination rates go down in brighter spots, proving through absence that moth pollination mattered.[11] To quote a common idiom, perhaps some things are best left in the dark.

CHAPTER 13

Butterflies, Bats, and Border Walls

Continent-Crossing Butterflies

It's fall in Toronto. Monarch butterflies, preparing to migrate south, sun themselves on the north shore of Lake Ontario. They don't look like they're in a hurry to go anyplace. They lounge in the sand, soaking up sunlight with their orange and black wings. Now and then, they flutter for short distances across the beach before they settle down and bask some more. Butterflies are living solar collectors. Their wings are covered in light-trapping cells. Along with moths, they belong to the order Lepidoptera, which roughly translates to "scaled wings." Up close, the scales look like overlapping shingles. These little tiles are so good at catching sunlight that engineers study them for photovoltaics research.[1] Once they are warmed up and ready, these monarchs will fly up to 140 kilometres per day on a two-month trip covering 5,000 kilometres – an incredible distance to push their delicate bodies. Their record is unmatched for longest insect migration.[2]

The Forgotten Pollinators is an important and influential book co-authored by botanist and science writer Gary Paul Nabhan and entomologist Steven Buchmann, who take turns trading facts and anecdotes about pollination. In a section concerning monarchs, Nabhan narrates what happens once the butterflies reach Mexico. He describes the ground at the foot of oyamel fir trees littered with exhausted monarchs. Some of them reach the mountain trees only to fall back out, too spent to recover. The ones on the ground flutter their wings, too weak to fly. Others have already died. Nabhan counts three dozen "dead or dying butterflies." Those that survived the journey cluster in branches like "flamboyant shingles of tens of thousands."[3]

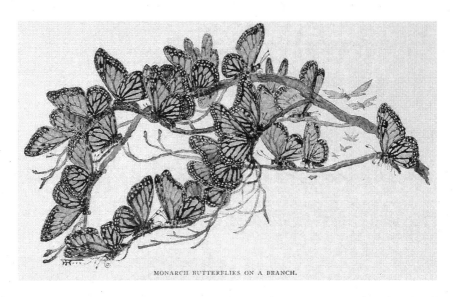

MONARCH BUTTERFLIES ON A BRANCH.

Monarchs on a branch: Landscape illustrator Harry Fenn's self-described "careful sketch" of monarch butterflies on a tree branch in Mexico. Millions of monarchs overwinter in fir trees in Mexico and parts of southern California. In the spring, this "super-generation," which migrated south in the fall, will begin the trip back. But it will take two more, shorter generations to complete the "return" trip to Canada and the northern United States – places they have never been. (Harry Fenn)

Those stolid survivors will rest in the trees until mating time in spring. When that time comes, they'll wing their way to someplace warmer, such as Texas, to copulate and lay eggs. When new monarchs, conceived by this "super-generation," come out of their chrysalises, they'll start heading "back" to where their parents once basked by Lake Ontario. They won't make it all the way; they lack the super-generation's longevity. It will take two more short-lived generations to finish the trek north.[4] In the end, they'll make it. What's remarkable is that no-one understands how, three generations later, these butterflies have any idea where to go. Monarchs have excellent on-board navigation, with a light-sensing "sun compass" in their antennae.[5] Yet how they're capable of finding a place they've never been with such accuracy is one of nature's great "how-did-they-do-that" moments.

The monarch butterfly's epic migration also powerfully illustrates the complexity of habitat. The eastern monarch's migratory "habitat" ranges from Canada to Mexico, with many flower patches in between.

Milkweeds: Noxious but Necessary

Monarchs sip nectar from a variety of flowers, maybe catching pollen with their bodies, although their long legs limit contact with anthers. Nectar-seeking monarchs don't necessarily return to the same flowers, so they're not the most consistent pollinators. However, one plant gets their constant attention. Monarchs always return to milkweeds.

A number of insects sample nectar from the milkweed's cluster of small flowers, called "florets." Stepping into a milkweed's florets can get sticky. An insect's leg might feel the tug of a small, toothy trap called a "stigmatic slit." While the insect struggles to free itself, two sticky clumps of pollen, called "pollinia" (see chapter 3), are pressed onto its limbs. Some victims of this floral assault end up permanently snared, but monarchs have enough leg power to pull away. However much milkweeds pull their legs, female monarchs seek them out, because these plants are where they come to lay their small, ovoid eggs.

When caterpillars hatch from these eggs, they feed voraciously on the milkweed plant's thick, veiny leaves. Caterpillars need plenty of nourishment as they molt through five discrete growth stages, called "instars." They increase from two millimetres to four centimetres – twenty times their original size – before they pupate into butterflies. To reach maturity, they must dine steadily on plant leaves that most creatures find poisonous. Leaves from milkweeds secrete a milky white sap full of toxic steroids known as cardenolides. This sap's effects on creatures that ingest it range from unpleasant to poisonous. Not so for monarch caterpillars. They have a mutation that makes them resistant to milkweed's noxious "milk" as it accumulates in their bodies.[6]

As the caterpillars start to gorge and grow, their bodies display bands of black and gold. These stripes send a message to birds and other predators that the caterpillars are bad to eat. As adults, their patterned wings vividly send the same message. People view monarch wings, with their painterly swirls of black and burnt orange, as living art. That might be because humans don't try to eat monarchs. Perhaps if people did, they might think more of their stomachs churning with toxins when monarchs fluttered past. The warning does not work equally well on every predator, and neither does the poison. Orioles and grosbeaks feed on monarchs, and seem to share the butterfly's tolerance for cardenolides. But for the most part,

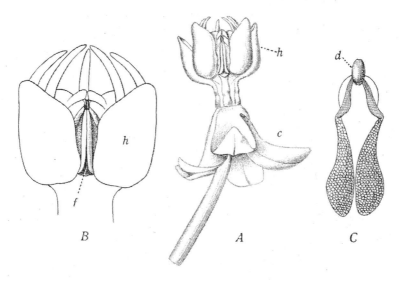

Pollen trap: Milkweed florets have five upward-pointing structures called "hoods," with toothy parts called "horns." Narrow slivers of space between these pointy parts are the "stigmatic slits." A nectar-sipping insect might get its leg caught in one of these slits. The flower presses two sticky pollen sacs called "pollinia" onto the trapped insect's leg. (Internet Archive Book Images)

its wing markings confer such a survival edge that two non-poisonous butterflies, viceroys and queens, mimic the monarch's appearance.

Yet, while humans love monarchs (and their lookalikes), we haven't always loved milkweeds. In the past, the plant's noxious nature has triggered efforts to cull them. Farmers disliked their cows getting sick from eating milkweeds, and urbanites found them unpleasant. For years, milkweeds were classed as noxious weeds, and were culled around cities and farmland, radically reducing their numbers.

But then it became increasingly clear that when milkweeds went away, so did monarchs. Worried conservationists started campaigns to turn perceptions around, such as "Got Milkweed," a charm offensive by the David Suzuki Foundation that encouraged people to plant milkweed. Several American and Canadian cities declared themselves monarch-friendly and encouraged gardeners to grow milkweeds. When Toronto campaigned for people to plant milkweeds in 2018, the city's residents put an estimated 25,000 plants in the ground. Now, even people who don't like milkweeds plant them. One neighbour told me she found the flowers un-attractive but grew them anyway, out of concern for monarchs.

Such devoted acts might benefit monarchs within cities, but their migrations must also cross wilderness, as well as farmland where milkweeds are 80 per cent less common since the 1990s, thanks to aggressive weed management.[7] Some research suggests weed-killers such as Roundup™ destroy milkweeds near Roundup-resistant plants. By one estimate, a staggering 850 million milkweeds perished in proximity to Roundup-Ready corn and soybeans since 1999.[8] Some experts counter that such declines were underway before Roundup-Ready crops existed.[9] In any case, 11 million milkweeds have vanished from former grassland converted to farmland. Facing this reality, some scientists suggest to farmers that they plant milkweeds around their fields.[10]

In North America, monarch numbers have not improved all that much; in fact, they've been doing the opposite. In the twenty-first century's first couple of decades, the eastern monarch, which migrates from to Mexico from southeastern Canada and the northeastern United States, declined by 80 per cent. Western monarchs, which overwinter in southern California, have dropped by 99 per cent since the 1980s. In 2019, western monarchs hovered around 30,000, close to extinction.[11] Their apparent bounce-back in 2021 only managed to inspire cautious optimism in ecologists, badly stung by past losses. In a blog for the Xerces Society, conservation biologist Emma Pelton warned, "It's crucial to remember that the modest uptick we're seeing is not population recovery or even evidence of an upward trajectory."[12]

Butterfly Border Problems

Replanting scores of milkweeds in cities and even around farms might not be enough to restore the world's most-travelled butterfly. People also cut down trees where monarchs overwinter, to harvest wood or clear land. In 2021, the World Wildlife Fund (WWF) in Mexico reported oyamel firs occupied just 2.1 hectares of the mountains where eastern monarchs overwinter. The WWF finds this amount of space concerning. Its experts claim monarchs need at least six hectares of habitat with oyamel firs and other conditions — natural shelter from the elements, sufficient water, and enough nectar sources.[13] With less available living space, more monarchs cluster around fewer trees, which intensifies every risk they face. Monarchs forced into fewer locations are more vulnerable to calamities such as droughts, flash frosts, and forest fires, which can potentially wipe out more of them at once. Climate change, unfortunately, raises the likelihood of fires and storms.

Some Mexican ecologists propose planting oyamel firs farther up mountainsides to increase their presence. But critics of such plans worry that up-mountain tree plantings will disrupt other habitats.[14] Mexican lawmakers try to protect existing trees from being cut down, but illegal logging still happens. Loggers sometimes attack conservationists. In 2020, Homero Gómez González, who managed El Rosario Monarch Butterfly Preserve, was strangled to death and dumped in a well. Days later, tour guide Raúl Hernández Romero was fatally stabbed.[15]

Cross-border politics also disrupt monarch migrations. Between 2016 and 2020, during Donald Trump's presidency, crews started work on a barrier meant to span all 1,954 miles (3,145 kilometres) of the United States–Mexico border, purportedly to stop illegal human migrations. According to US Customs and Border Protection, 452 miles (727 kilometres) of "border wall" were completed during Trump's tenure. An anti-immigration non-profit in Texas, called We Build the Wall, raised funds to construct three additional miles (four kilometres) of steel and concrete barrier near Mission, Texas. We Build the Wall's founder, Brian Kolfage, and its chairman, political firebrand Steve Bannon, later faced fraud charges and then charges of tax evasion around their handling of donations. In 2022, Kolfage pleaded guilty to wire fraud and filing false tax returns. Two other We Build the Wall associates were found guilty of similar crimes.[16] As of this writing, Bannon's case is ongoing.

Two years prior to that, a butterfly sanctuary took the right-wing charity to court. In December 2019, the National Butterfly Center filed a suit against Kolfage, We Build the Wall, and its contractors for attempting to build "an unpermitted and potentially illegal barrier on the banks of the Rio Grande River." The wall would cut through the butterfly sanctuary, potentially causing "irreparable damage to the Plaintiff's property." The plaintiffs castigated Kolfage and his allies for falsely claiming the Butterfly Center engaged in sex trafficking and drug smuggling. They declared wall construction would destroy large amounts of vegetation necessary to migrating monarchs. Marianna Treviño-Wright, the National Butterfly Center's executive director, lamented to media, "We could see the end of migration in my lifetime."[17]

The Butterfly Center protects more than just monarchs. The 100-acre (40-hectare) preserve hosts between two and three hundred butterfly species. Some, such as the dark kite swallowtail (*Eurytides philolaus*), pale-banded crescent (*Phyciodes tulcis*), and pale-spotted leafwing (*Anaea pithyusa*), are seen nowhere else in the United States besides the Rio Grande Valley. At least fifty species of wild bees frequent these flowers, including the rare red-legged Toluca leafcutter (*Megachile cf. toluca*), the endangered American bumblebee (*Bombus pensylvanicus*), and Strand's carpenter bee (*Xylocopa strandi*), which is only found in Texas. Sadly, border wall construction cuts through the ranges of host plants they depend on.

"Each species is intimately tied to one or two plant species," Treviño-Wright told the *National Geographic*. "If their host plant disappears, they disappear."[18]

In February 2020, the National Butterfly Center filed a restraining order against the Department of Homeland Security to stop construction on six miles of planned border wall, which included a 30-foot-tall (9-metre) concrete and steel wall, patrol roads, and a 150-foot (45-metre) "enforcement zone," cleared of vegetation.[19] The Center got something of a reprieve when the US changed presidents in 2021. A government funding bill put a stop to wall-building through parts of the Lower Rio Grande Valley. However, President Biden's transition team seemed ambivalent over whether they would dismantle the existing wall.[20] When I reached out to the Butterfly Center in 2021, they replied, "We are still fighting private property seizure for border wall," adding, "Biden's executive order 'pausing' border wall construction for 60 days is now more than 120 days old, with no permanent directive or cancellation of contracts, so the battle is not won."

In June 2021, the Department of Homeland Security announced it was "deobligating funds" and suspending "performance of all border barrier contracts and southwest border barrier construction activities." However, some work would continue, ostensibly for physical safety reasons.[21] In September, heavy equipment was seen in the Rio Grande Valley, at work on "discrete projects" reinforcing levees to prevent flooding. Activists called this designation a loophole to build shorter border walls.[22] Language on the Butterfly Center's website remained adversarial, claiming Biden was in fact continuing border wall construction.

In February 2022, the Center announced its indefinite closure, citing threats to its personnel. We Build the Wall's ongoing rumour campaign about smuggling illegal immigrants and child sex trafficking culminated in an altercation with Virginia congressional candidate Kimberly Lowe, who demanded entry to the Center's property to "watch the illegals crossing on rafts." Treviño-Wright claimed she was physically thrown to the ground in the encounter.[23] In an op-ed piece for *Scientific American*, Jeffrey Glassberg, president of the North American Butterfly Association (the Butterfly Center's parent organization), wrote, "Misinformation and political conspiracy theories can seriously threaten conservation and education."[24]

Border Walls versus Bats

While the Butterfly Center might not be sneaking people across the Mexican border, it has been hospitable to migrating winged mammals, such as silver-haired bats (*Lasionycteris noctivagans*), hoary bats (*Aeorestes cinereus*), and Mexican free-tailed bats (*Tadarida brasiliensis*). Bats consume three-quarters of their body weight in insects each night and pollinate night-blooming plants such as the cereus cactus and jimsonweed, plus popular food plants that include bananas, avocados, and agave. In Texas, bats congregate in large numbers, gathering under such structures as the Congress Street bridge in Austin or the Expressway 83 overpass near the Butterfly Center. Their social nature, unfortunately, makes them vulnerable to habitat disruptions. They convene in large numbers at relatively few spots.

Mexican long-nosed bats (*Leptonycteris nivalis*), known for their long muzzles and seven-centimetre tongues, migrate 1,200 kilometres through Mexico and the southwestern United States each year, chasing blooms of paniculate agaves. Some ecologists call this long migration an "endangered phenomenon" because of all the hazards along the complex route. Threats they face involve everything from unfriendly locals confusing them with vampire bats to climate-driven stress on wild agave.[25]

Border-crossing bat: Mexican long-nosed bats (*Leptonycteris nivalis*) migrate 1,200 kilometres from the south of Mexico to the southwestern United States, seeking the nectar-rich flowers of paniculate agaves, which they pollinate. Some ecologists call their long migration an "endangered phenomenon." (National Park Service)

The International Union for the Conservation of Nature (IUCN), the state of Texas, and two national governments consider the bats endangered. Populations of long-nosed bats are half what they were when the twenty-first century started.[26] Sections of border wall block migration routes in Texas and other border states, including Arizona, where a thirty-foot (nine-metre) steel wall cuts through the San Bernadino Valley. With its powerful searchlights, the wall's apparatus disturbs nocturnal wildlife and places huge obstacles between agave patches on both sides of the US-Mexico border.

Like other succulents, agave's spear-shaped leaves are fused into hardy, thick masses that photosynthesize and respire like other plant leaves, while retaining much-needed moisture. Clusters of hairy-looking flowers shoot up from these pointy leaves on stalks up to four and a half metres tall. The flowers open at night, wafting odours akin to rotting fruit, which tempt bats to their plentiful nectar. Bats and agave plants both have big needs. Bats need copious nectar for their energetic bodies and agaves need high inputs of pollen, which bats can provide. This creates a fragile ecological balance. When one organism suffers, the other one falls hard.[27]

A number of humans crave agave in its fermented form, tequila. In June 2014, for International Pollinator Week, science writer Gwen Pearson tried making an ecology case to alcohol drinkers in *Wired*. Pearson enthused that by talking up pollination's importance to tequila fans, her post would make "Pollinator Week Relevant to Pretty Much Everyone." She took a bold stab at making bat conservation speak the language of dude culture, while slipping in some nerdy science, and concluding that bats "are ADORABLE."[28]

Unfortunately, saving bats is not as simple as buying shooters. Tequila production methods can potentially harm the bat/agave situation more than they help. Commercial agave growers usually cut down plants before bats are able to forage on them. On plantations, agaves are propagated through cloned plant cuttings, not pollination and seeds. And since the limited gene pools of cloned crops make them vulnerable to fungus and disease, growers heavily resort to pesticides.[29]

Bats have at least some industry allies in the Tequila Interchange Project, a well-meaning collaboration between bartenders, businesspeople, supportive tequila drinkers, and scientists. This alliance promotes "bat-friendly" brands of tequila and mescal, made by companies with practices kinder to bats.[30] For example, some agave growers let sections of their plantations grow wild, for bats to feed on.

Whether or not eco-friendly drinking is ultimately the best way to conserve bats, it seems unavoidable that long-distance pollinators are at the mercy of human actions, over their perilous, lengthy migrations. Humanity's footprint is long, and habitat is complex for creatures whose territories traverse national borders. Their journeys become especially fraught as their migrations intersect with human habitats – where our species eats, drinks, and makes politics.

CHAPTER 14

A Few Degrees in the Future

Wired-Up "Floral Furnaces"

I struggle to insert two naked wires into the stems of black-eyed Susans (*Rudbeckia hirta*) so the scientist with me can record their temperatures with a gadgety kind of thermometer called a "thermocouple." Thermocouples measure temperatures based on voltage differences between two dissimilar metals, so both wire ends need to make it in. Hopefully they'll both penetrate this time and not just bend out of shape again. Peter Kevan, a retired professor from Guelph University, wants to compare temperatures inside the flower stems with air temperatures outside. He has me recite readings on the machine's display, which keep changing from second to second. Small changes in our surroundings, like passing clouds or momentary breezes, make the numbers jump. It's hard to keep up. Still, I've probably got it easy with this device, compared to past versions. Kevan remembers having to make his own thermocouples while roughing it in the Canadian Arctic, decades ago.

"They were a bit cumbersome," he recalls. "You could only take one reading at a time and had to write it down. All the recordings were made in millivolts and had to be translated into degrees Centigrade."

In the sixties and seventies, Kevan stuck thermocouple wires into the corollas of flowers blooming near Lake Hazen, the largest lake north of the Arctic Circle, on Ellesmere Island. Kevan wanted to know how flowers passively heated themselves with sunlight, and how that helped them live. Ellesmere Island's low precipitation makes it technically a polar desert, despite its frigid lake. Yet 125 flowering plant species defiantly bloom during the Arctic island's short, chilly summers.[1] Kevan noticed a number of Arctic flowers had parabolic shapes, which concentrated the sun's rays into their centres and heated their reproductive parts.

"Bowl-shaped flowers work like headlights, but in reverse," he explains. "It's just like a parabolic antenna for a television or a radio telescope, or anything like that."

Some of these so-called "floral furnaces" keep themselves heated by tracking the sun. "Heliotropic" flowers pivot slowly, changing orientation through small increments of stem growth.

"They grow faster on the shaded side than on the sunny side, which causes the stems to bend," says Kevan. This trick keeps flowers facing sunward. "They are reacting to the sun. If the sun isn't shining, they don't track."

Continuously tracking the sun is a useful adaptation for plants in a habitat with twenty-four hours of daylight, April through August.[2] Kevan recorded temperatures inside heliotropic flowers up to 10 degrees Celsius warmer than the ambient air around them. This captured heat could warm plant ovaries, where seeds need to mature before chilly summers give way to frost. Kevan wondered whether insects visiting the flowers preferred their warmth. Insects need shelter as well as food, and balmy flowers offer them warm havens. However, when Kevan started his research, scientists weren't sure whether Arctic plants had pollinators.

"The general view was that there weren't enough insects to do pollinating and that most Arctic plants did not require pollination," says Kevan. "Some of the very common plants were, in fact, being extensively pollinated by insects. That was all contrary to the general dogma at the time."[3]

Bees are not plentiful in high Arctic places. Only hardy bumblebees such as *Bombus polaris* and a couple of cousin species inhabit Ellesmere Island. The island also supports butterflies and moths, which warm up by spreading their wings to collect sunlight, not unlike sun-tracking flowers.[4] Mostly, though, the Arctic has a lot of flies. Around the time of Kevan's early Arctic excursions, researchers mainly studied biting flies. Kevan set out to prove that flies also pollinated flowers on Ellesmere Island. To confirm this, he used his cumbersome thermocouples to measure the body temperatures of flies, midges, and other insects to see how much heat the cold-blooded arthropods soaked up as they basked in bowl-shaped blossoms such as Arctic avens (*Dryas integrifolia*) and purple saxifrage (*Saxifraga oppositifolia*). Insects that lounged in these flowers absorbed heat very well, Kevan found. Some insects he measured were twice as warm as the flowers they basked in.[5]

Sun-tracking flower: Mountain avens (*Dryas integrifolia*) keeps itself warm by tracking the sun. This Arctic flower's stem grows by small amounts throughout the day, orienting the flower to keep it pointed sunward. By constantly collecting sunlight, the plant warms its reproductive parts. The flower's warmth also attracts insects such as flies, midges, and butterflies, which pollinate it. (Denali National Park and Preserve)

During the 1970s, Kevan paid only brief attention to plant stems. He took just a small number of readings before turning to other research. Four decades later he took an interest in "sneezeweed" (*Helenium autumnale*), a tall-stemmed sunflower near Churchill, Manitoba, just inside the Arctic Circle. The flower's especially rapid growth surprised him. Within six weeks, sneezeweed shot up a full metre, he found.

"This is a fantastic growth rate," says Kevan. He wondered where the energy came from for such rapid growth. The plants had to be heating up somehow. "In order to grow fast, you need to be warm."

Kevan wondered whether sneezeweed's hollow stems trapped heat, similar to the way greenhouses do. Out came the thermocouples. Fortunately, such devices had improved since the seventies. Their apparatus for recording temperatures had been miniaturized, and the devices were now handheld. Kevan now also had access to infrared sensing. Years ago, during his graduate work, he had no instruments to visualize heat.

"That instrumentation was just not available when I was up in the Arctic," he recalls. "It just wasn't there." Kevan could now back up his temperature readings with infrared photography. He travelled to parts of the Canadian Arctic and eastern Siberia, armed with his new tools, to test his hunches about stem temperatures in polar plants such as this-tles, louseworts, campions, and Arctic fernweed. As he suspected, hollow plant stems experienced a kind of "micro-greenhouse effect," which made them up to 10 degrees Celsius warmer. Sun-heated stems also sent heat to the ground. The warmer soil lengthened their growing days as much as 25 per cent. Having greenhouses inside their stems seemed to help plants grow.[6]

Micro-Weather in Plant Stems

Under close scrutiny, plant stems revealed small atmospheric events similar to large weather systems, where bodies of moving air exchange heat. Kevan describes this type of scaled-down stem weather as "micro-meteorology." Each stem has its own miniature climate, subject to green-house effects.[7]

"It's the same thing with global warming," Kevan says. "It's a wide-spread phenomenon."

In Earth's atmosphere, the "macro" greenhouse effect raises the world's average temperature. Heat from the sun is trapped by greenhouse gases such as CO_2, methane, nitrous oxide, and water vapour. This additional heat adds energy to the roiling roller-coaster of air and water circulating round the planet, intensifying all types of weather. It's hard to miss huge climatic events such as record-setting hurricanes, vast destructive wild-fires, and ice sheets large as cities cracking off of polar landmasses. Yet climate change also plays out in smaller, more localized "microclimates." Such small-scale happenings don't make the weather reports. Weather satellites don't record a few cubic millimetres of temperature change in plant stems. But Kevan wonders what impact larger climate events may have on these tiny, self-contained weather systems.

"That's where we're asking the questions, yes," he agrees. "If tempera-tures of the general atmosphere rise two or three degrees Centigrade above where they'd been for the last couple of hundred years, then you would expect the temperature in these microenvironments to also in-crease by that amount, if not more."

More heat in the atmosphere means plants having more heat to absorb. But when metabolisms absorb heat, they also have to shed it. In the trop-ics, where it's already hot, plants may soak up more heat than they can shed, which could have deadly implications as the world keeps warming. Things might hit a point where plants perish from heat waves within their own stems.

"Maybe one can get sort of excessive heat buildup in things," says Kevan. "And global climate change and global warming is going to push that envelope."

The locale where I spend one windy afternoon sticking wires into daisy stems is not at the equator, but in southern Quebec. While it might be a warm fall, temperatures don't reach any dangerous extremes, inside or outside flower stems. Still, it's possible to see the interiors of stems react to small, momentary shifts in air temperature. These tiny, interior weather events might hold clues about the bigger climate picture, but Kevan cautions that the science is still pretty new.

However, he thinks micro-warming might soon affect agriculture. He foresees repercussions for crop plants with hotter stems. They might, for instance, attract more pests. Kevan presumes that pest insects probably enjoy warmed-up plants as much as pollinators do. Bug infestations could increase, and crops could take huge hits from invaders. Still, Kevan also expects many plants will flourish (at least for now) as the world warms, including Arctic flora. Growing seasons will last longer, and springs will come sooner. "One expects the flowers to open earlier," he says. "One of the things that's been suggested is that Arctic plants are just going to do a little bit better."

Arctic Temperature Time Machines

In its annual report for 2021, the United Nations Intergovernmental Panel on Climate Change (IPCC) warned that Arctic temperatures were spiking four times faster than the global average.[8] Some impacts of these temperature spikes are visible from space. Greg H.R. Henry, an Arctic researcher at the University of British Columbia, compares satellite data with his on-the-ground observations at Ellesmere Island. What he sees, from both vantage points, is new plants invading. The "treeline," a frigid northern limit past which trees won't grow, has been shifting, even on Canada's northernmost island.

"The whole place is becoming woodier," says Henry. "Trees are being found further north, even in the high Arctic." The effect of more trees is more warming. As trees and shrubs creep north, they darken the tundra. Less sunlight bounces off dark scrubland than shiny sheets of ice and snow. "That actually speeds up the melt of the snow, if there's a bigger area of dark stuff," says Henry. "That's what the satellites are seeing very clearly."[9] Satellites show the Earth's reflective power, its "albedo," decreasing. A less reflective Earth will get hotter, faster.

When I chat with Henry in 2020, he's anxious about getting back to Ellesmere Island. Like other scientists trying to do field research in 2020, he and his students find their travel plans blocked by the COVID-19 pandemic. A sudden surge of the virus in Nunavut cuts down time available for fieldwork to a couple of weeks. Even that small window could shrink if winter comes early. The Arctic may be warming, but it still has plenty of cold weather. Work is always limited, says Henry, by "how far you can walk from your tent."

He's in a hurry to visit a patch of land by Lake Hazen that he's observed since the 1990s. He calls this research site "the longest-running warming experiment in Canada." The experiment sounds a lot like gardening, except half the plots are inside small roofless greenhouses. These Plexiglas pods, called "open-top chambers," passively warm the air inside them. They block wind and let in sunlight, creating bubbles of air balmier by about 3 degrees Celsius. The chambers produce miniature climates predictively ahead of present Arctic warming. These warmed-up mini-gardens are like long-running movies of near-future climate conditions. Some of what they predict is obvious. Plants in the chambers grow more, which is not totally surprising.

"When you warm them up, they grow bigger," Henry notes, a little wryly. "Anybody could have predicted that. 'Okay, spectacular result, there, Greg.' But what is remarkable is just how the species are playing out in the warming."

What intrigues Henry is which species turn up in the chambers. He encounters plants he wouldn't expect that far north. Seeds from shrubs normally found a thousand kilometres south blow into his chambers and grow there with abandon. "They are now taking over the plots," he observes. These Arctic newcomers drop leaves, altering the ground's carbon content and the makeup of soil bacteria. They literally change the land. Meanwhile, climate change is catching up in the control plots. The regular environment now looks like things did inside the chambers, just a

Time machines: These Plexiglas structures, called "open-top chambers," heat the ambient air inside them. They block wind and let in sunlight, creating bubbles of air balmier by about 3 degrees Celsius, slightly ahead of warming trends in the Arctic. These warmed-up mini-gardens are like long-running movies of near-future climate change. (Cassandra Elphinstone)

few years ago. As a scientist, Henry is pleased to see his predictions confirmed, but as a citizen concerned about climate change, he is frightened to be so correct.

"The scary part is just the speed," he says. "You shouldn't be seeing this woodification, or shrubification of the Arctic over less than a lifetime. You should not see this. It's just unprecedented anywhere in the paleo record."[10]

Fossil records from the Arctic show that the north got very warm millions of years ago. It became not only shrubby, but heavily wooded. It had lush forests with trees suitable to temperate North America: birch, alder, elm, sycamore, and horse chestnut. Ellesmere Island even once hosted tropical species such as dawn redwood, Chinese swamp cypress, and ginkgo.[11] However, it took several millennia for the Arctic to become a jungle, whereas current warming could reach the same place in a century or two. Henry finds the difference jarring.

"We're seeing, in my lifetime, changes that would take, normally, tens of thousands of years to see," he says. "It's pretty scary, actually, is what it is."[12]

Forecasting Arctic Pollination

In 2011, Henry tapped one of his graduate students to study how climate change could affect Arctic pollination. Logistically, it's not hard to research pollination inside open-top chambers, since insects can fly in and out. The difficult part was finding someone willing to sit there and observe. Samuel Robinson, now at the University of Calgary, agreed to peer inside Henry's experimental plots to see how plants and pollinators reacted to climate change in the Arctic's sparsely populous ecosystem.

"Strictly speaking, the stuff I studied is probably some of the lowest diversity pollination systems," says Robinson.

As Kevan's Arctic research revealed decades earlier, flies did most of the pollinating, and did so without prejudice. They visited every type of flower, with little to no preference. They behaved like complete generalists. But then, so did other pollinators. Flexibility makes sense on Ellesmere Island, where plant life is relatively sparse compared to warmer climes, and flowering times are short.[13] Options are few and there is little time to seek better ones.

"In the Arctic, it's all the flies, all the butterflies, all the moths," says Henry. "As long as there's flowers, they're happy."

While Robinson monitored Henry's open-top chambers, he looked to see whether temperatures in the near future would upset the balance of pollinators and plants. Some scientists fear climate change could create mismatches between plants and pollinators. Pollination depends on timing. If a plant is not flowering when its pollinator comes around, it loses its chance to be pollinated. Likewise, the pollinator leaves unrewarded. Such missed opportunities might happen if unseasonably warm temperatures cue insects to forage days or weeks before sunny spring mornings cue plants to bloom, for example. Ecologists reason that speedy shifts in climate could knock pollination cycles out of sync. However, Robinson witnessed no such cross-species confusion in Henry's open-top chambers. A few degrees in the future, pollination still took place, with no significant mismatches.[14]

"In the Arctic, that idea of mismatch is not as critical," says Henry. "That might change in a hundred years or so from now, but right now it doesn't seem to be a big issue." What makes Arctic communities vulnerable, he says, is their sparse diversity. "The biological diversity is low, but the functional diversity is pretty much the same. It's just that the number of components in that puzzle is fewer. I guess the danger, then, is lower redundancy in each of those functional pieces." Climate change not only warms the planet, it raises the likelihood of chaotic climate events. Freak weather becomes more common. For example, the number of Arctic lightning storms shot up from their previous normal of practically nil to over 7,000 in 2021. Henry wonders whether more extreme weather could jeopardize the Arctic's limited diversity. Not just yet, he says, with qualified optimism. "So far so good. But are they going to be flexible enough to allow them to survive, ultimately?"

Microclimates on Mountainsides

Jessica Forrest at the University of Ottawa (see chapter 7) studies how pollination occurs in habitats many kilometres south of Ellesmere Island. Forrest conducts field research on both sides of the Canada-US border, in places where species are more diverse and pollination systems more complex than those in the high Arctic. She has investigated whether pollinators experience "phenological mismatches" in environments such as Colorado's alpine ecosystem. She's actively searched for signs of "asynchrony" between pollinators and plants.[15] Her results make Forrest question whether pollination's clockwork is as delicate as some scientists think.[16]

"There is some truth to it," she says. "I guess I just think it's messier." In Forrest's experience, nature is unpredictable, so organisms evolve to deal with the unexpected. Clock parts can't modify their habits, but living things can. Through the day, plants adjust to small changes in light and temperature. An insect such as a foraging bee has to traverse numerous "microhabitats," each with its own "microclimate." Even just going a short distance, a bee crosses shady spots, sunny clearings, damp gloomy spaces, and so forth. Bees encounter many such microclimates on mountainsides in the Colorado Rockies.

"There are north-facing slopes and south-facing slopes that are going to have wildly different thermal environments," she says. "Even just in the shade of a tree versus outside the forest, the thermal environment is quite different."

Pollinators and plants must also adapt to seasonal cycles. But even with climate-related surprises, such as unusually warm springs, they seem to adjust on more or less the same schedule.

"To some extent, everything has to come out in the summer," she says. "And all organisms have some way of controlling when they become active or when they begin to flower, or whatever it is. After a certain amount of heat has accumulated in a season, bees will come out and flowers will bloom."

Yet different organisms still react to different cues. Young bees waiting to crawl out of their cocoons and hibernating adults, such as bumblebee queens, respond to heat, since they overwinter in dark places where light can't reach. Conversely, plants respond to periods of sunlight, or "photoperiod," to cue their growth. The length of time between sunrise and sunset is based on the Earth's axial tilt and position in its orbit, whether spring comes early or not. Forrest says her evidence still suggests that bees and flowers heed climate cues with similar timing.[17] They stay more or less in sync because light and heat are complementary. Those effects work in tandem.

"These cues interact," she explains. "A plant might only really become responsive to warm temperatures if, for example, days are long, and it's experienced a certain duration of chilling. Or it might not require so much chilling if days are already really long. So, all of these cues can influence sensitivity to the other cues."

One of the bees Forrest studies has climate flexibility built into its life cycle. The solitary bee, *Osmia iridis*, has no common name, but is a near relative of blue orchard bees (see chapter 8). This bee's offspring delay their emergence as adults in response to seasonal warmth. *Osmia iridis* larvae spin cocoons, and wait through the winter, emerging full-grown and ready to forage the following year. But if their first summer is too cool and brief, they skip that season and wait another year.

"In most years, either [their eggs will] be laid too late in the season or it's just going to be too cold for them to develop that quickly," explains Forest. "If they're partway through metamorphosis when winter hits, they're dead. So, what we mostly see is that they play it safe."

However, if one warm year follows another, bees from this species emerge two years in a row. After experimentally forcing this result in her lab, Forrest saw it happen naturally, during field studies in 2018 and 2019.

"We had this very hot, dry year," she says. "And in fact, we did, then, get emergence of bees in 2019, showing that they had responded to the heat and warmth of 2018. They were able to speed up development. It's all good for them."[18]

Still, Forrest isn't totally certain all species will adapt so smoothly. With luck, plants and pollinators will stay in sync. But times are uncertain. The world is warming quickly.

"Maybe everybody is going to come out earlier, and so there's not going to be a problem," she says. "Or maybe there will be a mismatch."

In some climate change scenarios, pollinators become climate refugees. They're driven into new habitats as their current ones get too hot. This might be happening already to creatures adapted for chilliness, such as North American bumblebees.[19] Relocation involves risk. It's not simply a matter of buzzing north. New territory might be clogged with competitors, or be unliveable for other reasons. However, if conditions to the south have gotten too hot, retreat is no good either. The range of a species just shrinks. This sort of shrinkage could easily happen on a mountain, says Forrest. The only way to migrate is up. That won't be so bad at first, for bees making the climb.

"They're not at their thermal tolerance limit. They're nowhere near it," says Forrest. "Warming means they can be more active. Their larvae can develop more quickly. That's all good." However, if bees are forced even further up-mountain, conditions may be less tenable. If a bee's species nests in fallen trees, for instance, she might not find any tree trunks to inhabit. "There's no trees above treelines, certainly no dead trees," says Forrest. "I think that's the situation we're getting into. With change being so rapid we're likely to just run into circumstances where bees can't move upward." Regrettably, if it's too hot further down the mountain, they can't retreat downward either. "If things are getting better at the high elevations, they're probably getting worse at the low elevations." Squeezed from both sides, the bee's range compresses.

Forrest feels optimistic that many species will adapt, but maybe not all of them will. "How much adaptive capacity do the bees have at that point?" she wonders. "Can they respond evolutionarily to whatever new changes we're throwing at them? I guess that's what worries me the most. We're throwing all of these stressors on pollinator populations at once.

We're reducing their capacity to respond evolutionarily to the changes that at this point are basically inevitable."[20]

Gardening for Future Climate

Some conservationists hope they can help pollinators deal with the inevitable by planning – and planting – for the future. Clement Kent, an adjunct professor at York University, decided to make small efforts in this direction. As a scientist, he spent years getting to know the evolution of bee traits by understanding their genomes. He's also long indulged a passion for community gardening. In 1987, Kent helped co-found the Parkdale Horticultural Society, which a year later merged with the Toronto Horticultural Society, a century-old organization whose motto was "beautify Toronto." The group's meetings are pleasant, neighbourly gatherings where people trade gardening lore and discuss favourite plants. There is also a subtle flavouring of activism, with native plant giveaways, lectures on ecology, and the occasional slideshow on guerilla gardening.

"I often ended up being a speaker, and so one of the things I tried to do was to bring watered down horticultural science into the talks and explain it in a way that gardeners could relate to and enjoy," he says. Kent was not above using theatre in his talks. He once wore a hazmat suit to a presentation on pesticides.

· In 2017, one of the society's founding members and its past president, Katherine Andrachuk, passed away. To honour her, members decided to plant a community garden in Stanley Park – which should not be confused with Vancouver's much larger Stanley Park. The modest sward of green space in Toronto's downtown lacked the scale of Vancouver's 400-hectare oasis, but it still had room to garden in. The proposed plot, called "Kathy's Grove," offered an opportunity to replace standard-issue turf grass with flora native to southern Ontario. Volunteers installed eleven flowering trees to host caterpillars, and planted native perennials, such as bluestars, white Agastache, and hairy beardtongue, to attract bees, butterflies, and other local pollinators.

Kent had an additional goal. He wanted Kathy's Grove to be a "sideways" act of preparation for climate change. He thought the garden's plants should not just be resilient enough to meet urban challenges, but be fit enough to weather future climate. Plants in city parks need to be tough;

they face hardships from vandalism to neglect. Also, there was no hookup for a hose in Stanley Park, so plants there had to be drought-tolerant. Additionally, their climate zone is shifting. Southern Ontario is the northern tip of the "Carolinian life zone." This biodiverse region reaches south through the eastern United States into the Carolinas, hence its name. It contains much of Canada's agriculture and most of its urban sprawl. It has many forests, dominated by predominantly broad-leafed, "deciduous" trees. Carolinian trees have crept gradually north, beyond their previous limits. At the turn of the twentieth century, basswoods reached no further than the shores of Lake Erie. Now they're up by Lake Nipissing, four hundred kilometres north.[21]

Shifting tree ranges raise ecological questions, such as which trees will be most fire-prone in the future.[22] In a number of newsworthy cases, that fiery future has already arrived. In late 2019 and early 2020, bushfires ripped through Australia's New South Wales region, laying waste to 18.6 million hectares of forest. Australians now call this calamity the "Black Summer." In July 2016, wildfires devastated half a million hectares of forest in Northern Alberta, forcing the oil town of Fort McMurray to evacuate 88,000 citizens. The fires took a year to fully extinguish. Extremely hot and exceptionally dry summers helped bring on Alberta's and Australia's blazes. Southern Ontario is known for its moist, mild climate, which helps dampen the prospect of forest fires. But hotter, drier summers could change that, especially for fire-prone trees such as spruces and pines.

"Evergreen woods in a drought become just a giant fire hazard," says Kent. Evergreens in Alberta's boreal forests accelerated 2016's wildfires. Conversely, what slowed down the burning was deciduous aspens. "It stopped, because those trees were nowhere near as flammable as the spruce and firs around."

In Stanley Park, two sickly pines barely clung to life. But the park's deciduous beech tree didn't look so well, either. It suffered from beech bark disease, caused by scale insects and canker fungus. This fungal tree killer is expected to plague many more beeches, as mild winters go soft on its carriers.[23] Volunteers replaced the dying trees with serviceberries, redbuds, sweetgums, and a tulip tree. These deciduous trees were well-adapted for heat, and just a little north of their traditional ranges. Kent's rule of thumb for the project was "plant for at least one climate zone south of what our gardening books and maps tell us, especially for flowering trees and shrubs." Yet despite careful attempts to plant with climate-minded foresight, two sweetgum trees died during an exceptionally dry summer in 2018. So did two serviceberries, a couple of shrubs, and several perennial plants.

"Those trees shouldn't have croaked," says Kent. "They normally would have been okay." Kent says the trees were taken out by "one of these climate excursions of a super-hot period."

Kent admits that planting predictively for climate involves guesswork, whether for one year ahead or two decades. "We don't know what our climate will be in twenty years. One year is going to have floods and the next year will have droughts and so on." He anticipates more plants, even formerly resilient ones, succumbing to tough seasons. "We're going to have some species reduced to very small numbers, if not driven extinct. And we have to look at how to help them or find their replacements."

There are those who voice concerns around this kind of speculative gardening. Some objections are emotional. A lot of gardeners don't want to give up on their favourite plants.

"It can become controversial," Kent admits. "Some people are sentimentally attached to the trees and the shrubs that they grew up with, and I completely understand that."

Ecologists also worry about disrupting habitats and disturbing vulnerable niches by planting species outside of their old ranges.

"It's a big debate," says Kent. "I'm sure that there's no right answer, but I think we need lots of different diversity in our landscape, because we don't know what the right answer is going to be. We need lots of possible solutions."

Kent insists on the necessity of taking action, even before all the research is done. "You know, you ask an academic, they'll always say it needs more study. Because that's their way of pitching the next grant. But the reality is we've had plenty of study on this. We pretty well know what to do. We've just got to do it. We don't need more study."

CHAPTER 15

Last Flowers? Shrinking Pollination Options

Berries "Not as Sweet"

What's in a name? Sometimes not what we think. When you call something a berry, it's not always a berry. Strawberries and blackberries are "aggregate fruits": several small fruits clustered together. Saskatoon berries are "pomes," closer in nature to apples. Because of their big pits, cherries are called "drupes." Some are actual "true berries," such as gooseberries, currants, persimmons, bananas, blueberries, and (oddly) tomatoes. Botanical hair-splitting aside, over two hundred species of small, fleshy fruits that range from sweet to sour, edible to poisonous, grow wild in North America.

Berries have names given to them in languages other than English and the scientific creole of Latin used by botanists. *The Berry Book*, published in 2016, names several berries in English, Linnaean taxonomic language, and Inuinnaqtun, spoken by Inuit communities in western Nunavut. You can read about aqpiit, or cloudberry (*Rubus chamaemorus*); paun'ngat, or crowberry (*Empetrum nigrum*); kingmingnat, or cranberry (*Vaccinium vitis-idaea*); kablat, or Alpine bearberry (*Arctostaphylos alpina*); and kigu-tigirngnat, or blueberry (*Vaccinium uliginosum*). *The Berry Book* combines science, stories, recipes, and cultural lore, such as when bearberries turn red char will be spawning, cloudberries are good for treating heartburn, and crowberry freezer jelly is delicious.[1]

The book emerged from in-depth interviews with elders and youth in the hamlet of Kugluktuk in Nunavut, conducted by José Gérin-Lajoie from Université du Québec à Trois-Rivières (UQTR) and Sarah Desrosiers from the University of British Columbia (UBC). The project started off as an effort to involve Northern communities in research around environmental change. School students learned environmental monitoring while collecting, counting, and weighing berries from research plots in Kugluk/Bloody Falls Territorial Park. Elders shared observations about environmental changes gleaned from years of berry-picking. The community had goals of its own, such as preserving oral history and language. Nunavut schools now use *The Berry Book* as a manual to teach the Inuinnaqtun language, while explaining the cultural and ecological value of berries.

In a related effort, scholars from UBC, UQTR, and Memorial University interviewed 145 Inuit elders and knowledge holders from nineteen northern communities across Nunavut, the Northwest Territories, northern Quebec, and Labrador. Between 2007 and 2010, scholars heard accounts in four Inuit dialects about impacts that ecological change has on berry collecting and other parts of local life.[2] These interviews resulted in a second multilingual book, *The Caribou Taste Different Now*. Some oral accounts concerned land-use changes, such as houses being built on land where people used to berry-pick. Others shared observations about changing weather, invasive plants, and bothersome animals such as geese, which folk accused of robbing berries. Some said biting insects, including blackflies, were increasing, while bumblebees were more scarce. Blueberries and cloudberries were less abundant, while other berries were too small or just not as tasty.

"The taste is different," one elder complained. "They are not as sweet."[3]

Anecdotes of berries losing abundance are troubling, since historically, berries (and berry-ish fruits) are common in the Northern Hemisphere. They're well-adapted to the north's cooler climate, since they take less time to mature than larger fruits. In climates with fewer warm months, little flowers with small, fast-growing fruits make biological sense. Botanist Jana Vamosi curates the University of Calgary's herbarium, its library of plant specimens. She is well-acquainted with smallish flowers and their berry-like fruits.

"Most of the species that I am looking at now, lots of them are really nothing to write home about," she says. "They're not really that pretty. We have a lot in our Canadian climate. There's a short growing season and so there's not a lot of time in the Canadian environment to make a really big, showy display, get it pollinated, and start fruit development, all before the frost and the snow comes."

Scary Statistics: Plant and Pollinator Declines

Along with minding the herbarium, Vamosi uses its specimens to track the abundance of plant species. An herbarium is a library of plants, but it's also an evidence room where botanical detectives piece together past scenarios of plant survival and extinction. Sometimes Vamosi looks for signs of plant extinctions that might be imminent.

"Because you have the physical specimen of a plant that grew at some place at some time in the past, you can then sort of collate and collectively look at what that plant's range was, say, at the turn of the century," she says. "Then you can compare it to where that plant lives now. And if the range is continually shrinking, then that is cause for alarm, and you might even want to flag in a status report that maybe that species is going extinct."

For Vamosi, plant populations are trending the wrong way.

"I'd say extinction rates are increasing throughout Canada." Some rare species, she laments, are "just sort of hanging on by their fingernails." Losing habitat adds to their problems. "Species recovery is going to be tough because areas that probably used to have the suitable habitat just no longer exist. It's a shopping mall now or something like that. So, you're not going to be able to do any restoration efforts. The opportunity is long gone. It's tough."

Pollinators have also become fewer. For years, ecologists have warned that many more plants could disappear due to "extinctions of mutualist partners." Loss of pollination is not easy to prove, however. Plants that have lost their pollinators give no outward signs they are "widow" species.[4] They live out their lives in apparent good health, while producing no heirs. Since non-pollination is hard to directly observe, scientists look to statistics. Agriculture shows worrisome signs. A US-wide study in 2020 reported five out of seven crops, including apples, watermelons, and almonds, lost millions of dollars because pollination by native bees and insects has dropped.[5]

Natural ecosystems are less easy to quantify, but a worldwide survey in 2021 set out to calculate the value of pollinators ecologically, to help measure the harm of losing them. The study was led by mathematician James G. Rodger at Stellenbosch University in South Africa. Its contributors hailed from nations such as Australia, Germany, China, Brazil, the United States, and Canada. Vamosi was among the scientists who gleaned data from more than 1,500 papers on pollination from the mid-1970s up to now, from every continent besides Antarctica. The global team surveyed survival rates of flowering plants and what bearing pollination had on staving off their demise. The study's final figures were stark. Without animal pollinators, a third of flowering plants would make no seeds and half of them would suffer an 80 per cent drop in fertility.[6]

Plants have ways to reproduce without pollinators. They may propagate asexually, by cloning new plants from parts of themselves. Farmers and horticulturalists exploit this trait, generating hundreds of plants from one original. About 12 per cent of plants reproduce through wind pollination. And when other options are scarce, plants with hermaphroditic flowers may pollinate themselves.[7]

"That ends up being a bit of an insurance measure for them, that they can essentially have sex with themselves," says Vamosi. "They can't move. They have to just sort of sit and wait. Being able to just exchange gametes with yourself is a handy trick for something that has to stay still."

Self-Pollination's Endgame

Charles Darwin was so fascinated with self-pollination as an evolutionary oddity, he wrote a book about it. He examined plants such as the bee orchid (*Ophrys apifera*), which (despite having "bee" in its common name) preferentially pollinates itself. Darwin concluded that plants evolved this tendency when forced to by lack of pollinators. "Under these circumstances," he wrote, "it would manifestly be more advantageous to a plant to produce self-fertilised seeds rather than none at all."[8] He named this survival strategy "reproductive assurance."

Self-pollination might beat extinction, but it doesn't produce the best genetic outcomes, any more than inbreeding does in animals. Darwin was one of the first biologists to describe inbreeding depression, long before anyone knew its underlying genetics. In one of his efforts to understand self-pollination, Darwin used experimental trickery to keep pollinators away from flowers, leaving plants no option but to self-pollinate. Their offspring were visibly sickly.[9]

Present-day biologists tend to concur with Darwin, such as Dan Schoen, a plant geneticist at Montreal's McGill University. Schoen says genetic evidence, not attainable in Darwin's time, backs the famous scholar's observations.

"Certainly, there are hundreds of examples documented in the literature of inbreeding depression in plant populations and in animal populations too," says Schoen. "So yeah, you can see that things get worse."

In 2013, Schoen and his then graduate student Kyle Bobiwash (now a professor at University of Manitoba) tried to see what inbreeding looked like in blueberries. Blueberries, and their plant genus, *Vaccinium*, are almost completely immune to self-pollination. However, the matter can be forced by determined experimenters.

"There is some so-called 'leakiness' to the system, where the occasional self-pollinated grain does manage to squeak by," says Schoen. Experimenters can basically torture plants into accepting their own pollen, he explains. "You can stress it out a bit – high temperature, high CO_2. This is one way people try to get around the system."

Maybe not everything that can be done should be done with plant mating. When Schoen and Bobiwash induced blueberries in New Brunswick to self-pollinate, the next generation of plants was so unhealthy that many failed to set fruit.[10] To avoid such unhappy results, many plants protectively deny their own pollen, when pollen grains land on their own flower's stigma.

"It's a bit akin to self-recognition in humans, I guess," says Schoen, citing the body's ability to recognize its own cells and reject foreign organisms. "But in this case, plants have evolved ways to reject their own pollen. Once there is a recognition, then a cascade of events happens."

When a flower's recognition system activates, its so-called "self-pollen" meets with resistance when it tries to send a pollen tube down the style. The pollen tube might make a promising start, but it never reaches the ovary. Chemical defences cause it to dry up and wither on the way down.

"It will lose the ability to become hydrated and it just won't make it," says Schoen. "You can see, in those situations, pollen tubes that have partially germinated and then stopped halfway – or not even halfway, sometimes really close to the top of the stigma or style. These things are easy to see with a microscope."

However, a number of plant species lose this biochemical self-defence, becoming "self-fertile," as botanists say. It actually happens quite a lot.

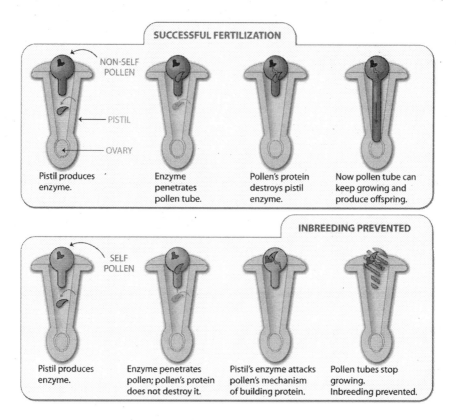

NON-SELF POLLEN

PISTIL

OVARY

Pistil produces enzyme.

Enzyme penetrates pollen tube.

Pollen's protein destroys pistil enzyme.

Now pollen tube can keep growing and produce offspring.

INBREEDING PREVENTED

SELF POLLEN

Pistil produces enzyme.

Enzyme penetrates pollen; pollen's protein does not destroy it.

Pistil's enzyme attacks pollen's mechanism of building protein.

Pollen tubes stop growing. Inbreeding prevented.

Defence against self: For plants, self-pollination carries genetic risks akin to inbreeding depression in animals. To prevent this, many plants use biochemical defences that prevent pollen tubes from reaching the plant's ovaries. (National Science Foundation)

"This is probably one of the most common evolutionary transitions in the flowering plants," says Schoen. "Maybe 40 or 50 per cent of plants may be self-compatible." Most plants don't self-pollinate exclusively, though. They keep themselves open to animal pollination. It is rare to find species that are 100 per cent self-fertilizing.

Plants from Brassicaceae, the mustard family, are highly self-fertile. Insects pollinate their flowers, but mustards are enthusiastic self-pollinators. Their family includes many food plants such as cabbage, cauliflower, and broccoli; oil plants such as rapeseed; and the familiar condiment mustards, white mustard (*Sinapis alba*), black mustard (*Brassica nigra*), and brown mustard (*Brassica juncea*). People who farm these plants must be vigilant to make sure crops don't fertilize themselves and start behaving like weeds.

What farmers see as a nuisance, Schoen saw as an opportunity to understand plant genes that control self-compatibility. He has deeply studied the "S-locus," a pair of tightly linked genes that trigger self-recognition. Mustard plants lack this gene; they are comparatively defenceless against self-pollination.[11] However, their offspring are not chronically unhealthy. Unlike blueberries, the progeny of self-pollinated mustard plants seem robust. The reason why is, so to speak, "generational." Plants that transition to self-pollination get over the worst effects of inbreeding after a few generations, Schoen explains.

"Some populations go through a kind of stage where they shed these deleterious alleles during this inbreeding process," he says, "and that could come out favourably."

Some agricultural scientists have thought about genetically modifying crop plants such as fruit trees to self-pollinate.[12] If the bad effects of inbreeding taper off after a few generations, perhaps apple trees that fertilize themselves could prove useful, for example. But not so fast, says Schoen. Species don't escape the consequences of self-breeding perpetually. They eventually backslide.

"You have to recall that mutation is an ongoing process," he says. Bad genes eventually reassert themselves. A lot of self-pollinating plants have become dead branches on their evolutionary tree. "The tips have been pruned. They haven't survived to the present day. It looks like the rate of extinction in plants that have evolved self-pollination is higher than it is for plants that cross-pollinate. It's not generally considered favourable for long-term survival."

At first, plants on this trajectory don't look bound for extinction; quite the opposite, they seem to thrive. Since they self-fertilize, they breed quickly, and it doesn't take long for them to dominate habitats.

"They're often weedy," Schoen explains. "They're good at getting around."

But even as they flood through locales, their gene pools are shrinking. They lose things, such as their looks, as they stop selecting for showiness. They produce less pollen and offer less nectar, so pollinators lose interest. They end up locked in a vicious cycle. Over time, as self-breeding continues, bad genes build up.

"Self-pollination increases the level of inbreeding," says Schoen. "It may cause the population's growth rate to decline below replacement level. And then the population can go locally extinct."

Self-pollination can buy time for plants short on mating options, but ultimately, they doom themselves genetically, if they keep going it alone.

CHAPTER 16

Sunflowers and Space Invaders

Writing the Book on Invasive Plants

We all know what weeds are. We see them in gardens, pull them up, and then later on they usually come back. But when it comes to defining what weeds are specifically, things get more complex. Since weedy plants have a kind of negative social status, "weed" can almost be considered a political term. They are plants deemed unwelcome in society. Governments have official language around the status of these *plantae non grata*. Section 403 of the US Department of Agriculture's (USDA) *Plant Protection Act* (PPA) defines a "noxious weed" as "any plant or plant product that can directly or indirectly injure or cause damage to crops ... public health, or the environment."[1] The European Union tracks "invasive alien species of union concern."[2] The Canadian Food Inspection Agency oversees national policy around suspicious botanicals termed "invasive" plants, while each province keeps its own database of weedy flora. Ontario's Ministry of Agriculture, Food, and Rural Affairs has a Schedule of Noxious Weeds for policing leafy undesirables. It has rap sheets for weeds of interest such as smooth bedstraw, common crupina, tansy ragwort, and woolly cupgrass.[3]

Science has its own words for weediness, explains plant geneticist Loren Riesberg at the University of British Columbia. He acknowledges some so-called weeds are "just things that occur where you don't want them." But that isn't the whole story. "There are traits associated with these things," he adds.

Weeds have particular weedy powers, such as an ability to thrive in degraded places. "A variety of them are plants that are successful in disturbed habitats." Humans are talented at disturbing habitats, often on staggering scales, with activities including industry, agriculture, and urban expansion. As a result, weeds tend to follow us. "If it wasn't for humans," says Riesberg, "a lot of these things wouldn't have habitats to invade. In some ways, invasiveness wasn't very advantageous until humans sort of began to completely change our landscapes."

Rieserg credits influential botanist Herbert George Baker for literally writing the book on weedy plants. In his writing, Baker compiled traits common to what he termed "colonizing plants."[4] While local plants can get out of hand and become weedy, plants we call weeds often come from away. They are imported, either by accident or on purpose, as horticultural or agricultural plants. Whether a plant's presence was originally desired or not, once it gets out of bounds and takes over spaces it doesn't belong in, it's invasive. "Invasive" and "weedy" are two different definitions, but they overlap quite a lot, since invasive plants are often weedy, and vice versa.

"Invaders, in general, are found in regions where they're not native but also result in large and abundant populations that have negative effects on other species," Riesberg elaborates.

Invasives are good at breeding faster and more widely than local plants. Their defining traits vary but may include long roots, extreme "seediness" (producing many seeds quickly), "ecological competence" (tolerance for changing environmental conditions), and long reproductive seasons; a lot of them bloom earlier than local plants and may still be flowering when others have quit. Invasive plants tend to be pollination generalists. They avail themselves of many pollinators – including themselves, through self-pollination. Some invasives succeed through prettiness. People like their showy blossoms and happily plant them, not knowing what they've unleashed.

"There is a whole horticulture industry that has created invaders," says Riesberg. "'Oh, this is a beautiful plant.' And then they plant it everywhere." Scotch broom (*Cytisus scoparius*), with its sunny yellow and candy-red petals, is one example. This pretty flowering shrub is one of British Columbia's most notorious plant invaders. Europeans, who grow Scotch broom as ornamentals, first brought them over to beautify gardens in North America. "It's beautiful. But my god, it kills everything else around it."

Pollen Crossing Species Boundaries

Riesberg's research concerns a trait common to invasive plants: their ability to hybridize with other species. "Often, successful invaders do have some kind of a hybrid ancestry," he points out.

Biologists are not totally comfortable around the concept of species hybrids because hybrids blur the line between one species and another. One accepted cut-off biologists use to define separate species is reproductive isolation. Different species should not be able to breed with each other. Reasons for this vary. Some animals have unique genitalia that make sex outside their species physically impossible. Some animal species can physically mate with each another but don't produce viable offspring. Others simply lack opportunity. Lions and tigers are both big cats, but tigers live in Bengali jungles and lions roam African grasslands; they would never meet in the wild. But lions and tigers have mated in captivity and conceived hybrid offspring, known as "ligers" (from a male lion and a tigress) or "tigons" (from a lioness and a male tiger).

Plants have no way to stop pollen from other species landing on their stigmas, so they rely on biochemical defences to keep foreign pollen from germinating. Such defences work most of the time, but nature's not always keen on absolutes. Flowers sometimes drop their defences and hybridize. A number of hybrids are intentional, and even popular. Horticulturalists crossbreed plants to produce flashy, fuchsia stargazer lilies or Toscana strawberries, edible ornamentals with red flowers instead of white ones. Food-growers breed hybrids such as sweet corn and Meyer lemons, which mix traits of lemons and mandarin oranges.

Riesberg studies sunflowers, which are prolific at making natural hybrids. In the world of plants, sunflowers tick off several boxes. People love them as garden flowers. They are farmed for food oil and their snackable seeds. They are widespread as wildflowers; birds eat their seeds and insects harvest their pollen and nectar. Sunflowers can be nuisance plants for wheat, corn, soy, and sugar beet crops, so sometimes they're even weeds. For Riesberg, they are a fascinating test case for what happens genetically when plants hybridize.

"They become a really useful way of studying how plants can diverge and adapt in the presence of gene flow," Riesberg says.

He recalls, as a graduate student, his professor handing him a textbook on plant speciation and asking him to pick a research focus. The big-headed, yellow-petalled flowers caught his attention. "Sunflowers were in there as one of the classic examples of hybridization. I said, 'Okay, this is going to be it.'"

Riesberg is fascinated with the resilience of sunflowers. They are gifted at thriving in hostile environments. "You can grow them in some pretty bad soil and they will do fine," he says. "They're tough." Sunflowers tend to be drought-tolerant and do just fine in salty ground. Riesberg has found them in sand dunes, and in marshes with higher salt content than oceans. Some of the most hardy sunflowers are hybrids. Their toughness runs counter to long-held ideas about hybrids being genetically weak.[5]

"They take advantage of genes from other [species] to colonize novel habitats, it seems like," he says.

Curiously, sunflowers are not all that easygoing about receiving strange genes. They reject more pollen than they accept from other species.

"It's a bit of a paradox," Riesberg notes. "Their reproductive barriers are fairly strong. They're blocking about 99 per cent of geneflow or more. It's kind of a trickle of genes, rather than sort of a wholescale swamping of the genome."

The reason sunflowers produce so many hybrids is persistence; they make multiple attempts. Since sunflowers grow well in different soil types, they fill a number of so-called "micro-niches." This gives them repeated chances to share pollen between species. After many tries, some of their spikey yellow pollen survives rejection and spreads genes. Products of this gene-mixing are found at the boundaries of different habitats. For instance, the common prairie sunflower (*Helianthus annuus*) grows well in clay-heavy ground, while its near relative *Helianthus petiolaris* prefers sandy soil. In spots where these soil types border one another, results of cross-species mating can clearly be seen. "It's really remarkable," says Riesberg. "There will be a ditch along the road. And you'll have *annuus* at the bottom of the ditch, *petiolaris* at the top of the ditch and hybrids in the middle."[6]

Breeding opportunism doesn't only happen in dunes and ditches. Wild sunflowers trade gametes with farmed sunflowers, and vice versa. It's not always the best exchange. Riesberg suspects that genes from domestic sunflowers reduce the fitness of wild species. Traits growers select for

Persistent pollen: Although they hybridize quite a lot, sunflowers don't easily accept pollen from other species; they reject 99 per cent of foreign pollen. However, because sunflowers adapt so well to different habitats and soil types, different sunflower species end up blossoming near one another. They exchange pollen often enough for hybrids to sometimes result. (Louisa Howard)

in crops aren't always optimal for plant survival off the farm. Domestic sunflowers have huge floral heads, excellent for producing sumptuous, large seeds. But big-faced flowers are wide open to pests, pathogens, and seed-stealing birds.

"Blackbirds love them," says Riesberg. "They just sit there and eat."

Riesberg suspects commercial sunflowers might need more wild genes. He fears the crop plants are wearing thin, genetically.[7]

"Modern breeding has certainly greatly reduced the diversity that farmers grow," he says. "We are focused on a fairly small number of crops and varieties and plant millions of acres. So, there's not that much diversity on a farm. There is a huge amount of diversity to be tapped from wild species."

Many sunflowers: The huge floral faces of agricultural sunflowers produce sumptuous seeds for snacking and food oil production. But these big flowers are vulnerable to diseases and seed-stealing by birds and other animals. These are not viable traits for wild species. (Laslo Varga)

However, not all wild traits are good for domestic plants. For instance, seed dormancy is advantageous for wild species but not for farmed breeds. During harsh seasons, seeds in wild plants go dormant and wait for better conditions to germinate. This keeps an unfortunate year from wiping them out. But farmers can't profit from seeds that won't sprout. More genetically obscure problems plague hybrids too, such as strands of incompatible RNA that interfere with protein coding and potentially stunt plant growth.[8]

"When you bring in these alleles from wild species, you're bringing in all sorts of crap," says Riesberg. "This is probably truest for tomato and sunflower."

Custom-Built Hybrids

These days, biotechnicians use genetic science to create hybrids more predictably than randomly sprinkled pollen. They insert selected strands of genetic code into plant cells. They even add genes from non-plants to introduce novel traits. As with pollination, the goal is to produce seeds. In the 1990s, the chemical and seed company Monsanto inserted genes from an agrobacterium into corn, canola, and other crop plants, conferring resistance to glyphosate, the herbicide sold commercially as Roundup™.[9] Roundup-Ready seeds sold well, as did genetically enhanced hybrids with other traits, such as drought-resistance and the power to kill pests without spraying. Genetically modified organisms (GMOs) have since been widely adopted – and widely resisted. They have penetrated agribusiness faster than any food technology in modern agriculture.[10] Yet since the first GMO seeds hit markets, critics have challenged the ethics of altering genomes and questioned the safety of genetically modified foods. Some governments have echoed this caution and legislated against such products. Mexico refuses to cultivate genetically modified corn and the European Union strictly regulates or outright bans several GMO crops.

Opponents of GMOs question the legality of owning and patenting organisms and claiming their traits as intellectual property. Monsanto (acquired by the German chemical giant Bayer in 2018) has aggressively defended its ownership of seeds. Farmers who buy new seeds from Monsanto cannot save them, breed new strains from them, or plant them without contracts. Monsanto has filed acrimonious lawsuits against farmers with unlicensed crops in their fields. Not all farmers facing Monsanto's lawyers say they planted its seeds on purpose. One farmer sued by Monsanto insisted their seeds blew uninvited onto his land.

In 1997, Monsanto's Roundup-Ready canola became the first genetically modified canola to be sold commercially. Canola's spherical, one-millimetre seeds are light enough to blow easily between one farm field and another, and it's common for them to fly off of seed trucks. Plants that sprout from these wayward seeds are called "volunteer canola." In rural western Canada, volunteer canola is currently the fourth most common weed.[11] In the 1990s, one persistent patch of volunteer canola made considerable trouble for Percy Schmeiser, a western Canadian farmer.

Schmeiser faced Monsanto's lawyers in court between 1997 and 2004, when the company sued him for unlicensed use of its seeds. Schmeiser insisted he tried to get rid of the unwanted plants, and even sprayed them with herbicide before seeding his own crop. However, their engineered resistance to herbicide stymied his efforts. Monsanto argued that it deserved compensation, whether Schmeiser intended to plant its canola seeds or not. In the end, Monsanto won its intellectual property case, but Schmeiser paid no damages. The story didn't quite end there. In 2005, Schmeiser found more volunteer canola in his fields and billed Monsanto CAD$660 for the cost of removing the plants. He was paid the money after filing a small claims suit in 2008. Schmeiser's battle with the seed and chemical giant has taken on David-versus-Goliath stature and become a modern parable about corporate greed.

As a plant geneticist and agricultural researcher, Riesberg kept an eye on Schmeiser's case. He describes Monsanto's tactics as heavy-handed. "Monsanto way overplayed their hand. They were so over-the-top."

Why There Are No GM Sunflowers

Riesberg has butted heads with biotech, himself. During the 1990s, his lab collaborated with scientists at Ohio State University to analyze transgenic sunflowers, which never made it to market. The plants he and others tested were modified with the Bt transgene, which introduced traits from a soil bacterium, *Bacillus thuringiensis* (Bt). The Bt bacterium excretes a natural toxin fatal to insects, and so do Bt plant hybrids. Riesberg and his colleagues learned the Bt transgene had a strong chance of migrating from farmed sunflowers to wild species through pollen, the usual way plants trade genes.

"It would not only escape, but it would increase at quite a high frequency because selective advantage is strong," says Riesberg.

His work was not well-received by the seed industry. "It was not a very popular paper because this is exactly what the folks that were pushing GM did not want to find."

After considerable pushback, Riesberg and his collaborators finally published in a smaller journal, *Ecological Applications*.[12] The paper's appearance in a less prestigious publication nonetheless garnered attention and became part of a conversation around whether or not to grow transgenic sunflowers. Riesberg credits Europe's caution about transgenic crops as much as his research for putting the brakes on genetically modified sunflowers.

"The sunflower community was going through a lot of thinking about how to capture as much of the oil market as they could," he recalls. "They realized that Europe was more and more highly opposed to anything GM. And so they decided as a global community they were going to go non-GM. It was partly because of the Bt paper that we did, but it was more because they wanted to capture the oil market in Europe."

Riesberg feels this result had been a mixed blessing. Europe became a robust market for GMO-free sunflower products, but sunflower oil fell behind other food oils in North America.

"It can't compete with Roundup-Ready soy and Roundup-Ready canola," he says. "So yeah, it has huge consequences."

Riesberg says run-ins such as the Schmeiser case caused reputation damage to Monsanto (which has let some of its seed patents expire since 2015) and hurt biotech's image. However, he doesn't think fewer GMO sunflowers necessarily means greater food safety.

"There's really no evidence, I don't think, of any direct harm from any transgene in plants, at least not that I'm aware of," he says. "But the way Monsanto introduced transgenic crops kind of has killed the industry, so speak. And it's made it very difficult to ever use biotechnology again in crop plants."

Riesberg feels his hands are now tied if he wants to use newer gene-splicing techniques such as CRISPR-Cas9 to enhance genetic diversity in sunflower crops. His work is currently limited to conventional cross-breeding, as he tries to finesse wild genes into farmed sunflowers.

"What we're trying to do is to look for natural variants," he says. Riesberg feels this work is important. He feels crop plants in general have gotten too gene-poor. "Modern breeding has certainly greatly reduced diversity."

Part of the problem, he says, is agri-food monopolies concentrating very few seed varieties among a handful of big suppliers. "There has been indirect harm through greater aggregation of the market to a small number of cultivars and a small number of companies," he says. "So, it's all been kind of these indirect consequences. You have less agricultural biodiversity."

CHAPTER 17

Pollination Influencers and Urban Prairies

Deep-Rooted Problems in Manitoba's Prairies

On the Manitoba Museum's blog, its botanical curator, Diana Bizecki Robson, poses with a specimen of white prairie clover (*Dalea candida*). The victory shot celebrates a difficult dig to extract the plant, roots and all, from sandy ground in south-central Manitoba. Held level with her head, the whole plant, flower to root, reaches her feet. Most of its 160 centimetres is roots. Bizecki Robson's team took great pains to recover as much of the plant's delicate root system as possible.

"That wasn't even the whole thing," she tells me. "It started to get finer and finer roots as you go further and further down."

Bizecki Robson also obtained roots-and-all specimens of June grass (*Koeleria macrantha*) and big bluestem (*Andropogon gerardii*), Manitoba's provincial grass, for an attraction titled *Anchoring the Earth* in the museum's New Prairies Gallery. These long-rooted plants show off their subterranean parts in a glass cabinet, among curios from the Canadian prairies – a log cabin, a diorama of grazing pronghorns, and pinned prairie insects such as the clearwing moth, a charismatic bee mimic. The clover and tall grasses have their own earthy sort of appeal. The big bluestem's long, lanky roots resemble tawny, tangled hair. The exceptional length of these naked roots demonstrates how much goes on underground for prairie plants. Just outside the museum, tall fescues shoot up through packed December snow. Their yellowed stems and seed heads suggest the grasses are dead, but their lower parts are still cozily alive down below, where temperatures remain above freezing.

Endangered prairie flower: The prairie fringed orchid (*Platanthera praeclara*) is listed as endangered by the Committee on the Status of Endangered Wildlife in Canada and the Manitoba *Endangered Species Act*. (William Hamilton Gibson)

"Grasses are really, really good at getting down into the deep layers of the soil and sucking up all that moisture," says Bizecki Robson. "They're better at that than the trees typically are." These deep-rooted plants are comparable to trees as important, often-overlooked carbon sinks, she tells me. "We spend a lot of time talking about planting trees to soak up carbon dioxide in the atmosphere. You want something that sequesters carbon? Native prairie will do that." She laments there is seemingly little alarm over how endangered prairies are, compared to forests. "There's been a lot of concern in the news lately," she notes. "People talking, 'Oh, the rainforest is burning down, this is terrible.' And I'm kind of like, you know what? We destroyed 99 per cent of all wild prairie here in Manitoba. Nobody feels bad about that."

Saving prairies is not always an easy sell, because they're not overtly picturesque. Bizecki Robson admits prairies have a charisma problem. "Prairie is a little hard to appreciate," she says. "It's usually flat. I get it." The fertile flatness of prairies inspires farmers and land developers more than tourists. It's hard to keep their utilitarian interests at bay. Bizecki Robson remembers trying to save a plot of prairie land from a coal mine's expansion, back when she worked as a consultant.

"There were some rare species there, so I suggested, 'Hey, can you maybe not dig it up?'" she recalls. "But that wasn't going to fly. 'Or can you leave at least a little bit more of a buffer and not go quite so far?' They weren't really interested in that either. So, their solution was, 'Well, why don't we just take some seeds of those rarer plants, and we'll grow them in a restored area where we've already removed the coal?' So that's what they ended up doing. But you know, it always kind of bugged me afterwards."

Prairie quietly harbours diversity. It is inhabited by large and small mammals, from meadow voles to deer; birds such as the yellow rail and sandhill crane; and over two hundred plant species, such as blazing star and the extremely rare fringed orchid (*Platanthera praeclara*). Prairies accommodate vibrant insect communities that feed, hunt, and pollinate amid fescue, brome, and other tall grasses.

"You need to sort of stop and pay attention," says Bizecki Robson. "You need to watch. You need to be quiet. Nature has kind of got a slower pace. Just watching things go by can be really good for people, and a good way to gain an appreciation of some of these more subtle features of the prairie."

Pollination Networks and Influencers

A short video made by the museum shows Bizecki Robson sitting on a stool, watching things go by at Bird's Hill Provincial Park, a little north of Winnipeg. In the video, she explains to museum staffer Melissa Pearn that she's monitoring one group of western silvery asters (*Symphyotrichum sericeum*) – designated a species of concern since 1988, then upgraded to threatened in 2021.[1] Bizecki Robson relates how she has counted twenty-one insects coming and going from the flower patch. She keeps an eye on them after they quit the silver asters, curious to see what other flowers they go to.

"The interesting thing is that those same insects are actually visiting a wide variety of plants in the park before this plant even flowers in late August," she states. "Everything in the park is connected to each other in some way. It's like a giant interaction web, kind of like a computer network."[2]

In a minute and forty-five seconds, Bizecki Robson lays out the basics of "pollination facilitation," the process of plants sharing pollinators. Western silvery aster is "self-incompatible" — it is unable to pollinate itself — so it needs outside pollinators. But that one plant on its own can't attract the quantity of pollinators it needs. It requires allies, preferably fellow plants similar to its own species, to bring in more insects. Hopefully these insects will want to also visit silvery asters. It would be best if the other plants had slightly different blooming periods. If they bloom a little earlier or later than silvery aster, they won't be direct competitors. Instead, they'll be collaborators, helping maintain a pollinator community beneficial to all the plants. Bizecki Robson estimates the silvery aster's network has twenty-two mutually dependent species in it. Protecting one flower's survival calls for preserving its neighbours.[3]

"If you want to conserve a rare species, it's not just that you can take that rare species and you can plunk it down somewhere and it will be fine," she tells me. "There's this whole suite of species that you probably need there. They're actually evolving through time together and influencing each other. People don't always think about those connections."

When species disappear, they take parts of their network with them. How much of that network goes away depends on how much influence a species has with its neighbours. Some species are like social media stars, says Bizecki Robson. "You know, where you have those people who are super-influencers who are connected to all sorts of people, and they can actually really make or break your media campaign?" Others, she says, are more like lurkers and occasional commenters. They play a part, but not as large. When rarer species disappear, their loss is felt, but the loss makes fewer ripples, whereas more common species make serious waves when they vanish. "Once you start to lose those common ones, those creatures that are sort of linking lots of species to each-other …" She makes a cut-neck gesture.

Bizecki Robson doesn't have an exact count for how many influential species an ecosystem can lose before it hits a fatal tipping point. Networks are all different, and chance plays a part. She drops the internet comparison and switches to 1970s board games. "Have you ever played Kerplunk? Or Jenga? Any of those games with the blocks? How many blocks do you have to remove before the whole thing collapses? Maybe if you lose ten blocks it'll collapse, in one game. Maybe you can lose twenty. Maybe even thirty. I don't know. We know that these tipping points are out there, but we don't know exactly when it's going to happen." Key pollinators such as bumblebees are like Jenga pieces that support several other ones. If they're taken out, they might topple the whole tower. "Certain bees are really kind of the linchpin of these ecosystems," says Bizecki Robson. "It's often these bees that are the ones visiting lots and lots of species of flowers."

Prairies need more than just plants and pollinators to keep them functioning. It may sound counterintuitive, but they also need disrupters. Disturbance is not merely destructive; it's nature's way of switching things up. One common disturbance is grazing animals, such as bison. In prairies, buffalo grass flourishes when bison and other grazers clear taller grass around it. Grazers influence pollinators too. Bizecki Robson saw their influence at work in one of Manitoba's prairie parks, the Yellow Quill Prairie Preserve. The grazers were not buffalo but cattle. A local rancher frequently brought his cows to graze. In springtime, their grazing opened up spaces for flowers to bloom, and bees took advantage of the bounty.[4]

Fire is another form of disturbance. While massive, out-of-control wildfires are simply destructive, a certain amount of fire is tolerable, even useful, in ecosystems. When tall grasses dry out, they ignite easily and blaze bright. But their long roots survive and the grasses grow back quickly. Meanwhile, fire has cleared dead matter and released soil nutrients. Fires even trigger the flowering of certain plants, such as narrow-leaved purple coneflower (*Echinacea angustifolia*).[5] As coneflowers burst into bloom, pollinators appear. The buzzing of bees follows a prairie fire.

Living Prairie Museum

Cities don't have room for grazing cows or bison, but some municipalities have patches of remaining prairie within them. Sarah Semmler manages the Living Prairie Museum, thirteen hectares of native tallgrass prairie within Winnipeg, Manitoba's capital and Canada's seventh largest city. The museum, actually more of a park and nature preserve, is just a short drive from James Armstrong Richardson International Airport. Signs of urban encroachment, such as a construction crane, intrude on the vista.

"Farther north, you're getting close to the airport and things are being developed," says Semmler. "It is expanding. Winnipeg's notorious for urban sprawl."

Despite its suburban surroundings, the Living Prairie Museum replicates natural disturbance as best it can. It has a pilot program to bring in grazing sheep, which might be as close as an urban park/museum gets to grazing bison. In springtime, staff also do controlled burns on different sections of land.

"It's just that mass removal of vegetation that allows things to rejuvenate from the roots," Semmler explains. "It removes the thatch layer, increases sunlight. It warms the soil and really gets things growing."

A growing city such as Winnipeg is a constant source of disturbances, but not necessarily healthy ones. Invasive plants are one recurring headache. It takes a lot of hand-weeding to keep this patch of native prairie intact. Invasive trees, such as non-native aspens, need girdling, a technique involving cuts to a tree's midsection so nutrients are choked off and its roots eventually starve. Native plants need care, maintenance, and sometimes replanting. Simply letting nature take its course is not an option.

"It's such a small fragment with so many pressures around it," Semmler says. "In this site, hands-off would mean the loss of it entirely."

In the museum's main building, seedlings await planting next spring. They germinate in cone-shaped containers, called "conetainers."

"They're a root trainer," she explains. "You end up with a nice root mass that you can put into the ground. They come back every year from the roots and they store their energy in there. They hold tons of carbon that way."

Semmler sometimes copes with misplaced good intentions from people who want to plant trees in native prairie, unaware how much carbon sequestration plants there already do.

"When we hear people wanting to do tree planting projects on the prairies, we at least let them know that there's other options," she says.

Winnipeggers seem attached to their disappearing prairies, at least as an idea. An afternoon's stroll through the Forks, the city's beloved meeting place and shopping centre, reveals a lot of prairie-centric branding. Shop names include Tall Grass Prairie Bread Company, Prairie Sunshine Honey, and Prairie Potions, a store selling natural health products. A touristy-looking store sells coffee table books with art shots of prairies. One book on display opens on a two-page splash of a canola field, its colours saturated to maximize yellowness. The image's unintended irony is that canola fields have supplanted numerous acres of natural prairie.

The city of Winnipeg has more prairie remnants than just the Living Prairie Museum. The Assiniboine Forest, a natural woodland within the city, has substantial sections of native prairie. Semmler knows of just under a thousand hectares of additional prairie, "of varying degrees of quality." Some succeed at holding off the city's encroachment. Others have lost the battle, including a struggling swath of grassland near the airport. Museum staff had to go in and rescue what plants they could.

"They went in and harvested the seeds and planted those plants in our seed plots," Semmler says. "Now those are cross-pollinating with plants from other areas. So, the genetics are still there somewhere."

Restoring some areas means starting over from scratch. Such efforts are dauntingly labour-intensive. First, restorers bake weedy ground to death under black plastic, in a process called "solarization." If that fails to smother every weed, they sometimes spray with herbicides. In some cases, topsoil is totally replaced before replanting starts.

"We've had developments where they've scoured the surface and removed everything down to the clay," says Semmler. "In some cases, you don't start a restoration in the first year because you're just busy prepping the soil." Semmler doesn't prefer this approach. "I think most people are inclined to try to conserve intact prairie and keep it at a decent quality than they are to completely start from scratch."

Despite such efforts, these pieces of reclaimed prairie aren't sufficient for some endangered species, such as the Poweshiek skipperling (*Oarisma poweshiek*), a small, critically imperilled butterfly.[6] The Poweshiek hangs on to habitat in prairies across Michigan, Wisconsin, and Minnesota, but its only Canadian refuge is the Tallgrass Prairie Preserve in Manitoba. The orange and brown butterfly's total population might be no more than two hundred adults, it's estimated. The Poweshiek depends on such plants as prairie dropseed (*Sporobolus heterolepis*) and black-eyed Susans, where they might also lay their eggs. Winnipeggers often approach Semmler asking how they can help the threatened butterfly, but there isn't much they can do locally.

"People ask, 'What can I do? Can I plant this species in my garden?' That butterfly would probably never have a chance out here. The conditions just aren't the same." The Poweshiek requires a certain mix of wet and dry conditions. Winnipeg's scattered patchwork of prairie spaces would be too fragmented, anyway, for the butterfly's fragile habitat needs. "It's a poor disperser. You can put the perfect mix of plants and grasses in your garden but it's just not going to make it there. That's the bummer of prairie fragmentation."

Calgary Bee Corridor

Elsewhere on the Canadian prairies, another city labours to merge habitat creation with urban planning. In Calgary, efforts have been underway since 2017 to make a flower-filled freeway for local pollinators called a "pollination corridor." The Canyon Meadows Bee Boulevard covers a three-kilometre stretch along a roadside in southwest Calgary. The scrubland bordering Canyon Meadows Drive used to be described as "rundown," until Dave Misfeldt, a planner for the city's Roads and Parks department, took it upon himself to repurpose the area's "unfunctional landscaping." Misfeldt managed to acquire resources – and allies, such as the David Suzuki Foundation and two academic partners, Mount Royal University and the University of Calgary.

One of the project's scientific advisors is Lincoln Best, an independent bee biologist affiliated with the University of Calgary. Best was approached by Misfeldt, who wanted scientific credibility behind planting choices so that his "bee boulevard" would have more than just pretty flowers. Misfeldt struck Best as "a bit of an instigator," who had a vision to change the boulevard into "something much better." Best, Misfeldt, and Jenna Cross, a botanist from the city's Parks Department, set to work rehabilitating the site. While Misfeldt allocated personnel and equipment to develop the space, Best did bee inventories to see what species were active in the city. He stumbled across surprising diversity.

"I think there's around two hundred species of bees within the municipality," he says. Best thinks the diverse set of land types that make up Calgary are why its bees are so varied. "We have prairie, parkland, and montane (mountain slope) ecosystems."

Best worked with Cross selecting native plants for the space. Best is passionate about planting just the right flowers for the right pollinators. As an entomologist, he has learned the best way to find bees is to look for flowers and soils that support them. "I don't go looking for bees, I go looking for plants and soil types, because those are the two things which really are the most important for supporting diversity and abundance of bees," he says.

Best tried to see if his plant knowledge, acquired from years of bee-hunting, could work in the other direction. He tried to work out, from what bees he found in Calgary, which flowers should be planted.

"If I can look at a bee sample and understand what the site looks like, then I can do that in reverse," he says. "I can go to a site and identify a bunch of small changes that make a massive difference, whether that's reconditioning the soil or whether that's planting a particular suite of native plants or woody shrubs. You can kind of look at this from both sides."

With help from 300 schoolchildren (to Misfeldt's pleasant shock, two local schools sent all their students), volunteers and city staff planted shrubs, grasses, and flowers meant to be salt-tolerant, drought-resistant, and good for native pollinators. The team added sand beds for ground-nesting, "bumblebee houses" for bumblebees to nest in, milkweed for butterflies, and domiciles for solitary tunnel-nesting bees. Then they waited for pollinators to come. In 2019, there was one (and then another) notable "plant-it-and-they-will-come" moment, which seemed to confirm the project's success. While doing follow-up surveys, Best found a gypsy cuckoo bumblebee (*Bombus bohemicus*), listed as endangered and feared extinct. Then he found another one.[7]

Best believes cities have great potential as refuges for native bees and plants. Despite weediness and sprawl, cities are potentially more diverse than farmland, he thinks. "Where you have large regional scale agriculture, there's nothing but crops, which is kind of a horrifying prospect. But green spaces in the municipalities could, or might have to, serve as a reservoir for these things."[8]

Sprawl remains a challenge. Calgary has consistently been ranked among Canada's fastest-growing cities. Yet enthusiasm for pollinator gardening remains high among Calgarians and Calgary's city council.

"New sites have been popping up around the city," Best reports. "Every community wants to have their own native plant gardens and so on. There's an enormous amount of support in the city."

In 2020, Calgary moved forward with a pilot project to plant wildflowers and native grasses along Calgary's 16th Avenue N.E. Bland-looking turf grass, which had to be cut four times a season, was replaced with low-maintenance native plants. Wooden boxes for wild bees to nest in were hooked onto chain link fences between roadsides and residences. This effort is meant as a first step in a larger "Roadside Naturalization Project" to refurbish roadsides and make them catalysts for biodiversity, while saving on maintenance costs, like mowing.[9]

Unfortunately, someone didn't get the "no-mowing" memo about one of Calgary's other bee corridors. Coventry Hills Bee Boulevard, in north central Calgary, was mysteriously mowed down in 2021, wiping out three years of volunteer gardening and $10,000 of city funds. One volunteer called the guerilla landscaping incident "heartbreaking."[10] Whoever razed the fledgling meadow in road medians ignored, or failed to notice, signs displaying pictures of bees, big-lettered admonitions such as "nature at work," and printed appeals to specifically not mow. The city managed to rule out its own staff as culprits, but the mystery mower's identity remains unknown.

This incident highlights the chaos inherent in cities. Cities can surprise us with hidden gems of biodiversity, but random human acts can also unnerve us. Still, Best feels upbeat about people's potential to naturalize cities. Furthermore, he sees it as necessary, going forward, to actively maintain the spaces we inhabit.

"I think in the future, we're going to have to take a more active approach in managing the landscape," he says. "Not just crops, but ecosystem fragments as well. Ensuring that those fragments are protected, healthy, and maintained is going to be more and more important."

CHAPTER 18

Bees and Neighbours

Guelph: Pollination City

In March 2020, as COVID-19 swiftly graduated from mysterious new virus to worldwide pandemic, many parts of public life were suddenly put on hold. Planned events were hastily cancelled, including Pollination Guelph's annual symposium. It seemed like the yearly meetup of polli-nation experts and enthusiasts would be going ahead until just a couple of days before, when organizers messaged attendees to let them know the symposium was not happening, at least the scheduled live event. Three months later, with quarantine measures fully in place, Pollination Guelph's co-chair, Victoria MacPhail, gave her opening address via Zoom, kicking off a series of webinars based on the symposium's speakers list. MacPhail updated her virtual audience about Pollination Guelph's pol-linator gardens, maintained through volunteer effort, "from the north end of the city, through the south end of the city, east through west." She asked people to stay tuned about the native plant sale, hosted online by the Guelph Wildflower Society. Fundraising must continue, even during a pandemic.[1]

Pollination Guelph's largest gardening effort has been to convert the decommissioned Eastview landfill to a natural meadow, now named the Eastview Pollinator Park. Since its first hectare was seeded in 2013, the 45-hectare space has been gradually "re-naturalized." Most of the re-wilding takes place behind a fence, where ecologists labour to transform wasteland to pollinator habitat. Outside the fence, artist Christina Kings-bury engages people through creativity by sewing a quilt, on-site, from 2,500 square feet (232 square metres) of homemade paper embedded with seeds. As the paper quilt disintegrates, the ground is seeded with

Bee hotel: This "air bee and bee" is a hotel for wild bees to nest in, which sits atop Guelph's City Hall. While inspiring and attractive, it is not a universal solution. "It's not the best design for pollinators," says Pollination Guelph co-chair MacPhail. "Even if it's a catchy design." MacPhail, a pollination biologist, says making space in parks and gardens for bees to nest in naturally is more important. (Pollination Guelph)

goldenrod, yellow coneflower, coreopsis, and other wildflowers. Titled "ReMediate," the living artwork comes with an audio installation featuring poems with titles such as "Pins and Needles" and "How To Love a Landfill," by Kingsbury's collaborator, Anna Bowen.[2]

Remediating the Eastview site will take years to fully realize, but in the meantime, other Pollination Guelph projects have taken root in different parts of the city. One of its gardens now graces the headquarters of Alectra Utilities, Guelph's power supplier. There, a 1,500-square-foot (457-square-metre) drainage swale was seeded with pollinator-friendly shrubs and perennials such as blue flag iris (*Iris versicolor*), Canada anemone (*Anemone canadensis*), and swamp milkweed (*Asclepias incarnata*). Flowerbeds run along Guelph's section of the Trans Canada Trail, a nationwide system of walking trails. Another project, the Food Forest, mimics a woodland ecosystem while producing edible plants. In Riverside Park, three flowerbeds bloom along a trail near Guelph's Speed River, with signs informing strollers about native bees and how to plant pollinator gardens.

Pollination Guelph's labours started in 2008, when the non-profit began to promote pollinator conservation as an urban issue. At the time, there were not many groups mentioning pollination in cities.

"We were one of the first," says MacPhail. "I would say probably the first for Canada and one of the first in North America. Especially considering we're a local, community-based grassroots group focused just on pollinators and the different aspects of pollinators. I should say *pollination*. We're *Pollination* Guelph."

MacPhail leans into this word to emphasize how her organization does not just support pollinators, but pollination's networks of pollinators and plants. Another dimension of pollination networks is landscape. Pollinators have a variety of habitat needs to consider.

"A lot of insects will just kind of fly a couple of hundred metres from their nest site," MacPhail explains. "A larger bee can go a few kilometres. The more habitat you create, the more pollinators you support." Spaces next to pollinator habitats also matter, she says. "What pollinators will arrive when you plant and when they will arrive does vary, depending what the neighbourhood is." As in human real estate, *location*, *location*, *location* has value. Curb appeal counts for pollinators.

Bringing Bee Facts to City Hall

Pollinators appreciate good neighbours as well. Pollinator parks do better when they're near yards with healthy gardens. The challenge around that piece is every yard belongs to someone, who makes their own gardening decisions. Big portions of urban land are privately held by homeowners, businesses, land trusts, and so on. Changing urban land to pollinator habitat necessarily involves numerous private decisions. MacPhail and her colleagues work hard to develop messaging that will reach the most city-dwellers. In 2018, MacPhail described the need for "steppingstones across the city," at a ceremony where Guelph branded itself Canada's nineteenth Bee City. Signalling their desire for bee-friendliness, city administrators voted unanimously for the initiative, spearheaded by Pollination Guelph. Mayor Cam Guthrie dressed as a bee for the send-off.[3]

Bee Cities began in the United States as the brainchild of Phyllis Stiles, a citizen ecologist and pollinator advocate, from Asheville, North Carolina. The campaign she started in 2012 took off nationwide. As of this writing, there are 147 Bee Cities and 126 Bee Campus affiliates across forty-four American states. In 2016, Toronto became the first Canadian Bee City, an effort championed by citizen naturalist Shelly Candel. The Bee City declaration promised bee and pollination advocates more tools to focus attention and funds on education campaigns and ecology work.

In 2019, the city launched a PollinateTO Community Grants program for creating pollinator habitats.[4]

With a mandate to support bees in Toronto, questions revolved around not just how to help, but which bees needed help. "Bees" for many people means honeybees. Before Phyllis Stiles founded Bee Cities U.S.A., she was inspired to become a hobbyist beekeeper after reading about colony collapse in 2007. Stiles is not the only person who heard the "call of the bees" this way.[5] Since 2007, a number of urbanites started their own back-yard hives to help "save the bees." A lot of bee experts question whether the best move is to put more honeybee hives in cities. In its annual *State of the World's Plant and Fungi* report in 2020, Kew Gardens in the UK flatly warned, "Campaigns encouraging people to save bees have resulted in an unsustainable proliferation in urban beekeeping." The report went on to say such campaigns overlooked "how honeybees interact with other, native species."[6]

One of Bee City Canada's first expert participants, York University professor and bumblebee researcher Sheila Colla, found it challenging at first to educate Toronto's city councillors about bee diversity. When council first considered the Bee City proposal, word reached Colla that one councillor was fixated on honeybees. "That councillor went to the city staff and said, 'Okay, we need to do this honeybee program in Toronto to save the bees.'" Hearing this, Colla and other Bee City advisors scrambled to broaden the messaging. With Colla's input, language around pollinator protection steered toward "conserving habitat and enhancing habitat so it promotes wild bees." Her group's proposal described Toronto as "home to over 300 species of bees and hundreds more non-bee pollinator spe-cies, making it home to one of the most diverse pollinator populations in Canada."[7]

A few years later, Colla and other scientists got curious over what the general public knew about bees. They decided to phone people and ask. Through telephone surveys, they learned public awareness was low around bee diversity. Just 10 per cent of respondents could name one more wild bee species and half of those questioned thought European honeybees were native to Canada. On the other hand, people's hearts were largely in the right place. Respondents were well-disposed to bees, felt concerned for their well-being, and strongly favoured "conservation work for all at-risk species, including pollinators."[8]

Bees on a hotel: Members of the Toronto Beekeepers Cooperative (since renamed the Toronto Beekeepers Collective) keeping hives atop the Fairmont Royal York in downtown Toronto. The Fairmont's Bee Sustainable program maintains twenty rooftop honeybee apiaries at its hotel locations, along with "bee hotels" for wild bees. Some bee ecologists question whether keeping hives in cities is the best approach to urban bee conservation. (Stephen Humphrey)

Bee ecologist Charlotte de Keyzer, at the University of Toronto, feels some businesses too often seize on goodwill toward bees for monetary gain. De Keyzer's website, bee-washing.com, calls out companies that promote themselves as "bee-friendly" without necessarily helping bees. Food companies, in particular, use honeybee imagery to make their products seem benign. Some businesses market directly to hobbyist beekeepers. There are enough hobbyists in cities to support a niche market for beekeeping supplies. Alvéole, a Montreal-based company, markets gear to amateur beekeepers and installs hives, which it manages, for schools and businesses.

Customers post glowing testimonials on the company's webpage, but it receives bad reviews on de Keyzer's site. "The work this company does is not beneficial to conservation, yet they continue to use the #SaveTheBees tag on social media," reads bee-washing.com's critique.[9] Despite being panned by de Keyzer, Alvéole does brisk business. The company sells its beekeeping supplies and services in several Canadian and American cities. Its prestige clients include the Canadian embassy in Washington, DC. During a radio interview in 2020, de Keyzer referenced honeybees as "essentially livestock managed by people." She likened backyard bee-keeping to saving wild birds by keeping chickens.[10]

Evidence from Europe suggests honeybees might not be the best neighbours to other city-dwelling bees. In 2019, French scientists noticed a significant drop in wild bee visits within 500 metres, and even 1,000 metres, of urban beehives in Paris. The French study's authors encouraged cities to plant more flowers to feed native species and to offset the appetites of honeybees. They also recommended reducing the quantity of urban hives. A Swiss study from 2022 concurs. It states specifically that cities should limit the number of hives allowed in urban locations, based on the quantity of nearby greenspace.[11]

Provincial Bee Act in Limbo

While Toronto and Guelph promote the importance of native pollinators, neither city has rules limiting how many beehives to keep in one place. Ontario, home province to both cities, has some regulations around where to put urban hives. The *Ontario Bees Act* advises beekeepers to set their hives at least thirty metres back from the property lines of dwellings, public buildings, or parks. Also, hives should come no closer than ten metres to highways. The act advises beekeepers to register their hives with the province, report and treat pests and diseases, correctly dispose of dead colonies, and post proper signage for bee yards.

However, those regulations might be lifted. In 2019, Ontario's Progressive Conservative government announced that, "on a day to be proclaimed," it would repeal the *Bees Act*, which had become part of Bill 132, the *Better for People, Smarter for Business Act*. Other laws related to agriculture were swept into the bill, such as the *Livestock Community Sales Act* and the *Livestock Medicines Act*.[12] However, since the province's announcement, the situation has been in a holding pattern. Ontario's lawmakers have not yet proclaimed a specific day to repeal the *Bees Act*, so for the moment, it's business as usual. Just after the repeal was announced, the Ontario Beekeeper's Association (OBA) drafted an open letter. It expressed surprise at the government's plan to reverse Bill 132 and asked leaders to respond about their "unilateral decision to repeal the Bees Act."

In 2020, I chatted briefly by phone with OBA president Bernie Wiehle. I heard the occasional high-pitched whine as bees flew near his phone, since Wiehle was out with his hives. He informed me that Ontario's government, to date, had not replied to the letter.

"Yeah. That one came as quite a bit of a surprise to us, quite obviously," he said. "They made it one of their campaign issues to get rid of a whole lot of what they considered unnecessary legislation or legislation that was harmful to business. And without consulting us, they announced that they were going to throw the Bees Act into that." Wiehle personally reached out to the province's agriculture ministry, the Ontario Ministry of Agriculture, Food and Rural Affairs (OMAFRA), which knew nothing more about the decision's status than he did. "Obviously the message didn't get all the way up and down the chain, there. It kind of surprised everybody. But they've said, 'As far as we're concerned, we're still operating as if the Bees Act is in force.'"

As long as beekeepers follow the rules and come forward to register their hives, Wiehle views the *Bees Act* — at least while it's in force — as a tool to help limit the spread of disease and parasites among honeybees, and hopefully prevent pathogens from spilling over to wild bees.

"There are certain diseases, certain issues that transcend just beekeeping," he says. "What's good for honeybees is good for native bees and other pollinators."

There Goes the Neighbourhood

If there is one thing that experts all seem to agree on, it's that planting more flowers is good for bees and other pollinators. When they have access to floral abundance, their populations increase, often quickly. But as fast as they rise, they can be driven down. Miriam Richards at Brock University saw this quick reversal of fortunes in a site she has monitored for two decades in St Catharines, Ontario. Like Guelph's Eastview Pollinator Park, the Glenridge Quarry Naturalization Site used to be a landfill. After it was closed and capped in 2001, the site was rehabilitated and reopened in 2004 as pollinator habitat. Ever since that transformation, Richards has gone there to count bees. She was curious about the time it took to repopulate such a heavily disturbed space. It actually didn't take long for pollinators to flock there. Within three to five years, it had a diverse, vibrant community. Then, in 2017, Richards was unpleasantly surprised by a sudden drop in numbers at Glenridge Quarry. At the time, when interviewed, Richards described a bad feeling in the pit of her stomach.[13]

At first, she had no idea where all the bees had gone. Richards thought maybe the previous dry summer had been too much. Then she started to suspect a rash of home-building near the park had overstressed its resident pollinators. Despite a well-curated selection of native plants to feed on, Glenridge Quarry's pollinators were devastated by disturbance from the next neighbourhood over. Neighbourhoods are landscapes as much as wild areas are. Upheaval in one habitat is felt by adjacent ones.[14] The good news, Richards says, is that when conditions improve, communities bounce back, with encouraging speed.

"When environments are degraded, they decline quickly," she says. "But as long as you don't wipe them out altogether, if you fix their environments, they start responding quickly as well."

Ups and downs like these demonstrate how precarious restoring habitats can be. Recovery can turn to loss, sometimes in the blink of an eye.

"You can fix things quite effectively," says Richards. "But you can wreck them really effectively, too."

CHAPTER 19

Turning Over New Leaves

Nature's cycles involve disturbance and recovery. It's full of innumerable accidents waiting to happen. Disturbance can be small and slight. A fallen leaf blocks light that would otherwise reach a germinating plant. That same leaf offers an insect shelter and extends its life. When a tree falls it destroys an animal's burrow, but then becomes home for several more species. Disturbances can be worldwide: an asteroid hurtles from the heavens and triggers a cascade of extinction. Such an event happened 66 million years ago, ending the time of dinosaurs. But the demise of these giant beasts cleared the way, eventually, for humans, with their big brains, nimble thumbs, and unprecedented learning power. Learning, itself, is a succession of large and small shocks. The mind has its own cycles of disturbance and recovery. If untouched by new knowledge, it repeats familiar patterns, which become fixed over time. It takes the jolt of discovery to shake a mind out of its rut. The process can be unsettling, embarrassing, even painful. But that's how we learn.

Some insights are harder to process because their scope is too big or too small. Perhaps both. Climate change is a global calamity set in motion by an incalculable number of tiny events. Gas molecules, so small they're invisible, saturate the atmosphere, trapping heat. This happens over timespans too short for many living things to adapt to but too slow to trigger human threat responses, which evolved for Paleolithic threats. People are semantic and social, so we build narratives and form groups around them. Facts are filtered through politics, and scientific consensus gets batted around as "controversy," even as proof piles up. Some clues are huge and obvious, such as an entire town in British Columbia destroyed by fire. Some are personal and small, such as my mom calling from Alberta to tell me, yet again, about once-in-a-century weather.

Most of my labours on this book happened during the COVID-19 pandemic, when minuscule foes caused a worldwide disruption. The pandemic's instigators were beings so biologically basic they could not reproduce without hijacking human cells to make proteins they couldn't. Rudely simple creatures deftly exploited our species' technology-driven mobility to gain rapid, global reach, before we even noticed. Humans were mere vectors in a virus's network, which swiftly went global.

In much the same way, invasive plant species, originally rooted in soil an ocean away, turn up in the garden, frustrating my efforts to grow native plants. Invaders take root and colonize before I know what's happening. When at last I catch on, the revelation impertinently spoils my self-image as an ecological ally. No matter how much my mind absorbs about insects, plants, and pollination, I'm a hapless gardener. However much ecology I cram in my head, my thumb doesn't turn green.

My partner, Christina, and I have been trying to convert our overgrown, neglected lawn into an eco-friendly garden. We started with golden intentions, and scarcely any clue what to do. Our thoughts aglow with notions of bringing nature home, we acquired native plants (or plants we thought were native), dug up scruffy turf grass, and fired seedlings into the ground. While we floundered away, the garden gradually took shape. The parts Christina planted look aesthetic and orderly. The parts looking thrown together in mad haste were no doubt my doing.

The sunflowers surprised both of us. I was dazzled by how many of them burst from the ground. Christina thought they were clownish, but I insisted they were magical. Bumblebees, syrphid flies, and other six-legged flower feeders cavorted inside their huge floral heads, and flew away sprinkled with sunny pollen. When their seeds matured, goldfinches flew in and pecked at them, so we had birds to entertain us too. In the summer of 2020, when people were cautioned to stay home, I seldom journeyed further from our front door than this forest of sunflowers. If I wasn't inside the house, at my desk, mostly in my head, I had likely popped outside to glory in their bright, yellow bigness. I'd flit back inside to write about pollination, pleased at how well the garden had flourished from our benign neglect.

It took until August for me to notice that beneath the yellow blaze of sunflowers, the rest of the garden was overgrown and weedy to the point of confusion. I couldn't tell where one thing ended and another began, what most of our uninvited plants were called, or where they came from. However, I couldn't miss the weeds, spilling into the street. Suddenly, my simplistic (and apparently wrong-headed) credo about letting nature run its course had blown up in my face, in a profusion of mystery plants. We had no clue at first which plants were even weeds. I thought daylilies were native plants, since the fiery orange flowers bloomed so beautifully, without any encouragement. I thought the same about goutweed, and their handsome two-coloured leaves. We made little stabs at cutting those back now and then, but otherwise let them be, convinced they were naturally occurring. Neighbours colluded in this denial. The nice people next door had a well-trimmed, presentable garden plot, chock-full of invasives. English ivy from their side crept over, under, and through the fence, attempting to strangle our plants.

Things that looked lovely in our garden were virulent plant foes elsewhere. The goutweed that seemed so pretty at our place looks less cute blanketing an entire slope of a ravine.[1] In her webinar, invasive plant expert Colleen Cirillo selects a slide featuring fully "naturalized" goutweeds, which dominate a Toronto hillside. Their leaves have lost the variegated colour that made them nice in our garden. In Cirillo's picture, the plants are a wash of solid green. Below ground, their roots discharge chemicals that change the soil in ways that sicken native flora.

Toronto's ravines are one of the world's most spacious urban ecosystems. They cover 11,000 hectares, roughly 17 per cent of the city. In 2017, Eric Davies, a graduate student at University of Toronto, co-authored the *Toronto Ravines Study*, an exhaustive survey of life in Toronto's ravines, based on four decades of data. It is the largest biodiversity study in the city's history. The report describes ravines as "the primary source of habitat for Toronto's terrestrial biodiversity," and warns of threats to that diversity by invasives such as Japanese knotweed, garlic mustard, and dog-strangling vine, which clog 95 per cent or more of the city's forest floors.[2]

I find one of those invasives, garlic mustard, lurking beneath our largest stand of sunflowers. The ground-hugging plant comes away easily when I rip it out. That's good, because I have plenty of ripping out to do. Garlic mustard has a savoury, aromatic smell, and its leaves are tasty. I have a bag of garlic mustard I "harvested" in the fridge, and it's not bad in salads. Using humour as a recruiting tool, artist and nature activist Echo

Railton installed signs that read "EAT ME" around the city in patches overgrown with garlic mustard, urging foodies to help fight invasives.

While every little bit (or bite) counts, Eric Davies is pushing for more far-reaching responses to Toronto's ravine problem. He advises city staff on urban forestry policy and solicits public and private funds to "re-wild" Toronto's ravines with indigenous trees. Trees themselves are miniature ecosystems. They support diverse insect communities. Davies spent four years trapping and counting bugs from different trees in neighbourhoods near his university, to learn how much life those trees supported. According to that research, native trees support at least twice as much diversity as introduced species.

Thirty per cent of Toronto is tree canopy.[3] Unfortunately, the city's urban forests are besieged by invasive trees, such as Norway maple. These non-native maples were imported from Europe to North America as street trees. They do the job well: they are hardy, they tolerate poor soils, and they lack native pests. However, what makes them good decorative trees makes them virtual dead zones for local fauna. According to Davies, in just about any Canadian city, one in four trees is now a Norway maple. In a television news clip, Davies names off trees while hiking through one of Toronto's ravines. "Norway maple, Norway maple, Norway maple," he repeats with growing exasperation. Finally, with relief, he happens upon an indigenous white pine.

Of course, there's a Norway maple in front of my place. A skinny tree, with deep green, many-pointed leaves, leans awkwardly against the house. It stands in a spot where no-one would have planted a tree on purpose, so it probably seeded itself. Even if it was not invasive, the tree would eventually damage the house. I don't have the heart to kill it at first. I'm used to thinking all trees are good. Trees battle climate change. Trees are lovely poems. But it's got to go – I'm resolved. Christina can't bear to watch it destroyed, so she has me wait until she's visiting her friend's family cottage. The job of taking down the tree is actually easy. Even at its base, the trunk isn't much thicker than my wrist. I demolish it in minutes, with clippers and a cheap saw.

I feel some remorse doing it. Sure, I felled an invasive tree, but aren't invasives just species that will be native one day? Perhaps. Some even fill useful niches. Bees forage on lots of "weedy" plants in front of the house, such as white sweet clover and lamiums, an introduced plant with bee-friendly purple blossoms. I don't get rid of all the lamiums because they bloom so well in early springtime. Hopefully next year, more of the native spring bloomers will succeed, such as columbines and geraniums. Dandelions, introduced to Canada by French colonists, supply soil with calcium. But even when introduced plants play nice, they have fewer connections established with local fauna. American biologist Douglas Tallamy researches the networks native plants foster. "Ecosystems built from indigenous plants are more species-rich than ecosystems infused with non-natives," he notes in *The Living Landscape*, a collaboration with author and landscape ethicist Rick Darke.[4]

Much of Tallamy's work centres on butterflies, which pollinate, though not as prolifically as bees and flies. Pollination is not their only ecological role. They're a necessary part of the food chain. Caterpillars are highly nutritious for birds and their chicks. No other meal packs as much fat and protein. Chickadees depend on caterpillars exclusively in springtime, when they mate. Native trees host a huge variety of caterpillars – especially oak trees. According to Tallamy, oaks alone support 557 caterpillar species.

Nearly one-third of all oak species are threatened with extinction. Black oaks (*Quercus velutina*) are highly endangered in Ontario. Less than a tenth of a per cent of their previous number remain. A third of High Park, near where I live, is black oak savannah. A couple of springs ago, I joined a conservation walk through that area. During an hour-long walkabout, our guide identified more than forty plants native to black oak ecosystems. The guide was a conservationist from Tallgrass Ontario, a project dedicated to preserving such spaces. He compared the majestic trees to pillars in a cathedral. Later, in a less poetic mood, he turned and ripped out a shoot of some plant invasive, annoyance crossing his face.

"Untouched wilderness" might be a dying idiom, since there is very little wilderness that's untouched anywhere, especially in cities, where most humans live. Currently, 55 per cent of all people are city-dwellers. That figure is projected to be 68 per cent by 2050. In many ways, that's good. Cities are resource- and space-efficient. They concentrate people together with things they all need, from food to entertainment. If we all fled cities for the country, we'd disturb even more wilderness. Where people go, roads are built – along with streetlights, gas stations, power

Native plants: Seedlings of evening primrose and upland white aster. These native plants were grown from seed to plant in my home garden and given away for Project Swallowtail, a citizen naturalist initiative that encourages private homeowners to plant butterfly- and pollinator-friendly gardens. (Stephen Humphrey)

lines, and so on. Instead of "getting back to the land," maybe we can look for ways to rewild cities.

Tallamy coined the term "homegrown national park," by which he means treating private green spaces as nature preserves. People with yards and gardens become ad hoc park rangers. It's a personal argument for nature: direct ecological democracy where citizens vote with shovels. Nature groups often give out lawn signs, like political campaigns. The David Suzuki Foundation adores signage. A house down my street displays a sign for one Suzuki Foundation project among many – Butterflyway, which promotes butterfly habitat.

Our front yard has a sign for Project Swallowtail, a local butterfly initiative. The sign signals our garden's intent to be butterfly- (and pollinator-) friendly. It broadcasts to passers-by that things in our garden were planted on purpose. Native plants are locally rare enough to look strange at first, compared to other garden plants. One Project Swallowtail participant, in the Toronto suburb of Etobicoke, fought in civil court to keep his garden full of native plants, after a neighbour complained. Another freelance park steward, author, and naturalist, Lorraine Johnson, has a campaign underway to change Toronto's criteria for well-kept yards, so native plant gardens can't simply be cancelled as eyesores. Apart from what it broadcasts to neighbours, our sign helps remind me and Christina to be conscious gardeners, now that we've got advertising to live up to.

Things we planted are not showy right away. That will change when coneflowers, vervain, primroses, bottle gentians, and other plants (including sunflowers) start blooming. If things go like previous years, our place should have exploded with pollinators by June. So far, I've seen mining bees come and go from their nest under a rock. I've seen bee-mimicking flower flies, and mud-dauber wasps, with long black bodies and waists slim as sewing needles. There were some beetles and a couple of moths. It's gratifying to recognize the species returning from previous seasons. They feel like neighbours.

Our human neighbours buzz by, with pleasant comments about the garden. Apparently, watching us putter around and get grubby makes people chatty. I bring out my camera to take photos, partly because I want to, but also so I don't look strange just standing there, staring at flowers and insects, as they drop in to sip nectar, bask in sunlight, or shelter from rain, using blossoms as umbrellas. I squint and hold my breath, struggling to hand-focus, so I can get one or two decent shots of sweat bees doing their circular sidestroke through flowers to pick up pollen.

I'm in a cosmic zoom moment, where the universe is reduced to centimetres. One garden is not the whole cosmos. It's just one node in a chain of parks, gardens, and green spaces, set between buildings and concrete. Where I'm standing, I can't see the full sweep of it, just bits and pieces. If I made a time-lapse film of these moments, it might show flowers in and out of bloom, pollinators coming and going, and the garden transitioning through seasons – midsummer's burst of colours, fall's shower of butter yellow as goldenrods bloom, supplanting sunflowers as those lose their looks, becoming gnarled, gothic husks. In that dead-looking state, their next generation prepares its return as seeds. We harvest food from some plants: a few tomatoes, strawberries, some lettuce and kale, a bit of sage and mint. A food garden this size can barely provision a salad. Edible plants are fun, but we won't save tons on groceries. We're gardening for diversity, not dollars. We're banking on the notion that nature itself has value.

Forester and conservation writer Aldo Leopold is remembered for *A Sand County Almanac*, published in 1949, a year after he died helping his neighbour extinguish a grass fire. The book chronicles Leopold's private project of restoring an old farm to its previous, natural state, and lays out Leopold's tenet of "the land ethic." He defines this as "an ecological conscience" and "a conviction of individual responsibility for the health of the land." He defines "health" as the land's ability to renew. Leopold suggests a kind of personhood for the natural world. He urges people to form relationships with nature, to engage with it and try to know it, like any person.

"We can be ethical only in relation to something we can see, feel, understand, love or otherwise have faith in," he writes.[5]

Seeing is believing, it's said. Seeing things in ways that help us understand them is tricky, though. We have many tools for seeing, so numerous perspectives are possible. Let's take a minute and try our own cosmic zoom. Here is our planet, seen from space. Earth observation satellites track the flow of seasons, shrinking ice sheets, land masses turning green with trees, others going brown with desert. Zoom in. We're in an aircraft, flying over jungle, forest, desert, tundra. Now we're on the ground, looking around a prairie, a park, a ravine. We see those habitats struggling with pressures such as the city's grey encroachment, incursions of exotic animals, the creeping conquest of invasive plants.

Since it's my imaginary movie, we'll focus on one plant in my garden. It's not moving, but in its own way, it's active in the world. It soaks in sunlight, inhales CO_2, and respires oxygen. It responds chemically to soil microbes, kinetically to gardeners' shovels and hoses, and reproductively to insects that come along to pollinate. Entomologist E.O. Wilson once called insects the "little things that run the world."[6] These buzzing, bustling creatures live short, frenetic lives, which nonetheless have purpose. In the struggle to meet their needs they become plant mating allies, and co-authors of seeds.

Finally, we zero in on one single grain of pollen – waxen, sculptural, coded with genetic data, unconsciously questing for connection, and continuation. The power of these minuscule grains scales upward to seeds, then plants, and then ecosystems. From space, we can see this process

Pollen-covered: A male bumblebee dusted with pollen, sipping nectar from a coneflower, in my garden. (Stephen Humphrey)

painting the Earth's continents green. But let's not finish there. *Cosmic Zoom*, Eva Szasaz's film, ends with a boy rowing a boat – one person doing something ordinary. So, let's conclude with one human, pausing to gaze at a flower, and then glancing down to notice a petal spattered with yellow grains, specks of life, smaller than grains of sand.

NOTES

Prologue

1 Philip Gingerich, "Temporal Scaling of Carbon Emission and Accumulation Rates: Modern Anthropogenic Emissions Compared to Estimates of PETM-Onset Accumulation," *Paleoceanography and Paleoclimatology* (2019), https://doi.org/10.1029/2018PA003379.

2 National Centers for Environmental Information, "What Are 'Proxy' Data?" NOAA, https://www.ncdc.noaa.gov/news/what-are-proxy-data (accessed 15 January 2022).

3 Nehemiah Grew, *The Anatomy of Plants with an Idea of a Philosophical History of Plants, and Several Other Lectures, Read before the Royal Society* (London: W. Rawlins, 1682; Ann Arbor, MI: Text Creation Partnership, 2022), http://name.umdl.umich.edu/A42100.0001.001.

4 Luciana Gatti et al., "Amazonia as a Carbon Source Linked to Deforestation and Climate Change," *Nature* 595 (2021): 388–93, https://doi.org/10.1038/s41586-021-03629-6.

5 Aelys Humphreys et al., "Global Dataset Shows Geography and Life Form Predict Modern Plant Extinction and Rediscovery," *Nature Ecology and Evolution* 3 (2019): 1043–7, https://doi.org/10.1038/s41559-019-0906-2.

6 United Nations Department of Economic and Social Affairs, Population Division, *World Population Prospects 2022: Summary of Results* (2002), 3, https://www.un.org/development/desa/pd/sites/www.un.org.development.desa.pd/files/wpp2022_summary_of_results.pdf.

7 Michiel van Dijk et al., "A Meta-Analysis of Projected Global Food Demand and Population at Risk of Hunger for the Period 2010-2050," *Nature Food* 2 (2021): 494–501, https://doi.org/10.1038/s43016-021-00322-9.

8 Intergovernmental Science-Policy Platform on Biodiversity and Ecosystem Services (IPBES), "Assessment Report on Pollinators, Pollination and Food Production," *Zenodo* (2016), https://doi.org/10.5281/zenodo.3402857.

9 Brooke Jarvis, "The Insect Apocalypse Is Here," *The New York Times*, 27 November 2018, https://www.nytimes.com/2018/11/27/magazine/insect-apocalypse.html.

10 Caspar Hallmann et al., "More than 75 Percent Decline over 27 Years in Total Flying Insect Biomass in Protected Areas," PLOS ONE 12, no. 10 (2017): e0185809, https://doi.org/10.1371/journal.pone.0185809.

11 Yue Wang et al., "Plant Biomes Demonstrate that Landscape Resilience Today Is the Lowest It Has Been since End-Pleistocene Megafaunal Extinctions," *Global Change Biology* (2020), https://doi.org/10.1111/gcb.15299.

Chapter One

1 Graham Dolby, Howard Falcon-Lang, and Martin Gibling, "A Conifer-Dominated Palynological Assemblage from Pennsylvanian (Late Moscovian) Alluvial Drylands in Atlantic Canada: Implications for the Vegetation of Tropical Lowlands during Glacial Phases," *Journal of the Geological Society* 168 (2011): 571–84, https://doi.org/10.1144/0016-76492010-061.

2 Philippe Marmottant, Alexandre Ponomarenko, and Diane Bienaimé, "The Walk and Jump of *Equisetum* Spores," *Proceedings of the Royal Society B: Biological Sciences* 11, no. 1770 (2013): 280, https://doi.org/10.1098/rspb.2013.1465.

3 James Brooks and Gordon Shaw, "Sporopollenin: A Review of Its Chemistry, Paleochemistry and Geochemistry," *Grana* 17 (1978): 91–8, https://doi.org/10.1080/00173137809428858.

4 Ruud Poort, Henk Visscher, and David Dilcher, "Zoidogamy in Fossil Gymnosperms: The Centenary of a Concept, with Special Reference to Prepollen of Late Paleozoic Conifers," *Proceedings of the National Academy of Sciences of the United States of America* 93 (1996): 11713–17, https://doi.org/10.1073/pnas.93.21.11713.

5 William Chaloner, "Spores and Land-Plant Evolution," *Review of Palaeobotany and Palynology* 1, no. 1–4 (1967): 83–93, https://doi.org/10.1016/0034-6667(67)90112-1.

6 Howard Falcon-Lang, Viola Mages, and Margaret Collinson, "The Oldest *Pinus* and Its Preservation by Fire," *Geology* 44, no. 4 (2016): 303–6, https://doi.org/10.1130/G37526.1.

7 Hong Fu Yin and Hai Jun Song, "Mass Extinction and Pangea Integration during the Paleozoic-Mesozoic Transition," *Science China Earth Sciences* 56 (2013): 1791–1803, https://doi.org/10.1007/s11430-013-4624-3.

8 Jun Shen et al., "Evidence for a Prolonged Permian-Triassic Extinction Interval from Global Marine Mercury Records," *Nature Communications* (2019), https://doi.org/10.1038/s41467-019-09620-0.

9 John Stevenson, "The Formation of Coal Beds. I. An Historical Summary of Opinion from 1700 to the Present Time," *Proceedings of the American Philosophical Society* 50, no. 198 (1911): 1–116, http://www.jstor.org/stable/983954.

10 International Energy Agency, "Coal," https://www.iea.org/fuels-and-technologies/coal (accessed 14 December 2021).

11 David Upton, "The Predictive Power of Palynology," GEO *ExPro* 11, no. 1 (2014), https://www.geoexpro.com/articles/2014/09/the-predictive-power-of-palynology.

12 Tania Hernández-Hernández and John Wiens, "Why Are There So Many Flowering Plants? A Multiscale Analysis of Plant Diversification," *The American Naturalist* 195, no. 6 (2020): 948–63, https://www.journals.uchicago.edu/doi/10.1086/708273.

13 Michael Zavada, "The Identification of Fossil Angiosperm Pollen and Its Bearing on the Time and Place of the Origin of Angiosperms," *Plant Systematics and Evolution* 263 (2007): 117–34, https://doi.org/10.1007/s00606-006-0495-9.

Chapter Two

1 Hannah Ellis-Petersen, "Flowers or Vaginas? Georgia O'Keeffe Tate Show to Challenge Sexual Cliches," *Guardian*, 1 March 2016, https://www.theguardian.com/artanddesign/2016/mar/01/georgia-okeeffe-show-at-tate-modern-to-challenge-outdated-views-of-artist.

2 Grace Glueck, "Art Notes: 'It's Just What's In My Head…'" *New York Times*, 18 October 1970.

3 Carl Linnaeus, *Systema Naturae*, vol. 10 (New York: Stechert-Hafner Service Agency, 1964).

4 Carl Linnaeus and Stephen Freer, *Linnaeus' Philosophia Botanica* (London: Oxford University Press, 2007).

5 Erasmus Darwin, *The Botanic Garden: A Poem, in Two Parts: Part I. Containing the Economy of Vegetation. Part II. The Loves of the Plants*, vols. 1–2 (New York: T. & J. Swords, 1807), canto 1, lines 3–8.

6 Jinyan Guo, "Comparative Micromorphology and Anatomy of Crested Sepals in Iris (*Iridaceae*)," *International Journal of Plant Sciences* 176 (2015), https://doi.org/10.1086/682135.

7 Adrian Dyer, Christa Neumeyer, and Lars Chittka, "Honeybee (*Apis mellifera*) Vision Can Discriminate between and Recognise Images of Human Faces," *Journal of Experimental Biology* 208, no. 24 (2005): 4709–14, https://doi.org/10.1242/jeb.01929.

8 Karl von Frisch, "Der Farbensinn und Formensinn der Biene," *Abteilung für allgemeine Zoologie und Physiologie der Tiere* 37 (1914): 1–238.

9 Yannick Klomberg et al., "The Role of Ultraviolet Reflectance and Pattern in the Pollination System of *Hypoxis camerooniana* (Hypoxidaceae)," *AoB PLANTS* 11, no. 5 (October 2019): plz057, https://doi.org/10.1093/aobpla/plz057.

10 Alfred Kühn, "Über den Farbensinn der Bienen," *Zeitschrift für vergleichende Physiologie* 5 (1927): 762–800.

11 Ewald Hering, *Outlines of a Theory of the Light Sense* (Cambridge, MA: Harvard University Press, 1964).

12 Lars Chittka et al., "Ultraviolet as a Component of Flower Reflections, and the Colour Perception of Hymenoptera," *Vision Research* 34, no. 11 (1994): 1489–1508, https://doi.org/10.1016/0042-6989(94)90151-1. PMID: 8023461.

13 Johann Wolfgang von Goethe and Gordon L. Miller, *The Metamorphosis of Plants* (Cambridge, MA: MIT Press, 2009), https://doi.org/10.1162/LEON_r_00059.

14 Johann Wolfgang von Goethe, *Poetry and Truth* (London: H.G. Bohn, 1848).

15 Marcelo Carnier and Dornelas Odair Dornelas, "From Leaf to Flower: Revisiting Goethe's Concepts on the 'Metamorphosis' of Plants," *Plant Physiology* 17, no. 4 (2005), https://doi.org/10.1590/S1677-04202005000400001.

16 Jonas Collen et al., "Genome Structure and Metabolic Features in the Red Seaweed *Chondrus crispus* Shed Light on Evolution of the Archaeplastida," *PNAS* 110, no. 13 (2013): 5247–52, https://doi.org/10.1073/pnas.1221259110.

17 Sarah Arnold and Lars Chittka, "Flower Colour Diversity Seen through the Eyes of Pollinators. A Commentary on: 'Floral Colour Structure in Two Australian Herbaceous Communities: It Depends on Who Is Looking,'" *Annals of Botany* 124, no. 2 (2019): 8–9, https://doi.org/10.1093/aob/mcz107.

18 Vera Vasas et al., "Multispectral Images of Flowers Reveal the Adaptive Significance of Using Long-Wavelength-Sensitive Receptors for Edge Detection in Bees," *Journal of Comparative Physiology* 203 (2017): 301–11, https://doi.org/10.1007/s00359-017-1156-x.

19 Jason Rae and Jana Vamosi, "UV Reflectance Mediates Pollinator Visitation in *Mimulus guttatus*," *Plant Species Biology* 28 (2013): 177–84.

20 Yannick Klomberg et al., "The Role of Ultraviolet Reflectance and Pattern in the Pollination System of *Hypoxis camerooniana* (Hypoxidaceae)," *AoB PLANTS* 11, no. 5 (2019): 57, https://doi.org/10.1093/aobpla/plz057.

21 Matthew Koski, Drew MacQueen, and Tia-Lynn Ashman, "Floral Pigmentation Has Responded Rapidly to Global Change in Ozone and Temperature," *Current Biology* 30, no. 22, e3 (2020): 4425–31, https://doi.org/10.1016/j.cub.2020.08.077.

Chapter Three

1 Heather Penney et al., "A Comparative Analysis of the Evolution of Imperfect Mimicry," *Nature* 483, no. 7390 (2012): 461–4, https://doi.org/10.1038/nature10961.

2 Christopher O'Toole and Anthony Raw, *Bees of the World* (New York: Facts on File, 2004).

3 Romina Rader et al., "Non-Bee Insects Are Important Contributors to Global Crop Pollination," *Proceedings of the National Academy of Sciences* 113, no. 1 (2016): 146–51, https://doi.org/10.1073/pnas.1517092112.

4 Dylan Hodgkiss, Mark Brown, and Michelle Fountain, "Syrphine Hoverflies are Effective Pollinators of Commercial Strawberry," *Journal of Pollination Ecology* 22 (2018), https://doi.org/10.26786/1920-7603(2018)five.

5 Michelle Locke and Jeff Skevington, "Revision of Nearctic *Dasysyrphus Enderlein* (Diptera: Syrphidae)," *Zootaxa* 3660 (2013): 1–80, https://doi.org/10.11646/zootaxa.3660.1.1.

6 Masumi Kono and Hiroshi Tobe, "Is *Cycas revoluta* (Cycadaceae) Wind- or Insect-Pollinated?" *American Journal of Botany* 94, no. 5 (2007): 847–55, https://doi.org/10.3732/ajb.94.5.847.

7 Chenyang Cai et al., "Beetle Pollination of Cycads in the Mesozoic," *Current Biology* 10, no. 17 (2018): 2806–12, https://doi.org/10.1016/j.cub.2018.06.036.

8 David Peris et al., "Generalist Pollen-Feeding Beetles during the Mid-Cretaceous," *iScience* 23 (2020), https://doi.org/10.1016/j.isci.2020.100913.

9 Peter Bernhardt, "Convergent Evolution and Adaptive Radiation of Beetle-Pollinated Angiosperms," *Plant Systematics and Evolution* 222 (2000): 293–320, https://doi.org/10.1007/BF00984108.

10 Tong Bao et al., "Pollination of Cretaceous Flowers," *Proceedings of the National Academy of Sciences* 116, no. 49 (2019): 24707–11, https://doi.org/10.1073/pnas.1916186116.

11 Timotheüs van der Niet, Dennis Hansen, and Steven Johnson, "Carrion Mimicry in a South African Orchid: Flowers Attract a Narrow Subset of the Fly Assemblage on Animal Carcasses," *Annals of Botany* 107, no. 6 (2011): 981–92, https://doi.org/10.1093/aob/mcr048.

12 Virgilio Vázquez and Ignacio Barradas, "Deceptive Pollination and Insects' Learning: A Delicate Balance," *Journal of Biological Dynamics* 11, no. 1 (2017): 299–322, https://doi.org/10.1080/17513758.2017.1337246.

13 Peter Bernhardt et al., "Global Collaborative Research on the Pollination Biology of Rare and Threatened Orchid Species (*Orchidaceae*)," *Annals of the Missouri Botanical Garden* 102, no. 2 (2017): 364–76.

14 Colin Bower, "Observations on the Pollination of *Calochilus campestris R.Br*," *Orchadian* 11, no. 2 (1993).

15 Marinus de Jager and Allan Ellis, "Costs of Deception and Learned Resistance in Deceptive Interactions," *Proceedings of the Royal Society B: Biological Sciences* (2014), https://doi.org/10.1098/rspb.2013.2861.

Chapter Four

1 Charles Darwin, "Letter no. 3272," Darwin Correspondence Project, 1 October 1861, https://www.darwinproject.ac.uk/letter/DCP-LETT-3272.xml. Also published in F. Burkhardt et al., eds., *The Correspondence of Charles Darwin* (Cambridge: Cambridge University Press, 1985–).

2 Thomas Barloon and Russell Noyes, "Charles Darwin and Panic Disorder," *JAMA: Journal of the American Medical Association* 277, no. 2 (1997): 138–41, https://doi.org/10.1001/jama.277.2.138.

3 Charles Darwin, *The Various Contrivances by which Orchids Are Fertilised by Insects* 2 (London: John Murray, 1877), 284.

4 Charles Darwin, "Letter no. 3411," Darwin Correspondence Project, 25 [and 26] January 1862, https://www.darwinproject.ac.uk/letter/?docId=letters/DCP-LETT-3411.xml&query=3411. Also published in F. Burkhardt et al., eds., *The Correspondence of Charles Darwin* (Cambridge: Cambridge University Press, 1985–).

5 Darwin, *The Various Contrivances*, 198.

6 Walter Rothschild and Karl Jordan, "A Revision of the Lepidopterous Family Sphingidae," *Novitates Zoologicae* 9 (1903): 32.

7 Alfred Russel Wallace, "Creation by Law," *Quarterly Journal of Science* (1867): 474, http://people.wku.edu/charles.smith/wallace/S140.htm.

8 Spencer Barrett, "Sexual Interference of the Floral Kind," *Heredity (Edinburgh)* 88, no. 2 (2002): 154–9, https://doi.org/10.1038/sj.hdy.6800020. PMID: 11932774.

9 Spencer Barrett, "'A Most Complex Marriage Arrangement': Recent Advances on Heterostyly and Unresolved Questions," *New Phytologist* 224 (2019): 1051–67, https://doi.org/10.1111/nph.16026.

10 Spencer Barrett, "The Evolution of Plant Sexual Diversity," *Nature Reviews Genetics* 3 (2002): 274–84, https://doi.org/10.1038/nrg776.

11 Spencer Barrett, "Darwin's Legacy: The Forms, Function and Sexual Diversity of Flowers," *Philosophical Transactions of the Royal Society of London. Series B, Biological Sciences* 365, no. 1539 (2010): 351–68, https://doi.org/10.1098/rstb.2009.0212.

12 Spencer Barrett et al., "The Evolution and Function of Stylar Polymorphisms in Flowering Plants," *Annals of Botany* 85, no. 1 (2000): 253–65, https://doi.org/10.1006/anbo.1999.1067.

13 Lucy Nevard et al., "Transmission of Bee-Like Vibrations in Buzz-Pollinated Plants with Different Stamen Architectures," *Scientific Reports* 11, no. 13541 (2021), https://doi.org/10.1038/s41598-021-93029-7.

14 José Neiva Mesquita-Neto et al., "Flowers with Poricidal Anthers and Their Complex Interaction Networks – Disentangling Legitimate Pollinators and Illegitimate Visitors," *Functional Ecology* 32 (2018): 2321–32, https://doi.org/10.1111/1365-2435.13204.

15 Daniel Newman and James Thomson, "Interactions among Nectar Robbing, Floral Herbivory, and Ant Protection in *Linaria vulgaris*," *Oikos* 110 (2005): 497–506, https://doi.org/10.1111/j.0030-1299.2005.13885.x.

16 Nathan Muchhala et al., "A Generalized Pollination System in the Tropics: Bats, Birds and *Aphelandra acanthus*," *Annals of Botany* 103, no. 9 (2009): 1481–7, https://doi.org/10.1093/aob/mcn260.

17 Nathan Muchhala and James Thomson, "Fur versus Feathers: Pollen Delivery by Bats and Hummingbirds and Consequences for Pollen Production," *The American Naturalist* 175, no. 6 (2010): 717–26, https://doi.org/10.1086/652473. PMID: 20408751.

18 Jessica Zung et al., "Bee- To Bird-Pollination Shifts in Penstemon: Effects of Floral-Lip Removal and Corolla Constriction on the Preferences of Free-Foraging Bumble Bees," *Evolutionary Ecology* 29 (2015): 341–54, https://doi.org/10.1007/s10682-014-9716-9.

19 Sarah Johnson and Ralph Cartar, "Wing Wear, but Not Asymmetry in Wear, Affects Load-Lifting Capability in Bumble Bees *Bombus impatiens*," *Canadian Journal of Zoology* 92, no. 3 (2013): 179–84, https://doi.org/10.1139/cjz-2013-0229.

20 Graham Pyke, "What Does It Cost a Plant to Produce Floral Nectar?" *Nature* 350 (1991): 58–9, https://doi.org/10.1038/350058a0.

Chapter Five

1 Ruby Pawankar et al., *White Book on Allergy* (Milwaukee, WI: World Health Organization, 2013), https://www.worldallergy.org/UserFiles/file/ExecSummary-2013-v6-hires.pdf.

2 Jeff Ollerton, Rachael Winfree, and Sam Tarrant, "How Many Flowering Plants Are Pollinated by Animals?" *Oikos* 120 (2011): 321–6, https://doi.org/10.1111/j.1600-0706.2010.18644.x.

3 Lewis Ziska et al., "Temperature-Related Changes in Airborne Allergenic Pollen Abundance and Seasonality across the Northern Hemisphere: A Retrospective Data Analysis," *The Lancet Planetary Health* 3, no. 3 (2019): 124–31, https://doi.org/10.1016/S2542-5196(19)30015-4.

4 Lauren Pelley, "'I Actually Had to Call In Sick': Why Seasonal Allergies Are Getting Worse for City Dwellers," *CBC News*, 29 August 2019, https://www.cbc.ca/news/canada/toronto/cities-seasonal-allergies-symptoms-worsening-climate-change-1.5256496.

5 Gennaro D'Amato et al., "Meteorological Conditions, Climate Change, New Emerging Factors, and Asthma and Related Allergic Disorders. A Statement of the World Allergy Organization," *World Allergy Organization Journal* 8, no. 1 (2015): 25, https://doi.org/10.1186/s40413-015-0073-0.

6 Lewis Ziska et al., "Recent Warming by Latitude Associated with Increased Length of Ragweed Pollen Season in Central North America," *Proceedings of the National Academy of Sciences of the United States of America* 108 (2011): 4248–51.

7 Yan Sun et al., "Rapid Genomic and Phenotypic Change in Response to Climate Warming in a Widespread Plant Invader," *Global Change Biology* 26 (2020): 6511–22, https://doi.org/10.1111/gcb.15291.

8 Vandana Prasad et al., "Dinosaur Coprolites and the Early Evolution of Grasses and Grazers," *Science* 310 (2005): 1117–80, https://doi.org/10.1126/science.1118806.

9 Vandana Prasad et al., "Late Cretaceous Origin of the Rice Tribe Provides Evidence for Early Diversification in Poaceae," *Nature Communications* 2 (2011): 480, https://doi.org/10.1038/ncomms1482.

10 Dori McCombe and Josef Ackerman, "Collector Motion Affects Particle Capture in Physical Models and in Wind Pollination," *American Naturalist* 192, no. 1 (2018): 81–93, https://doi.org/10.1086/697551.

11 David Timerman and Spencer Barrett, "Comparative Analysis of Pollen Release Biomechanics in *Thalictrum*: Implications for Evolutionary Transitions between Animal and Wind Pollination," *New Phytologist* 224, no. 3 (2019): 1121–32, https://doi.org/10.1111/nph.15978.

12 Jannice Friedman and Spencer Barrett, "Wind of Change: New Insights on the Ecology and Evolution of Pollination and Mating in Wind-Pollinated Plants," *Annals of Botany* 103, no. 9 (2009): 1515–27, https://doi.org/10.1093/aob/mcp035.

13 Shannon Datwyler and George Weiblen, "On the Origin of the Fig: Phylogenetic Relationships of Moraceae from NDHF Sequences," *American Journal of Botany* 91, no. 5 (2004): 767–77, https://doi.org/10.3732/ajb.91.5.767.

14 Peter Wragg and Steven Johnson, "Transition from Wind Pollination to Insect Pollination in Sedges: Experimental Evidence and Functional Traits," *New Phytologist* 191, no. 4 (2011): 1128–40, https://doi.org/10.1111/j.1469-8137.2011.03762.x.

Chapter Six

1 Merriam-Webster.com, s.v. "melittologist," https://www.merriam-webster.com/dictionary/melittologist (accessed 8 May 2022).
2 Harald Krenn, John Plant, and Nikolaus Szucsich, "Mouthparts of Flower-Visiting Insects," *Arthropod Structure & Development* 34, no. 1 (2005): 1–40, https://doi.org/10.1016/j.asd.2004.10.002. ISSN 1467-8039.
3 Jerome Rozen and Eli Wyman, "The Chilean Bees *Xeromelissa nortina* and *X. sielfeldi*: Their Nesting Biologies and Immature Stages, Including Biological Notes on *X. rozeni* (*Colletidae: Xeromelissinae*)," *American Museum Novitates* 3838 (2015), https://doi.org/10.1206/3838.1.
4 Amro Zayed et al., "Increased Genetic Differentiation in a Specialist versus a Generalist Bee: Implications for Conservation," *Conservation Genetics* 6 (2005): 1017–26, https://doi.org/10.1007/s10592-005-9094-5.
5 Bryan Danforth, Robert Minckley, and John Neff, *The Solitary Bees* (Princeton, NJ: Princeton University Press, 2019), 136–8.
6 Eduardo Almeida, "Colletidae Nesting Biology (Hymenoptera: Apoidea)," *Apidologie* 39 (2008): 16–29, https://doi.org/10.1051/apido:2007049.
7 Laura Fortel et al., "Use of Human-Made Nesting Structures by Wild Bees in an Urban Environment," *Journal of Insect Conservation* 20 (2016): 239–53, https://doi.org/10.1007/s10841-016-9857-y.
8 Andrew Forbes et al., "Quantifying the Unquantifiable: Why Hymenoptera, Not Coleoptera, Is the Most Speciose Animal Order," *BMC Ecology* 18, no. 21 (2018), https://doi.org/10.1186/s12898-018-0176-x.
9 Bryan Danforth and George Poinar Jr., "Morphology, Classification, and Antiquity of *Melittosphex burmensis* (Apoidea: Melittosphecidae) and Implications for Early Bee Evolution," *Journal of Paleontology* 85, no. 5 (2011): 882–91, https://doi.org/10.1666/10-130.1.
10 Danforth et al., *The Solitary Bees*, 9.
11 Kevin O'Neill, "Egg Size, Prey Size, and Sexual Size Dimorphism in Digger Wasps (Hymenoptera: Sphecidae)," *Canadian Journal of Zoology* 63 (2011): 2187–93, https://doi.org/10.1139/z85-323.
12 Gabriel Melo et al., "Origin and Occurrence of Predation among Hymenoptera: A Phylogenetic Perspective," in *Predation in the Hymenoptera: An Evolutionary Perspective* (Trivandrum, India: Transworld Research Network, 2011), 1–22.

13 Simone Cappellari, Hanno Schaefer, and Charles Davis, "Evolution: Pollen or Pollinators – Which Came First?" *Current Biology* 23, no. 8 (2013): 316–18, https://doi.org/10.1016/j.cub.2013.02.049.

14 Sandra Rehan, Remko Leys, and Michael Schwarz, "First Evidence for a Massive Extinction Event Affecting Bees Close to the K-T Boundary," *PLOS ONE* 8, no. 10 (2013): 76683, https://doi.org/10.1371/journal.pone.0076683.

15 Kirk Johnson, "Leaf-Fossil Evidence for Extensive Floral Extinction at the Cretaceous-Tertiary Boundary, North Dakota, USA," *Cretaceous Research* 13, no. 1 (1992): 91–117, https://doi.org/aryary10.1016/0195-6671(92)90029-P.

16 Minnae Mathiasson and Sandra Rehan, "Wild Bee Declines Linked to Plant-Pollinator Network Changes and Plant Species Introductions," *Insect Conservation and Diversity* 13 (2020): 595–605, https://doi.org/10.1111/icad.12429.

Chapter Seven

1 Christophe Praz, Andreas Müller, and Silvia Dorn, "Specialized Bees Fail to Develop on Non-Host Pollen: Do Plants Chemically Protect Their Pollen?" *Ecology* 89 (2008): 795–804, https://doi.org/10.1890/07-0751.1.

2 T'ai Roulston, James Cane, and Stephen Buchmann, "What Governs Protein Content of Pollen: Pollinator Preferences, Pollen-Pistil Interactions, or Phylogeny?" *Ecological Monographs* 70 (2000): 617–43, https://doi.org/10.1890/0012-9615(2000)070[0617:WGPCOP]2.0.CO;2.

3 Evan Palmer-Young et al., "Nectar and Pollen Phytochemicals Stimulate Honey Bee (Hymenoptera: Apidae) Immunity to Viral Infection," *Journal of Economic Entomology* 110, no. 5 (2017): 1959–72, https://doi.org/10.1093/jee/tox193.

4 Jonathan Giacomini et al., "Medicinal Value of Sunflower Pollen against Bee Pathogens," *Scientific Reports* 8 (2018), https://doi.org/10.1038/s41598-018-32681-y.

5 Steven Johnson, Andrew Pauw, and Jeremy Midgley, "Rodent Pollination in the African Lily *Massonia depressa* (Hyacinthaceae)," *American Journal of Botany* 88 (2001): 1768–73, https://doi.org/10.2307/3558351.

6 Shawn Steffan et al., "Omnivory in Bees: Elevated Trophic Positions among All Major Bee Families," *The American Naturalist* 194, no. 3 (2019): 414–21, https://doi.org/10.1086/704281.

7 Hoang Vuong and Quinn McFrederick, "Comparative Genomics of Wild Bee and Flower Isolated *Lactobacillus* Reveals Potential Adaptation to the Bee Host," *Genome Biology and Evolution* 11, no. 8 (2019): 2151–61, https://doi.org/10.1093/gbe/evz136.

8 Jason Rothman et al., "Diet Breadth Affects Bacterial Identity but Not Diversity in the Pollen Provisions of Closely Related Polylectic and Oligolectic Bees," *Insects* 11, no. 9 (2020): 645, https://doi.org/10.3390/insects11090645.

9 Hamutahl Cohen, Quinn McFrederick, and Stacy Philpott, "Environment Shapes the Microbiome of the Blue Orchard Bee, *Osmia lignaria*: RRH: Environmental Drivers of Bee Microbiome," *Microbial Ecology* 80 (2020), https://doi.org/10.1007/s00248-020-01549-y.

10 Rebecca Dew, Quinn McFrederick, and Sandra Rehan, "Diverse Diets with Consistent Core Microbiome in Wild Bee Pollen Provisions," *Insects* 11, no. 8 (2020): 499, https://doi.org/10.3390/insects11080499.

11 Megan McAulay and Jessica Forrest, "How Do Sunflower Pollen Mixtures Affect Survival of Queenless Microcolonies of Bumblebees (*Bombus impatiens*)?" *Arthropod-Plant Interactions* 13 (2019), https://doi.org/10.1007/s11829-018-9664-3.

12 Christian Westerkamp, "Pollen in Bee-Flower Relations Some Considerations on Melittophily," *Botanica Acta* 109 (1996): 325–32, https://doi.org/10.1111/j.1438-8677.1996.tb00580.x.

13 Gail MacInnis and Jessica Forrest, "Quantifying Pollen Deposition with Macro Photography and 'Stigmagraphs,'" *Journal of Pollination Ecology* 20 (2017): 13–21, https://doi.org/10.26786/1920-7603(2017)six.

14 Jessica Forrest, "Plant Size, Sexual Selection, and the Evolution of Protandry in Dioecious Plants," *American Naturalist* 184, no. 3 (2014): 338–51, https://doi.org/10.1086/677295.

Chapter Eight

1 Jordan Eamer et al., "Multi-Decadal Coastal Evolution of a North Atlantic Shelf-Edge Vegetated Sand Island – Sable Island, Canada," *Canadian Journal of Earth Sciences* (2020), https://doi.org/10.1139/cjes-2020-0194.

2 Paul Catling, Zoe Lucas, and Bill Freedman, "Plants and Insects New to Sable Island, Nova Scotia," *Canadian Field Naturalist* 123 (2009), https://doi.org/10.22621/cfn.v123i2.692.

3 Nova Scotia Department of Lands and Forestry, "Recovery Plan for the Sable Island Sweat Bee (*Lasioglossum sablense*) in Nova Scotia [Final]," *Nova Scotia Endangered Species Act Recovery Plan Series* (2020), https://novascotia.ca/natr/wildlife/species-at-risk/docs/Recovery-plan-Sable-Island-Sweat-Bee.pdf.

4 Charles Michener, *The Social Behavior of the Bees* (Cambridge, MA: Belknap Press, 1974).

5 Jason Gibbs, "Revision of the Metallic Species of *Lasioglossum* (*Dialictus*) in Canada (Hymenoptera, Halictidae, Halictini)," *Zootaxa* 2591 (2010): 283–6, https://www.mapress.com/zt/article/view/zootaxa.2591.1.1.

6 Martin Nowak, Corina Tarnita, and Edward Wilson, "The Evolution of Eusociality," *Nature* 466, no. 7310 (2010): 1057–62, https://doi.org/10.1038/nature09205.

7 Edward Wilson and Bert Hölldobler, "Eusociality: Origin and Consequences," *Proceedings of the National Academy of Sciences of the United States of America* 102, no. 38 (2005): 13367–71, https://doi.org/10.1073/pnas.0505858102.

8 Suzanne Batra, "The Evolution of 'Eusocial' and the Origin of 'Pollen Bees,'" *The Maryland Naturalist* 39, no. 1–2 (1995): 1–4.

9 Miriam Richards, Eric Wettberg, and Amy Rutgers, "A Novel Social Polymorphism in a Primitively Eusocial Bee," *Proceedings of the National Academy of Sciences of the United States of America* 100 (2003): 7175–80, https://doi.org/10.1073/pnas.1030738100.

10 Karl von Frisch, *The Dancing Bees*, trans. Dora Ilse (New York and London: Harvest/Harcourt Brace Jovanovich, 1953).

11 James Gould, "The Dance-Language Controversy," *The Quarterly Review of Biology* 51, no. 2 (1976): 211–44, http://www.jstor.org/stable/2823629.

12 Fan Han, Andreas Wallberg, and Matthew Webster, "From Where Did the Western Honeybee (*Apis mellifera*) Originate?" *Ecology and Evolution* 2, no. 8 (2012): 1949–57, https://doi.org/10.1002/ece3.312.

13 Thomas Seeley, "Honey Bee Colonies Are Group-Level Adaptive Units," *American Naturalist* 150, no. 1 (1997): 22–41, https://doi.org/10.1086/286048.

14 James Nieh, "Recruitment Communication in Stingless Bees (Hymenoptera, Apidae, Meliponini)," *Apidologie* 35, no. 2 (2004), https://doi.org/10.1051/apido:2004007.

15 Bernd Heinrich, *Bumblebee Economics* (Cambridge, MA: Harvard University Press, 1979, 2004), 142–3.

16 Natalie Boyle and Theresa Pitts-Singer, "Assessing Blue Orchard Bee (*Osmia lignaria*) Propagation and Pollination Services in the Presence of Honey Bees (*Apis mellifera*) in Utah Tart Cherries," *PeerJ* 7 (2019): 7639, https://doi.org/10.7717/peerj.7639.

17 Paige Embry, "A Promising Backup to the Honeybee Is Shut Down," *Scientific American* (March 2018), https://www.scientificamerican.com/article/a-promising-backup-to-the-honeybee-is-shut-down/.

18 Charles Michener, "Biogeography of the Bees," *Annals of the Missouri Botanical Garden* 66 (1979): 277–347.

19 Bryan Danforth, "Emergence Dynamics and Bet Hedging in a Desert Bee, *Perdita portalis*," *Proceedings of the Royal Society of London* B.266 (1999): 1985–94, http://doi.org/10.1098/rspb.1999.0876.

20 Taher Shaibi and Robin Moritz, "10,000 Years in Isolation? Honeybees (*Apis mellifera*) in Saharan Oases," *Conservation Genetics* 11 (2010): 2085–9, http://doi.org/10.1007/s10592-010-0088-6.

21 Thomas Seeley, *Wisdom of the Hive* (Cambridge, MA: Harvard University Press, 1996).

22 Thomas Seeley, *Honeybee Democracy* (Princeton, NJ: Princeton University Press, 2010).

23 Thomas Seeley, *The Lives of Bees* (Princeton, NJ: Princeton University Press, 2019).

Chapter Nine

1 Canadian Honey Council, "Industry Overview – Canadian Apiculture Industry" (2018), https://honeycouncil.ca/industry-overview/.

2 Global Industry Analysts, "Global Honey Market to Reach $10.9 Billion by 2026," *PR Newswire*, 1 October 2021, https://www.prnewswire.com/news-releases/global-honey-market-to-reach-10-9-billion-by-2026--301389000.html.

3 Food and Agriculture Organization of the United Nations, "Why Bees Matter" (2018), https://www.fao.org/3/i9527en/i9527en.pdf.

4 Diana Cox-Foster and Dennis van Engelsdorp, "Saving the Honeybee," *Scientific American* 300 (2009): 40–7, http://doi.org/10.1038/scientificamerican0409-40.

5 Riley Waytes, "Pollinator Movement and Pollen Transfer in Hybrid Seed Canola," Master's thesis, University of Calgary, 2017, http://doi.org/10.11575/PRISM/27379.

6 Daphne Fairey, J.A.C. Lieverse, and B.J. Siemens, "Management of the Alfalfa Leafcutting Bee in Northwestern Canada," Agriculture Canada, publication no. NRG 84–21, 1984, https://www1.agric.gov.ab.ca/$department/deptdocs.nsf/all/for10008/$FILE/nrg84-21_01-8.pdf.

7 Samuel Robinson, "Central-Place Foraging, Crop Yield, and Population Change in Bees: A Study in Canola Agroecosystems," doctoral thesis, University of Calgary, 2019, https://prism.ucalgary.ca/handle/1880/111128.

8 Al Mussell and Kevin Grier, "Ontario Processing Vegetables: An Economic Analysis," *Agri-food Economic Systems* (August 2017), http://www.omafra.gov.on.ca/english/farmproducts/misc/DirectiveUpdates/analysis.pdf.

9 Alison McAfee, "The Blueberries and the Bees," *American Bee Journal* (2018), https://americanbeejournal.com/the-blueberries-and-the-bees/.

10 George Hoffman, Claire Lande, and Sujaya Rao, "A Novel Pollen Transfer Mechanism by Honey Bee Foragers on Highbush Blueberry (Ericales: Ericaceae)," *Environmental Entomology* 47, no. 6 (2018): 1465–70, http://doi.org/10.1093/ee/nvy162.

11 Jason Gibbs et al., "Contrasting Pollinators and Pollination in Native and Non-Native Regions of Highbush Blueberry Production," *PLOS ONE* 11, no. 7 (2016): 0158937, http://doi.org/10.1371/journal.pone.0158937.

12 Matthias Albrecht et al., "The Effectiveness of Flower Strips and Hedgerows on Pest Control, Pollination Services and Crop Yield: A Quantitative Synthesis," *Ecology Letters* 23 (2020): 1488–98, http://doi.org/10.1111/ele.13576.

13 Rufus Isaacs et al., "Integrated Crop Pollination: Combining Strategies to Ensure Stable and Sustainable Yields of Pollination-Dependent Crops," *Basic and Applied Ecology* 22 (2017), http://doi.org/10.1016/j.baae.2017.07.003.

14 Lucas Garibaldi et al., "Wild Pollinators Enhance Fruit Set of Crops Regardless of Honey Bee Abundance," *Science* 339 (2013), http://doi.org/10.1126/science.1230200.

15 Rachael Winfree, Brian Gross, and Claire Kremen, "Valuing Pollination Services to Agriculture," *Ecological Economics* (2011), http://doi.org/71.10.1016/j.ecolecon.2011.08.001.

16 Christian Lippert, Arndt Feuerbacher, and Manuel Narjes, "Revisiting the Economic Valuation of Agricultural Losses Due to Large-Scale Changes in Pollinator Populations," *Ecological Economics* 180 (2020), http://doi.org/10.1016/j.ecolecon.2020.106860.

17 Aaron Hoshide et al., "What Is the Value of Wild Bee Pollination for Wild Blueberries and Cranberries, and Who Values It?" *Environments* 5, no. 98 (2018), http://doi.org/10.3390/environments5090098.

Chapter Ten

1 Alexei Barrionuevo, "Honeybees Vanish, Leaving Keepers in Peril," *New York Times*, 27 February 2007, https://www.nytimes.com/2007/02/27/business/27bees.html.

2 Diana Cox-Foster and Dennis van Engelsdorp, "Saving the Honeybee," *Scientific American* 300, no. 4 (2009): 40–7, http://doi.org/10.1038/scientificamerican0409-40.

3 Dennis van Engelsdorp et al., "An Estimate of Managed Colony Losses in the Winter of 2006–2007: A Report Commissioned by the Apiary Inspectors of America," *American Bee Journal* 147 (2007): 599–603.

4 "David Mendes Addressing Congressional Panel," in *Vanishing of the Bees*, dir. George Langworthy and Maryam Heinen, written by Maryam Henein, James Erskine, and George Langworthy (Hive Mentality Films, 2010), 52:49–53:27.

5 Noa Simon-Delso et al., "Systemic Insecticides (Neonicotinoids and Fipronil): Trends, Uses, Mode of Action and Metabolites," *Environmental Science and Pollution Research International* 22, no. 1 (2015): 5–34, http://doi.org/10.1007/s11356-014-3470-y.

6 Jennifer Bonnell, "Insecticides, Honey Bee Losses and Beekeeper Advocacy in Nineteenth-Century Ontario," *Ontario History* 112, no. 2 (2020): 139–56, http://doi.org/10.7202/1072234ar.

7 Cristobal Berry-Caban, "DDT and Silent Spring: Fifty Years After," *JMVH* 19, no. 4 (2011), https://jmvh.org/article/ddt-and-silent-spring-fifty-years-after/.

8 Rachel Carson, *Silent Spring* (New York: Mariner, 1962), 15.

9 Peter Kevan, "Forest Application of the Insecticide Fenitrothion and Its Effect on Wild Bee Pollinators (Hymenoptera: Apoidea) of Lowbush Blueberries (*Vaccinium* spp.) in Southern New Brunswick, Canada," *Biological Conservation* 7 (1975): 301–9, http://doi.org/10.1016/0006-3207(75)90045-2.

10 Mélanie Colin et al., "A Method to Quantify and Analyze the Foraging Activity of Honey Bees: Relevance to the Sublethal Effects Induced by Systemic Insecticides," *Archives of Environmental Contamination and Toxicology Springer Verlag* 47 (2004): 387–95.

11 Sainath Suryanarayanan and Daniel Kleinman, "Beekeepers' Collective Resistance and the Politics of Pesticide Regulation in France and the United States," *Political Power and Social Theory* 27 (2014): 89–122, http://doi.org/10.1108/S0198-871920140000027011.

12 Michael Gross, "Pesticides Linked to Bee Deaths," *Current Biology* 18, no. 16 (2008): 684, http://doi.org/10.1016/j.cub.2008.08.004.

13 Dennis van Engelsdorp et al., "Colony Collapse Disorder: A Descriptive Study," *PLOS ONE* 4, no. 8 (2009): 6481, http://doi.org/10.1371/journal.pone.000648.

14 Robyn Underwood and Dennis van Engelsdorp, "Colony Collapse Disorder: Have We Seen This Before?" *Bee Culture* 35 (2007): 13–18.

15 Peter Kevan et al., "Colony Collapse Disorder in Canada: Do We Have a Problem?" *HiveLights* (2007): 14–16, http://hdl.handle.net/10214/2418.

16 Ernesto Guzmán-Novoa et al., "*Varroa Destructor* Is the Main Culprit for the Death and Reduced Populations of Overwintered Honey Bee (*Apis mellifera*) Colonies in Ontario, Canada," *Apidologie* 41 (2010): 443–50, http://doi.org/10.1051/apido/2009076.

17 Julie Ferland et al., "Statement on Honey Bee Wintering Losses in Canada," *Canadian Association of Professional Apiculturists* (2021), https://capabees.com/shared/CAPA-Statement-on-Colony-Losses-2020-2021.pdf.

18 Christopher Ingraham, "Call Off the Bee-pocalypse: U.S. Honeybee Colonies Hit a 20-Year High," *Washington Post*, 23 July 2015, https://www.washingtonpost.com/news/wonk/wp/2015/07/23/call-off-the-bee-pocalypse-u-s-honeybee-colonies-hit-a-20-year-high/.

19 National Research Council, *Status of Pollinators in North America* (Washington, DC: The National Academies Press, 2007), http://doi.org/10.17226/11761.

20 Food and Agriculture Organization of the United Nations, "Crops and Livestock Products: Beehives All Countries 2020," FAOSTAT, https://www.fao.org/faostat/en/#data/QCL (accessed 9 May 2022).

21 James Cane and Vincent Tepedino, "Gauging the Effect of Honey Bee Pollen Collection on Native Bee Communities," *Conservation Letters* 10 (2017): 205–10, https://doi.org/10.1111/conl.12263.

22 Nadejda Tsvetkov et al., "Conservation Genomics Reveals Pesticide and Pathogen Exposure in the Declining Bumble Bee *Bombus terricola*," *Molecular Ecology* 30 (2021): 4220–30, https://doi.org/10.1111/mec.16049.

23 Dorothy Willis-Chan et al., "Assessment of Risk to Hoary Squash Bees (*Peponapis pruinosa*) and Other Ground-Nesting Bees from Systemic Insecticides in Agricultural Soil," *Scientific Reports* 9 (2019): 11870, https://doi.org/10.1038/s41598-019-47805-1.

24 Dorothy Willis-Chan and Nigel Raine, "Population Decline in a Ground-Nesting Solitary Squash Bee (*Eucera pruinosa*) Following Exposure to a Neonicotinoid Insecticide Treated Crop (*Cucurbita pepo*)," *Scientific Reports* 11 (2021), https://doi.org/10.1038/s41598-021-83341-7.

25 2020 Bee Vectoring Project, "Farmer-Cooperators Needed for Strawberry Fungal Control Trial," *Ecological Farmers Association of Ontario*, 13 January 2021, https://efao.ca/strawberry-disease-trial/.

Chapter Eleven

1 Sheila Colla and Laurence Packer, "Evidence for Decline in Eastern North American Bumblebees (Hymenoptera: Apidae), with Special Focus on *Bombus affinis* Cresson," *Biodiversity and Conservation* 17, no. 1379 (2008), https://doi.org/10.1007/s10531-008-9340-5.

2 Adrian Higgins, "Signs of Decline: First Honeybees, Now Bumblebees," *Washington Post*, 7 August 2008, http://www.washingtonpost.com/wp-dyn/content/article/2008/08/06/AR2008080600958.html.

3 Committee on the Status of Endangered Wildlife in Canada (COSEWIC), "COSEWIC Assessment and Status Report on the Rusty-Patched Bumble Bee *Bombus affinis* in Canada," 2010, www.sararegistry.gc.ca/status/status_e.cfm.

4 Rich Hatfield et al., "Rusty Patched Bumble Bee (*Bombus affinis*)," *The IUCN Red List of Threatened Species* (2015), https://dx.doi.org/10.2305/IUCN.UK.2015-2.RLTS.T44937399A46440196.en.

5 Shelby Gibson, Amanda Liczner, and Sheila Colla, "Conservation Conundrum: At-Risk Bumble Bees (*Bombus* spp.) Show Preference for Invasive Tufted Vetch (*Vicia cracca*) while Foraging in Protected Areas," *Journal of Insect Science* 19, no. 2 (2019), https://doi.org/10.1093/jisesa/iez017.

6 Amanda Liczner et al., "Training and Usage of Detection Dogs to Better Understand Bumble Bee Nesting Habitat: Challenges and Opportunities," *PLOS ONE* 16, no. 5 (2021): 0249248, https://doi.org/10.1371/journal.pone.0249248.

7 Stephanie O'Connor, Kirsty Park, and Dave Goulson, "Humans versus Dogs; A Comparison of Methods for the Detection of Bumble Bee Nests," *Journal of Apicultural Research* 51 (2012): 204–11, https://doi.org/10.3896/ibra.1.51.2.09.

8 Genevieve Pugesek and Elizabeth Crone, "Contrasting Effects of Land Cover on Nesting Habitat Use and Reproductive Output for Bumble Bees," *Ecosphere* 12, no. 7 (2021): e03642, https://doi.org/10.1002/ecs2.3642.

9 Elaine Evans, Michelle Boone, and Dan Cariveau, "Monitoring and Habitat Assessment of Declining Bumble Bees in Roadsides in the Twin Cities Metro Area of Minnesota. University of Minnesota Center for Transportation Studies," retrieved from the University of Minnesota Digital Conservancy, 2019, https://hdl.handle.net/11299/208533.

10 Xerces Society for Invertebrate Conservation, "Grab Your Camera ... Bumble Bee Watch Is Here!" news release, 22 January 2014, https://xerces.org/press/grab-your-camerabumble-bee-watch-is-here.

11 Victoria MacPhail et al., "Using Bumble Bee Watch to Investigate the Accuracy and Perception of Bumble Bee (*Bombus* spp.) Identification by Community Scientists," *PeerJ* 8 (2020): 9412, https://doi.org/10.7717/peerj.9412.

12 iNaturalist, "One Sixth of All Named Species Tallied!" 2 June 2021, https://www.inaturalist.org/blog/52872-one-sixth-of-all-named-species-tallied.

13 iNaturalist, "Backyard Bumble Bee Count, June 25, 2021, to September 01, 2021," 1 September 2021, https://www.inaturalist.org/projects/backyard-bumble-bee-count.

14 Grace Di Cecco et al., "Observing the Observers: How Participants Contribute Data to iNaturalist and Implications for Biodiversity Science," *BioScience* 71, no. 11 (2021): 1179–88, https://doi.org/10.1093/biosci/biab093.

15 Jason Daley, "The Bee That Breaks Your Heart," *Smithsonian Magazine*, 25 October 2016, https://www.smithsonianmag.com/science-nature/bee-that-breaks-your-heart-180960900/.

Chapter Twelve

1 Jesse McLean, "Meet the High Park Mothia – A Group of 'Insect Obsessives' Who Make Late-Night Treks to Study Toronto's Moth Species," *Toronto Star*, 24 August 2019, https://www.thestar.com/news/gta/2019/08/24/meet-the-high-park-mothia-a-group-of-insect-obsessives-who-make-late-night-treks-to-study-torontos-moth-species.html.

2 Robert Raguso and Olle Pellmyr, "Dynamic Headspace Analysis of Floral Volatiles: A Comparison of Methods," *Oikos* 81 (1998): 238–54.

3 Chuanying Fang, Alisdair Fernie, and Jie Luo, "Exploring the Diversity of Plant Metabolism," *Trends in Plant Science* 24 (2018), https://doi.org/10.1016/j.tplants.2018.09.006.

4 Robert Raguso and Mark Willis, "Synergy between Visual and Olfactory Cues in Nectar Feeding by Wild Hawkmoths, *Manduca sexta*," *Animal Behaviour* 69 (2005): 407–18, https://doi.org/10.1016/j.anbehav.2004.04.015.

5 Joaquín Goyret and Robert Raguso, "The Role of Mechanosensory Input in Flower Handling Efficiency and Learning by *Manduca sexta*," *Journal of Experimental Biology* 209 (2006): 1585–93, https://doi.org/10.1242/jeb.02291.

6 Renee Borges, Hema Somanathan, and Almut Kelber, "Patterns and Processes in Nocturnal and Crepuscular Pollination Services," *The Quarterly Review of Biology* 91, no. 4 (2016): 389–418.

7 Armin Tröger et al., "Tetranorsesquiterpenoids as Attractants of Yucca Moths to Yucca Flowers," *Journal of Chemical Ecology* (2021), https://doi.org/10.1007/s10886-021-01308-4.

8 Glenn Svensson et al., "Floral Scent of Joshua Trees (*Yucca brevifolia sensu lato*): Divergence in Scent Profiles between Species but Breakdown of Signal Integrity in a Narrow Hybrid Zone," *American Journal of Botany* 103, no. 10 (2016): 1793–1802, https://doi.org/10.3732/ajb.1600033.

9 Richard Walton et al., "Nocturnal Pollinators Strongly Contribute to Pollen Transport of Wild Flowers in an Agricultural Landscape," *Biology Letters* 16 (2020), https://doi.org/10.1098/rsbl.2019.0877.

10 Richard Walton et al., "Improving the Pollinator Pantry: Restoration and Management of Open Farmland Ponds Enhances the Complexity of Plant-Pollinator Networks," *Agriculture, Ecosystems & Environment* 320 (2021), https://doi.org/10.1016/j.agee.2021.107611.

11 Callum Macgregor et al., "The Dark Side of Street Lighting: Impacts on Moths and Evidence for the Disruption of Nocturnal Pollen Transport," *Global Change Biology* 23 (2017): 697–707, https://doi.org/10.1111/gcb.13371.

Chapter Thirteen

1 Radwanul Siddique et al., "Bioinspired Phase-Separated Disordered Nano-structures for Thin Photovoltaic Absorbers," *Science Advances* 3, no. 10 (2017): 1700232, https://doi.org/10.1126/sciadv.1700232.

2 Samantha Knight et al., "Radio-Tracking Reveals How Wind and Temperature Influence the Pace of Daytime Insect Migration," *Biology Letters* 15 (2019), https://doi.org/10.1098/rsbl.2019.0327.

3 Steve Buchmann and Gary Paul Nabhan, *The Forgotten Pollinators* (Washington, DC: Island Press/Shearwater Books, 1996), 119–20.

4 Jason Bittel, "Monarch Butterflies Migrate 3,000 Miles – Here's How," *National Geographic*, 17 October 2017, https://www.nationalgeographic.com/animals/article/monarch-butterfly-migration.

5 Patrick Guerra, Robert Gegear, and Steven Reppert, "A Magnetic Compass Aids Monarch Butterfly Migration," *Nature Communications* 5, no. 4164 (2014), https://doi.org/10.1038/ncomms5164.

6 Simon Groen and Noah Whiteman, "Convergent Evolution of Cardiacglycoside Resistance in Predators and Parasites of Milkweed Herbivores," *Current Biology* (2021), https://doi.org/10.1016/j.cub.2021.10.025

7 Amanda Martin et al., "More Milkweed in Farmlands Containing Small, Annual Crop Fields and Many Hedgerows," *Agriculture, Ecosystems & Environment* 319 (2021), https://doi.org/10.1016/j.agee.2021.107567.

8 Orley Taylor et al., "Evaluating the Migration Mortality Hypothesis Using Monarch Tagging Data," *Frontiers in Ecology and Evolution* 8 (2020): 264, https://doi.org/10.3389/fevo.2020.00264.

9 Tyson Wepprich, "Monarch Butterfly Trends Reported in Boyle et al. (2019) Are Sensitive to Unexamined Changes in Museum Collections over Time," *Proceedings of the National Academy of Sciences* (2019), https://doi.org/10.1073/pnas.1903511116.

10 John Pleasants, "Milkweed Restoration in the Midwest for Monarch Butterfly Recovery: Estimates of Milkweeds Lost, Milkweeds Remaining and Milkweeds That Must Be Added to Increase the Monarch Population," *Insect Conservation and Diversity* 10 (2017): 42–53, https://doi.org/10.1111/icad.12198.

11 Emma Pelton et al., "Western Monarch Population Plummets: Status, Probable Causes, and Recommended Conservation Actions," *Frontiers in Ecology and Evolution* 7, no. 258 (2019), https://doi.org/10.3389/fevo.2019.00258.

12 Emma Pelton et al., "The Bounciness of Butterflies," *Xerces Blog*, 12 November 2021, https://www.xerces.org/blog/bounciness-of-butterflies.

13 World Wildlife Fund Mexico, "Less Monarch Butterfly Presence and Increased Degradation in Its Hibernation Forests," news release, 9 March 2021,

https://monarchjointventure.org/images/uploads/documents/Monarch_
Butterfly_Monitoring_2019-2020_PressRelease_Final.pdf.

14 Giorgia Guglielmi, "Protecting Monarch Butterflies' Winter Home Could Mean Moving Hundreds of Trees," *Nature* (2019), https://doi.org/10.1038/d41586-019-00190-1.

15 Kevin Sieff, "Second Man with Ties to Mexico's Largest Monarch Butterfly Reserve Found Dead," *Washington Post*, 2 February 2020, https://www.washingtonpost.com/world/the_americas/second-man-with-ties-to-mexicos-largest-monarch-butterfly-reserve-found-dead/2020/02/02/d655c3b4-460b-11ea-91ab-ce439aa5c7c1_story.html.

16 Department of Justice, U.S. Attorney's Office, Southern District of New York, "Two Leaders of 'We Build The Wall' Online Fundraising Campaign Plead Guilty to Defrauding Hundreds of Thousands of Donors," news release, 21 April 2022, https://www.justice.gov/usao-sdny/pr/two-leaders-we-build-wall-online-fundraising-campaign-plead-guilty-defrauding-hundreds.

17 Joshua Hammer, "An Epic Monarch Migration Faces New Threats," *Smithsonian Magazine*, May 2021, https://www.smithsonianmag.com/science-nature/epic-monarch-butterfly-migration-faces-threats-180977449/.

18 Sarah Gibbens, "The Border Wall Is Set to Cut through a Butterfly Sanctuary," *National Geographic*, 13 February 2019, https://www.nationalgeographic.com/environment/article/border-wall-set-to-cut-through-butterfly-center.

19 Samuel Gilbert, "'Death Sentence': Butterfly Sanctuary to Be Bulldozed for Trump's Border Wall," *The Guardian*, 13 December 2018, https://www.theguardian.com/environment/2018/dec/13/butterfly-sanctuary-border-wall-mission-texas.

20 Simon Romero and Zolan Kanno-Youngs, "A Rush to Expand the Border Wall That Many Fear Is Here to Stay," *The New York Times*, 28 November 2020, https://www.nytimes.com/2020/11/28/us/trump-biden-border-wall.html.

21 Homeland Security, "Department of Homeland Security Border Wall Plan Pursuant to Presidential Proclamation," United States Department of Homeland Security, 9 June 2021, https://www.dhs.gov/sites/default/files/publications/21_0611_dhs_security_border_wall_plan.pdf.

22 Aaron Nelsen, "The Biden Administration Says It's Repairing Levees. Some South Texans Say It's Building a Border Wall," *Texas Monthly*, 18 September 2021, https://www.texasmonthly.com/news-politics/biden-border-wall-hidalgo-county/.

23 *CBC Radio*, "Texas Butterfly Centre Targeted by Far-Right Conspiracies Closes over Security Concerns," *As It Happens*, 7 February 2022, https://www.cbc.ca/radio/asithappens/as-it-happens-monday-edition-1.6342527/texas-

butterfly-centre-targeted-by-far-right-conspiracies-closes-over-security-concerns-1.6342535.

24 Jeffrey Glassberg, "Dangerous Lies Fuel a New Kind of Butterfly Effect," *Scientific American*, 18 February 2022, https://www.scientificamerican.com/article/dangerous-lies-threaten-the-national-butterfly-center/.

25 Héctor Arita and Karin Santos-del-Prado, "Conservation Biology of Nectar-Feeding Bats in Mexico," *Journal of Mammalogy* 80 (1999): 31–41.

26 Emma Gómez-Ruiz and Thomas Lacher Jr, "Climate Change, Range Shifts, and the Disruption of a Pollinator-Plant Complex," *Scientific Reports* 9, no. 1 (2019), https://doi.org/10.1038/s41598-019-50059-6.

27 Fabrizia Ratto et al., "Global Importance of Vertebrate Pollinators for Plant Reproductive Success: A Meta-Analysis[J]," *Frontiers in Ecology and the Environment* 16, no. 2 (2018): 82–90.

28 Gwen Pearson, "Tequila, Booze, and Bats," *Wired*, 18 June 2014, https://www.wired.com/2014/06/tequila-booze-and-bats/.

29 Neda Ulaby, "Bats and Tequila: A Once Boo-Tiful Relationship Cursed by Growing Demands," *Weekend Edition Sunday*, 29 October 2017, https://www.npr.org/sections/thesalt/2017/10/29/560292442/bats-and-tequila-a-once-boo-tiful-relationship-cursed-by-growing-demands.

30 Roberto-Emiliano Trejo-Salazar et al., "Save Our Bats, Save Our Tequila: Industry and Science Join Forces to Help Bats and Agaves," *Natural Areas Journal* 36 (2016): 523–30, https://doi.org/10.3375/043.036.0418.

Chapter Fourteen

1 Susan Aiken et al., "Flora of the Canadian Arctic Archipelago: Descriptions, Illustrations, Identification, and Information Retrieval," *National Research Council of Canada, Ottawa* (Ottawa: NRC Research Press, 2007), http://nature.ca/aaflora/data.

2 Peter Kevan, "Sun-Tracking Solar Furnaces in High Arctic Flowers: Significance for Pollination and Insects," *Science* 189 (1975): 723–6, https://doi.org/10.1126/science.189.4204.723.

3 Peter Kevan, "High Arctic Insect-Flower Visitor Relations: The Inter-Relationships of Arthropods and Flowers at Lake Hazen, Ellesmere Island, Northwest Territories, Canada," doctoral thesis, University of Alberta, 1970, https://www.si.edu/object/siris_sil_611663.

4 Peter Kevan and Joe Shorthouse, "Behavioural Thermoregulation by High Arctic Butterflies," *Arctic* 23 (1970): 268–79, https://doi.org/10.14430/arctic3182.

5 Peter Kevan, "Thermoregulation in Arctic Insects and Flowers Adaptation and Co-Adaptation in Behaviour, Anatomy, and Physiology," *Thermal Physiology* (1989): 747–53.

6 Peter Kevan, "Heat Accumulation in Hollow Arctic Flowers: Possible Microgreenhouse Effects in Syncalyces of Campions (*Silene* spp. (Caryophyllaceae)) and Zygomorphic Sympetalous Corollas of Louseworts (*Pedicularis* spp. (Orobanchaceae))," *Polar Biology* 43 (2020): 2101–9.

7 Charlotte Coates and Peter Kevan, "Exploring Micrometeorology in Plant Stems and Flowers," *Scientia* (2021), https://doi.org/10.33548/SCIENTIA666.

8 United Nations Intergovernmental Panel on Climate Change (IPCC), *Sixth Assessment Report*, 2021, https://www.ipcc.ch/report/ar6/wg1/downloads/factsheets/IPCC_AR6_WGI_Regional_Fact_Sheet_Polar_regions.pdf.

9 Sarah Elmendorf et al., "Plot-Scale Evidence of Tundra Vegetation Change and Links to Recent Summer Warming," *Nature Climate Change* 2 (2012): 453–7, https://doi.org/10.1038/nclimate1465.

10 Christiansen Casper et al., "Long-Term Deepened Snow Promotes Tundra Evergreen Shrub Growth and Ecosystem Net CO_2 Gain but Reduces Soil Carbon and Nutrient Pools," *Global Change Biology* 24, no. 8 (2018): 3508–25, https://doi.org/10.1111/gcb.14084.

11 Christopher West, David Greenwood, and James Basinger, "The Late Paleocene to Early Eocene Arctic Megaflora of Ellesmere Islands, Nunavut, Canada," *Palaeontographica Abteilung B -Stuttgart-* 300 (2019): 47–163, https://doi.org/10.1127/palb/2019/0066.

12 Elizabeth Bush and Donald Lemmen, eds., *Canada's Changing Climate Report* (Ottawa: Government of Canada, 2019), https://changingclimate.ca/CCCR2019/.

13 Samuel Robinson, "Plant-Pollinator Interactions at Alexandra Fiord, Nunavut," *Trail Six: An Undergraduate Journal of Geography* 5 (2011): 13–20.

14 Samuel Robinson and Gregory Henry, "High Arctic Plants Show Independent Responses to Pollination and Experimental Warming," *Botany* 96 (2018), https://doi.org/10.1139/cjb-2017-0200.

15 Jessica Forrest, "Plant-Pollinator Interactions and Phenological Change: What Can We Learn about Climate Impacts from Experiments and Observations?" *Oikos* 124 (2014), https://doi.org/10.1111/oik.01386.

16 Jonas Freimuth et al., "Climate Warming Changes Synchrony of Plants and Pollinators," *bioRxiv* (2021), https://doi.org/10.1101/2021.01.10.425984.

17 Jessica Forrest, "Complex Responses of Insect Phenology to Climate Change," *Current Opinion in Insect Science* 17 (2016), https://doi.org/10.1016/j.cois.2016.07.002.

18 Jessica Forrest, Regan Cross, and Paul Caradonna, "Two-Year Bee, or Not Two-Year Bee? How Voltinism Is Affected by Temperature and Season Length in a High-Elevation Solitary Bee," *American Naturalist* 193 (2019): 560–74, https://doi.org/10.5061/dryad.r2dm56s.

19 Catherine Sirois-Delisle and Jeremy Kerr, "Climate Change-Driven Range Losses among Bumblebee Species Are Poised to Accelerate," *Scientific Reports* 8, no. 14464 (2018), https://doi.org/10.1038/s41598-018-32665-y.

20 Jessica Forrest, "Insect Pollinators and Climate Change," in *Global Climate Change and Terrestrial Invertebrates*, edited by Scott Johnson and Thomas Jones (New York: John Wiley & Sons, Ltd, 2017), 69–91, https://doi.org/10.1002/9781119070894.ch5.

21 Stephen Colombo, *Ontario's Forests and Forestry in a Changing Climate* (Toronto: Ontario Ministry of Natural Resources, 2008), http://www.climateontario.ca/MNR_Publications/276928.pdf.

22 Michael Wotton, Kim Logan, and Rob McAlpine, *Climate Change and the Future Fire Environment in Ontario: Fire Occurrence and Fire Management Impacts in Ontario under a Changing Climate* (Toronto: Ontario Ministry of Natural Resources, 2005), http://www.climateontario.ca/MNR_Publications/276920.pdf.

23 Christopher Stephanson and Natalie Coe, "Impacts of Beech Bark Disease and Climate Change on American Beech," *Forests* 8 (2017), https://doi.org/10.3390/f8050155.

Chapter Fifteen

1 Sarah Desrosiers and Gregory Henry, *The Berry Book*, ed. Millie Kuliktana, trans. Rosemarie Meyok (Vancouver, BC: Department of Geography University of British Columbia, 2016).

2 Noémie Boulanger-Lapointe et al., "Berry Plants and Berry Picking in Inuit Nunangat: Traditions in a Changing Socio-Ecological Landscape," *Human Ecology* 47 (2019): 81–93, https://doi.org/10.1007/s10745-018-0044-5.

3 José Gérin-Lajoie, Alain Cuerrier, and Laura Siegwart Collier, eds., *The Caribou Taste Different Now* (Iqaluit: Nunavut Arctic College Media, 2016).

4 Clare Aslan et al., "Mutualism Disruption Threatens Global Plant Biodiversity: A Systematic Review," *PloS One* 8, no. 6 (2013): 66993, https://doi.org/10.1371/journal.pone.0066993.

5 James Reilly et al., "Crop Production in the USA Is Frequently Limited by a Lack of Pollinators: Pollination Limitation in US Crops," *Proceedings of the Royal Society B: Biological Sciences* 287 (2020), https://doi.org/10.1098/rspb.2020.0922.

6 James Rodger et al., "Widespread Vulnerability of Flowering Plant Seed Production to Pollinator Declines," *Science Advances* 7 (2021): eabd3524, https://doi.org/10.1126/sciadv.abd3524.

7 Mialy Razanajatovo et al., "Plants Capable of Selfing Are More Likely to Become Naturalized," *Nature Communications* 7, no. 13313 (2016), https://doi.org/10.1038/ncomms13313.

8 Charles Darwin, *The Correspondence of Charles Darwin*, vol. 14 (London: Cambridge University Press), 129.

9 Charles Darwin, *The Effects of Cross and Self Fertilisation in the Vegetable Kingdom* (London: John Murray, 1876).

10 Kyle Bobiwash, Stewart Schultz, and Dan Schoen, "Somatic Deleterious Mutation Rate in a Woody Plant: Estimation from Phenotypic Data," *Heredity* 111, no. 4 (2013): 338–44, https://doi.org/10.1038/hdy.2013.57.

11 Sier-Ching Chantha et al., "Secondary Evolution of a Self-Incompatibility Locus in the Brassicaceae Genus *Leavenworthia*," *PLOS Biology* 11, no. 5 (2013): 1001560, https://doi.org/10.1371/journal.pbio.1001560.

12 Juan Vicente Muñoz-Sanz et al., "Self-(In)compatibility Systems: Target Traits for Crop-Production, Plant Breeding, and Biotechnology," *Frontiers in Plant Science* 11, no. 195 (2020), https://doi.org/10.3389/fpls.2020.00195.

Chapter Sixteen

1 US Department of Agriculture (USDA) *Plant Protection Act* (PPA), U.S.C. 7702 (2004), Sec. 403, no. 7.

2 EU Regulation no. 1143/2014 of the European Parliament and of the Council of 22 October 2014 on the Prevention and Management of the Introduction and Spread of Invasive Alien Species (2019).

3 *Weed Control Act*, R.S.O. 1990, c. W.5. O., reg. 248/14 (2014), https://www.ontario.ca/laws/regulation/r14248.

4 Herbert Baker, *The Genetics of Colonizing Species: Proceedings of the First International Union of Biological Sciences Symposia on General Biology* (Cambridge, MA: Academic Press, 1965).

5 Loren Rieseberg et al., "Hybridization and the Colonization of Novel Habitats by Annual Sunflowers," *Genetica* 129, no. 2 (2007): 149–65, https://doi.org/10.1007/s10709-006-9011-y.

6 Richard Abbott and Loren Rieseberg, "Hybrid Speciation," *eLS* (2021), https://doi.org/10.1002/9780470015902.a0029379.

7 Susan McCouch et al., "Mobilizing Crop Biodiversity," *Molecular Plant* 13, no. 10 (2020): 1341–4, https://doi.org/10.1016/j.molp.2020.08.011.

8   Chris Smith et al., "Aberrant RNA Splicing Due to Genetic Incompatibilities in Sunflower Hybrids," *Evolution* 75 (2021), https://doi.org/10.1111/evo.14360.

9   Todd Funke et al., *Proceedings of the National Academy of Sciences* 103, no. 35 (2006): 13010–15, https://doi.org/10.1073/pnas.0603638103.

10 International Service for the Acquisition of Agri-Biotech Applications (ISAAA), "Global Status of Commercialized Biotech/GM Crops," 2019, https://www.isaaa.org/resources/publications/pocketk/16/.

11 Melanie Epp, "Keeping Canola Out of Your Soybean Fields," *Grainews*, 10 April 2018, https://www.grainews.ca/crops/keeping-volunteer-canola-out-of-your-soybean-fields/.

12 Allison Snow et al., "A Bt Transgene Reduces Herbivory and Enhances Fecundity in Wild Sunflowers," *Ecological Applications* 13 (2003): 279–86, https://doi.org/10.1890/1051-0761(2003)013[0279:Abtrha]2.0.Co;2.

Chapter Seventeen

1   Diana Bizecki Robson, "Webs of Western Silvery Aster," The Manitoba Museum, 2014, video, 1:46, http://www.prairiepollination.ca/videos/reseaux_de_laster_soyeux-webs_of_western_silvery_aster/.

2   Species At Risk Public Registry, "Species Profile: Western Silvery Aster," Government of Canada, 29 November 2011, https://wildlife-species.canada.ca/species-riskregistry/species/speciesDetails_e.cfm?sid=269.

3   Diana Bizecki Robson, "An Assessment of the Potential for Pollination Facilitation of a Rare Plant by Common Plants: *Symphyotrichum sericeum* (*Asteraceae*) as a Case Study," *Botany* 91, no. 1 (2013): 34–42, https://doi.org/10.1139/cjb-2012-0133.

4   Diana Bizecki Robson, Cary Hamel, and Rebekah Neufeld, "Impact of Grazing History on Pollinator Communities in Fescue Prairie," *Blue Jay* 77 (2019): 10–15, https://doi.org/10.29173/bluejay374.

5   Stuart Wagenius et al., "Fire Synchronizes and Boosts Reproduction in a Widespread but Declining Prairie Species," *Proceedings of the National Academy of Sciences* (2020), https://doi.org/10.1073/pnas.1907320117.

6   Emily Royer, "*Oarisma powesheik* (amended version of 2019 assessment)," The IUCN Red List of Threatened Species (2020), https://dx.doi.org/10.2305/IUCN.UK.2020-1.RLTS.T122914337A166163683.en.

7   "City Staff Buzzing about Endangered Bee Discovery as Boulevard Preps for Another Season," *CBC News*, 22 April 2019, https://www.cbc.ca/news/canada/calgary/calgary-bee-boulevard-discovery-endangered-1.5106593.

8 Andrea Burr et al., "Wild Bees in the City: Reimagining Urban Spaces for Pollinator Health," *Consilience: The Journal of Sustainable Development* 16 (2016): 106–31, https://doi.org/10.7916/consilience.v0i16.3916.

9 Naheed Nenshi and Druh Farrell, "Application for Council Innovation Fund. Roadside Naturalization Pilot," Roads/Calgary Parks Business Units, 21 January 2020, https://pub-calgary.escribemeetings.com/filestream.ashx? DocumentId=121458.

10 Adam Toy, "'Heartbreaking': Calgary Bee Habitat, Volunteer Project Mowed Down," *Global News*, 10 August 2021, https://globalnews.ca/news/8102336/calgary-bee-habitat-destroyed/.

Chapter Eighteen

1 Victoria MacPhail, "Pollination Guelph Updates from 2019 and Plans for 2020," Pollination Guelph, 7 June 2020, video, 16:04, https://www.youtube.com/watch?v=K2_VVUMUU3Q&t=5s.

2 Christina Kingsbury, "ReMediate, Installation, poetry and performance," http://www.christinakingsbury.com/remediate (accessed 12 January 2022).

3 Tony Saxon, "Creating a Buzz about Becoming a Bee City," *Guelph Today*, 13 June 2018, https://www.guelphtoday.com/local-news/creating-a-buzz-about-becoming-a-bee-city-5-photos-952838.

4 Bee City Canada, "Bee City Renewal 2020," City of Toronto, 2020, https://beecitycanada.org/wp-content/uploads/2021/01/Toronto-Renewal2020.pdf.

5 Aiyanna Sezak-Blatt, "The Call of the Bees: Phyllis Stiles on Founding of Bee City USA," *Mountain Xpress*, 19 March 2015, https://mountainx.com/living/the-call-of-the-bees/.

6 Alexandre Antonelli et al., "State of the World's Plants and Fungi 2020," *Royal Botanic Gardens, Kew* (2020), https://doi.org/org/10.34885/172.

7 Chief Corporate Officer, "Bee City Affiliation and Pollinator Protection Strategy Update," City of Toronto, 17 March 2016, https://www.toronto.ca/legdocs/mmis/2016/cc/bgrd/backgroundfile-91558.pdf.

8 Nyssa van Vierssen Trip et al., "Examining the Public's Awareness of Bee (*Hymenoptera*: *Apoidae*: *Anthophila*) Conservation in Canada," *Conservation Science and Practice* 2 (2020): 293, https://doi.org/ 10.1111/csp2.293.

9 Emily Chung, "Urban Beekeeping Can Be Bad for Wild Bees," *CBC News*, 7 August 2020, https://www.cbc.ca/news/science/what-on-earth-bees-urban-wild-1.5676777.

10 Charlotte de Keyzer, "A Collection of Bad Bee-Washing," https://www.bee-washing.com/bad (accessed 12 January 2022).

11 Joan Casanelles-Abella and Marco Moretti, "Challenging the Sustainability of Urban Beekeeping Using Evidence from Swiss Cities," *NPJ Urban Sustainability* 2, no. 3 (2022), https://doi.org/10.1038/s42949-021-00046-6.

12 *Ontario Bees Act*. R.S.O. 1990, chap. B.6. sec. 19 (2019), http://www.omafra.gov.on.ca/english/food/inspection/bees/beekeepingregulations.htm.

13 Samantha Craggs, "'A Bad Feeling in the Pit of My Stomach': Bees Vanish from Brock Research Project," *CBC News*, 24 November 2017, https://www.cbc.ca/news/canada/hamilton/bees-in-the-fight-of-their-lives-1.4411197.

14 Thomas Onuferko et al., "Rapid Initial Recovery and Long-Term Persistence of a Bee Community in a Former Landfill," *Insect Conservation and Diversity* (2017), https://doi.org/11.10.1111/icad.12261.

Chapter Nineteen

1 Collen Cirillo, "What's Wrong with Garlic Mustard? Managing Invasive Species in the Garden," Project Swallowtail Fall Webinar Series, 15 October 2020, https://www.youtube.com/watch?v=B5RvHodTb44, 1:05:28.

2 Eric Davies et al., "The Toronto Ravines Study: 1977–2017," Faculty of Forestry, University of Toronto (2018), https://torontoravinesdotorg.files.wordpress.com/2018/09/toronto-ravines-study-1977-to-2017-short.pdf.

3 City of Toronto, "2018 Tree Canopy Study," 2018, https://www.toronto.ca/legdocs/mmis/2020/ie/bgrd/backgroundfile-141364.pdf.

4 Rick Darke and Douglas Tallamy, *The Living Landscape: Designing for Beauty and Biodiversity in the Home Garden* (Portland, OR: Timber Press, 2014), 104.

5 Aldo Leopold, *A Sand County Alamanac* (London: Penguin Classics, 2020; first publication Oxford, UK: Oxford University Press, 1949), 155–73.

6 Edward Wilson, "The Little Things That Run the World (The Importance and Conservation of Invertebrates)," *Conservation Biology* 1, no. 4 (1987): 344–6, http://www.jstor.org/stable/2386020.